Riches *of* Faith

The First Principle of the Gospel in the Lives of the Prophets and Saints

Edited by

John K. Challis & John G. Scott

Salt Lake City, Utah

Riches of Faith

Library of Congress Cataloging-in-Publication Data

Riches of faith: the first principle of the gospel in the lives of the prophets and saints / edited by John G. Scott and John K. Challis.

p. cm.
Includes bibliographical references and indexes.
ISBN 1-56236-214-3
1. Faith. 2. Spiritual life–Mormon Church. 3. Mormon Church–Sacred books. I. Scott, John G. (George), 1958- . II. Challis, John Kevin, 1958- .
BX8656.R53 1995 95-6363
248.4'89332–dc20 CIP

Cover illustration: Detail from *Jesus Healing the Sick,* by Gustave Doré
Cover design: Brian Bean

This book is dedicated to the memory of David Carl Danielson who, like the ancients, exercised mighty faith.

Contents

INTRODUCTION

JOHN G. SCOTT

IN LATTER-DAY SAINT theology *faith* is not a passive construct. On the contrary, faith in Jesus Christ implies activity, commitment, allegiance, sacrifice, time, devotion, and worship. Joseph Smith said that faith is "the first principle in revealed religion and the foundation of all righteousness" (*Lectures on Faith* 1:1). For Latter-day Saints, faith is an essential element of gospel living in this life if we are to attain exaltation in the life to come.

Each chapter in *Riches of Faith* highlights the importance of faith in the lives of major characters in gospel history. More specifically, this book examines examples from the lives of the faithful of how faith is developed, nourished, tested, and rewarded. This book, of course, is in no way a complete treatment of all the major characters in gospel history who worked through the principle of faith; such a study would require volumes to complete. But a study of these select individuals offers an understanding of how we might develop faith ourselves.

The first chapter, *"Again in the Flesh I Shall See God": Adam Victorious,* the scholarship of John K. Challis, discusses the pivotal role which Adam played as head of the human family in the establishment of faith in the world. In this chapter, Brother Challis recounts Adam's "faithful step into mortality" and the powerful example of overcoming the world by faith provided by our first parents.

Philip Wightman highlights the faith of *Abraham–Father of the Faithful.* In a most insightful way, Brother Wightman underscores how Abraham's "life illustrates the pattern established by the Son of God that all must follow to obtain eternal life." This chapter dramatically chronicles Abraham's journey of faith and the eventual culmination of his faith with the command to sacrifice Isaac.

In chapter three, *Is Anything Too Hard for the Lord? The Faith of Sarah,* Audrey Godfrey tenderly describes the testing which Sarah endured with regard to the promises made to her by the Lord. Sister Godfrey concludes that "[w]e should remember that when we add our faith to God's power all things are possible to do and to bear."

Faithful Isaac is the topic of chapter four. James Carver details the primary role of the yet future atonement with regard to the command to sacrifice Isaac. Additionally, this chapter addresses the perplexing issue of the birthright blessing given to Jacob instead of Esau, and what part faith played in this gospel drama.

In his usual scholarly and interesting way, Stephen D. Ricks addresses the topic of *Jacob: Trial and Triumph* in chapter five. Beginning with the conflict and resolution leitmotif in the life of this prophet and concluding with a brief interpretation of Genesis 28-32 as a possible temple text, this essay provides some extraordinary insights into the blessings, challenges, and requirements that accompany a life of faith.

Chapter six, the work of John G. Scott, discusses *Joseph Who Was Sold Into Egypt: Faithful Student of Jesus Christ.* This essay underscores Joseph's deep and abiding faith in God. Because of his faith Joseph was given the gift of seership, and through the use of this gift Joseph has given hope, inspiration, peace, and ultimately faith to all of Israel.

In chapter seven, *Moses: Spiritual Preparation of a Mighty Man of Faith,* Robert J. Matthews recounts for the reader the dramatic events in the life of this lawgiver to Israel which led to his unconquerable faith in Jesus Christ. The author finally concludes that Moses was "like unto Christ," a blessing to all who, like Moses, are willing by faith to "forsake Egypt."

In chapter eight, *Ruth: Woman of Faith,* Linda Aukschun uncovers subtle ways in which this progenitor of Jesus Christ exercised her faith, insights often missed by a cursory reading of the short account of Ruth's life.

Richard Draper draws upon years of research in Ancient Scriptures to present *Peter: Fisher of Men* in chapter nine. In his creative style Brother Draper follows the development of Peter's faith from one degree to another. This chapter will forever alter the reader's view of Peter.

Paul: Growing Seeds of Faith is the work of Doug Reeder. This chapter outlines Paul's conversion, his missionary zeal, and the fruition of his faith in his beloved Jesus. Brother Reeder offers a lively and broad discussion of how Paul's faith developed and blossomed throughout his life as a devout follower of Jesus Christ.

Daniel C. Peterson draws on his knowledge and expertise, including much time spent in the Holy Land, to create *Lehi: A Spiritual Portrait*. This is a thoughtful essay full of new insight into the spiritual life and faith of one of the Book of Mormon's great patriarchs.

With his usual engaging style, Kenneth Godfrey discusses *The Mighty Power of Deliverance: How Nephi Grew Faith* in chapter twelve. Brother Godfrey combines stories from scripture and his own life to discuss attributes of a faithful life and to create a lasting impression for the reader of one of history's mighty men of faith.

Gerald Hansen Jr. has written several insightful essays on Book of Mormon topics. In chapter thirteen he provides an interesting look at the book of Ether and *Moroni: A Prophet Who Endured through Faith*. In his essay, Brother Hansen examines what Moroni chose to include in his record of a fallen society whose prophets had faith enough to see the Son of God while its people became so wicked they were destroyed off the face of the land.

In many instances the faith of Joseph Smith is mentioned as a passing commentary. However, Danel Bachman goes beyond the mere mention of Joseph's faith in his essay *Even the Faith of Elijah: Joseph Smith's Faith in the Lord Jesus Christ*. Through his weaving of Church History and scriptural examples, the author creates a dramatic portrait of the faith of the prophet who heads this dispensation.

Finally, Carol Cornwall Madsen writes in chapter fifteen about *Women of Early Mormonism: A Study in Faith*. This chapter provides a capstone to the entire book. Sister Madsen cites journal entries to provide personal accounts of how faith was developed and tried among many of the early women in this dispensation. In the end, she says that "[i]f their lives can speak to us of this generation of the power of faith, they are telling us that faith for them was always more than a passive belief."

Many books have been written about faith. However, this work attempts to combine the principle of faith with the real lives of characters from gospel history that illustrate, through the example of their lives, how faith was developed, tested, and ultimately strengthened. These people were real human beings, with real life problems, difficulties, and stressful circumstances. Their faith was not developed in a vacuum. On the contrary, they stand as an example to us that no matter what life's disadvantages may be, we too can develop great faith in Jesus Christ.

This book is the production of various religious educators who recognize the powerful message in the lives of these faithful brothers and sisters. It is the work of individual members of The Church of Jesus Christ of Latter-day Saints who have a testimony of the restored gospel and a love for the scriptures and the Lord, members who teach the gospel at numerous institutions and are faithful and committed to the Church and the Savior. The ideas and doctrines discussed in this edited volume are the sole responsibility of the various authors and editors. They are not to be considered a primary source of doctrinal statements of The Church of Jesus Christ of Latter-day Saints. Only the prophet and the presiding councils of the Church can reveal or speak for the Lord in relation to things of doctrine. If there are errors, they are only the manifestations of human limitations and are the sole responsibility of the writers of this volume.

Chapter One

"Again in the Flesh I Shall See God" Adam Victorious

John K. Challis

Introduction

Adam, "the first man…the '[Ancient] of Days'…the first and oldest of all,"[1] must have had unique faith because of the knowledge he brought with him from the Garden of Eden. Though none of our lives will begin quite as his did, we, as he did, must learn to live by faith in this mortal sphere. Two experiences from Adam's life are particularly instructive as we consider how he utilized faith to assist him in winning the day.[2] Both illustrate that our first parents included faith as a fundamental part of their lives.

The first of these two experiences is the marvelous spiritual outpouring and angelic ministration recorded in the fifth chapter of the Book of Moses. This experience solidified Adam's faith, gave him assurance, and led him to make what I refer to as his *affirmation of faith*. The second is an overt sign of Adam's victory over the world through faith: the gift of the Second Comforter, or the personal ministration of the Savior to him. This event, now recorded in Section 107 of the Doctrine and Covenants, clearly demonstrates the fulfillment of Adam's affirmation of faith.

To Him That Overcometh

Truman G. Madsen, in a beautiful essay entitled "The Temple and the Restoration," outlined seven promises available to those who overcome the world.[3] Each of these promises begins with the phrase "to him that overcometh," and all seven relate to one kingdom of glory—the celestial (D&C 76:50–70). For example, the "Tree of Life" promise (Rev. 2:7), the "Crown of Life" promise (Rev. 2:10), and the "Pillar in the Temple" promise (Rev. 3:12) all suggest blessings available to the faithful who overcome the world. They are symbols of exaltation, and their fulness is comprehended only by those who "see as they are seen, and know as they are known," having received of the Lord's "fulness and of his grace" (D&C 76:94).

Perhaps the most sublime of the seven promises Madsen lists is the blessing and promise of "a Feast," the "Marriage Supper of the Lamb." These are the words of the promise: "Behold, I stand at the door, and knock: if any man hear my voice, and open the door, I will come in to him, and will *sup with him, and he with me.* To him that overcometh will I grant to sit with me in my throne, *even as I also overcame,* and am set down with my Father in his throne" (Rev. 3:20–21; emphasis added).

Regarding this final honor, Brother Madsen offers the following insight:

> The promise is not for the lukewarm but for the fully regenerate. To be anointed is to have one's eyes opened "to the glory of the kingdom" and then to become partaker or "to share" thereof. Such promises are not made on faith alone, but to those whose faith has brought them the mark of the prize of the high calling of Christ.... Those who have come up through affliction, who have not been defiled, who have had their faith and love tested, are "called, and chosen and faithful." (Revelation 17:14)[4]

How does all of this relate to Adam? Joseph Smith taught that Adam had proved his valiance in heaven. He "obtained the first Presidency & held the Keys of it, from generation to Generation; he obtained it in the creation before the world was formed.... He is Michael, the Archangel, spoken of in the Scriptures."[3] Additionally, Adam "was called of God to this office & was the Father of all living.... [He] is the Father of the human family," and stands next in authority to Jesus only.[5] Inherent in Adam's calling as the first mortal was the charge to confront and overcome the world. As the title of this chapter declares, Adam was victorious over the world; he was born of God (Moses 6:64–65) and thus became "a new creature" of the Spirit (2 Cor. 5:17). As the ultimate sign of this, Adam was again permitted into the Lord's presence—this time as a mortal. It was faith which led to Adam's victory over the world: "For whatsoever is born of God overcometh the world: and this is the victory that overcometh the world, *even our faith*. Who is he that overcometh the world, but he that believeth that Jesus is the Son of God?" (1 Jn. 5: 4–5; emphasis added).

Overcoming the World—a Blessing of Faith

"This mortal life is designed as a time of testing and trial," Elder Bruce R. McConkie counseled.

> The Lord is letting us choose whether we shall succumb to the lusts of the flesh and live after the manner of the world, or whether we shall keep the commandments; put first in our lives the things of his kingdom; develop the character, perfections, and attributes which he possesses; and thereby qualify for eternal life with him in the kingdom of his Father. And he expects us to overcome, to conquer, to come off triumphant, to be victorious, to win the war with sin, even as he himself did.[7]

The Lord *expects* us to overcome the world!

In the preceeding passage, Elder McConkie noted three requirements for overcoming, which the Savior himself adhered to (see D&C 93:11–17). The third of these, that of developing "the character, perfections, and attributes" of God, President Ezra Taft Benson has linked with faith. He said, "Faith is the foundation upon which a godlike character is built. It is a prerequisite for all other virtues."[8] We become like God by using the creative quality of faith as our foundation. However, in order to experience a fulness of creativity, or obtain a "fulness of joy" (D&C 93:33–34), one needs a body. Joseph Smith emphasized that "all beings who have bodies have power over those who have not."[9] To be godlike, one must obtain a tabernacle of flesh for one's spirit. This step is essential to our progression.

If we remember that God's work and glory is bringing to pass our "immortality and eternal life" (Moses 1:39), then we had to be "freed," in a sense, from premortality. The need for Adam to leave Eden has been underscored by Elder George Q. Morris, who noted that "we can never attain immortality without dying."[10] Also, in order to develop and exercise faith, we had to leave God's presence.

Adam's Faithful Step into Mortality

"Adam became mortal." These three simple words employed by President J. Reuben Clark Jr. describe "the first great crisis in the history of mankind."[11] This "crisis" remains the catalyst for frequent debate. Some argue that as a result of the Fall, the glory days for the earth are over: *Sic transit gloria mundi*—thus passes away the glory of the world. Others just cannot seem to forgive Adam and Eve for their transgression—although the Lord did (see Moses 6:53). Meanwhile, some Latter-day Saints, says Marden J. Clark, often speak of the Fall "in rhapsodic terms that make cosmic heroes out of Adam and especially Eve, who was willing to take that first bite, that ultimate risk."[12] "How literally do we take the story of the Garden of Eden?" Joseph Fielding McConkie has queried. "This we know: Adam was real. He was as real as Christ. For if Adam was not real the Fall was not real; and if the Fall was not real the Atonement was not real; and if the Atonement was not real Jesus the Christ is not and was not necessary."[13]

The Prophet Joseph Smith placed it all in perspective when he said, "Adam was made to open the way of the world."[14] Adam's creation and subsequent placement in Eden, along with his helpmeet Eve, was "done in the wisdom of him who knoweth all things" (2 Ne. 2:24). In the events surrounding the Fall we see wisdom—a plan. It is true that "by man came death" and "in Adam all die"; however, Paul's declaration that "even so in Christ shall all be made alive" (1 Cor. 15: 21–22) unveils the plan. From death comes life. When Adam was driven from the Garden, he was the first to face the challenges the world would present, including death as a result of his transgression, but he was expected and prepared to overcome them. This Adam was able to do because of a belief in the plan of salvation.

Implicit in the gospel of the Restoration is the message that the fall of Adam was a progressive act. As Orson F. Whitney's familiar maxim heralds, "the fall had a two-fold direction, downward, yet forward."[15] The Fall was, for Adam and Eve, a positive transition; it was part of a plan.

The Lord "foreordained the fall of man," according to the Prophet Joseph Smith, "but all merciful as He is, He foreordained at the same time, a plan for redemption for all mankind."[16] Joseph's words imply that the plan was in effect as Adam and Eve fell in the Garden of Eden. Inherent in the plan was opposition, struggle, and suffering, the latter two being unknown to Adam and his wife. The Lord God said: "Because thou hast hearkened unto the voice of thy wife, and hast eaten of the fruit of the tree of which I commanded thee, saying—Thou shalt not eat of it, cursed shall the ground be for thy sake" (Moses 4:23). The life Adam would face would be one of struggle and growth—progress from opposition. To borrow an analogy: "Imagine a car with absolutely frictionless tires, and we can easily see that opposition becomes the means of movement, of progress."[17] In life, it is essentially as Elder George Q. Morris has taught: "We come to the earth with all these conditions arranged as they are so that we have to struggle constantly against evil, struggle to preserve our lives, struggle for everything of true value—that is the thing for us to understand—this is the course of life that is most desirable, and for our good."[18]

The words the scriptures use to characterize Adam's expulsion from Eden, *drove* or *driven*, are intriguing (see Gen. 3:24; Moses 4:31; 5:1). They conjure up images of a God casting our first parents out of the Garden much like the Lord cleansed the temple at Jerusalem (2 Jn. 1:13–17). However, the Hebrew word *garash*, translated for us as "driven," can also be translated as "to divorce" or "to put away." Adam and Eve were separated from the presence of God as a matter of law: "For as I, the Lord God, liveth, even so my words cannot return void, for as they go forth out of my mouth they must be fulfilled" (Moses 4:30). It was for Adam and Eve much as it is for children separated from one (or both) of their parents as a result of a legal divorce.

So we find Adam separated from the presence of his Father, alone in the world with his wife. And immediately we see Adam using his faith creatively. The Lord had given Adam three commandments. These were (1) to till the earth; (2) to have dominion over all the beasts of the field; and (3) to eat his bread by the sweat of his brow. These commandments were all obeyed by Adam according to Moses 5:1–2; "and Eve, also, his wife, did labor with him."

The Lord Jehovah[19] then gave Adam and Eve additional commandments. These commandments were to first, worship the Lord *their* God (this is important, because we cannot forget the presence of another "son of god" suing for attention—see Moses 5:13), and second, to "offer the firstlings of their flocks, for an offering to the Lord" (Moses 5:5). To these commandments, also, "Adam was obedient" (v. 5).

Robert J. Matthews offers the following insight into the offering of "firstlings" and faith:

> The word *firstlings* puts certain qualifications and restrictions and even determines the quality of faith that is used in offering the sacrifice. *Firstling* does not necessarily denote the oldest of the flock but the firstborn of a particular mother. A firstling is a male, the first "that openeth the matrix" of its mother (Exodus 34:19; 13:2). Each mother in her lifetime could produce only one firstling, but a flock of sheep could have several firstlings born each year. In order to know which lambs were acceptable for sacrifice, the owner would have to know his flock. Some notice would have to be made of mothers and of young. Otherwise, how could anyone know which mothers had produced offspring for the first time? There is no way that a man, Adam or anyone else, could know which males were firstlings unless a record and some identification of mothers and offspring were kept. This requirement removes the element of chance and of haphazard or sometime obedience.[20]

If we think of the offerings of Cain and Abel (Moses 5:16–38) we can see that the Lord pays very close attention to what is an acceptable sacrifice. Brother Matthews' teachings shed important light on faith as a multifaceted presence in Adam's life. It required "the intelligent and deliberate attention of those who are seeking salvation"[21] to make an acceptable offering. Such an offering was, in other words, an act of faith.

Adam's Marvelous Spiritual Outpouring: A Blessing of Faith

Many days after Adam and Eve had begun to offer sacrifice they were blessed with a profound spiritual experience. The Bible is silent concerning it, but the Book of Moses is not. Moses chapter five contains precious truths relating to fruits of faith. These truths center in what could be considered a "type" for future pentecostal-like episodes.[22]

The fifth chapter of Moses tells of a day of angelic ministration and a powerful outpouring of the Spirit upon Adam and Eve. But what had transpired in the lives of Adam and Eve that led to the great blessings of this day? They had been living the law of sacrifice as they had been commanded (Moses 5:5). By faith, Adam, as a wise shepherd and husbandman, selected the proper firstlings and sacrificed them. This he had been doing for some time when suddenly the veil was parted and an angel from God's presence "appeared unto Adam" (Moses 5:6). According to Moroni, angels appear to people as a blessing for strong faith, "for behold, they [angels] are subject unto [the Lord], to minister according to the word of his command, showing themselves unto them of *strong faith* and a firm mind in every form of godliness" (Moro. 7:30; emphasis added).

Adam might have been performing a sacred ordinance (much like Zacharias, his counterpart in the meridian of time [see Luke 1:5–21]) when he received this angelic ministration. Moses records: "And after many days an angel of the Lord appeared unto Adam, saying: Why dost thou offer sacrifices unto the Lord? And Adam said unto him: I know not, save the Lord commanded me" (Moses 5:6).

The angel then assisted Adam in finding a focal point for his faithful observance of the law of sacrifice. This focal point, according to the angel, was the "sacrifice of the Only Begotten of the Father," who, the angel continued, "is full of grace and truth" (Moses 5: 5–7). The angel concluded with a great doctrinal commandment: "Wherefore, thou shalt do all that thou doest in the name of the Son, and thou shalt repent and call upon God in the name of the Son forevermore" (Moses 5:8).

Because of this ministration, (1) our father Adam was filled with the Holy Ghost though he still had not yet received the gift of the Holy Ghost (see Moses 6:64–66); (2) he heard the voice of the Holy Ghost bearing record "of the Father and the Son" (Moses 5:9); (3) he received the testimony of Jesus (Moses 5:7, 9; Rev. 19:10). Adam was filled with the Spirit, a return, in part, to the feeling he surely enjoyed in Eden and a great blessing granted as a fruit of great faith. Our first parent, thus filled with the testimony of Jesus, prophesied in a great hosanna shout: "Blessed be the name of God, for because of my transgression my eyes are opened, and in this life I shall have joy, and again in the flesh I shall see God" (Moses 5:10).

Mother Eve, upon hearing all these things, "was glad" (Moses 5:10) and spoke eternal truths by the power of the Spirit she was enjoying. Eve said: "Were it not for our transgression we never should have had seed, and never should have known good and evil, and the joy of our redemption, and the eternal life which God giveth unto all the obedient" (Moses 5:11). Moses then records: "And Adam and Eve blessed the name of God, and they made all things known unto their sons and their daughters" (Moses 5:12). Adam and Eve shared their newfound joy and knowledge. In latter-day revelation, the Lord has said, "And as all have not faith, seek ye diligently and teach one another words of wisdom; yea, seek ye out of the best books words of wisdom; seek learning, even by study and also by faith" (D&C 88:118). Adam and Eve sought to increase the faith of their children by teaching them concerning their experience—and by teaching them to read and write, even out of one of the "best books," Adam's book of remembrance (see Moses 6:4–6).

Adam's Affirmation of Faith

According to Moses' account, as Adam was filled with the Spirit, he made an interesting declaration. I call it his "affirmation of faith." He declared: "In this life I shall have joy, and again in the flesh I shall see God" (Moses 5:10).

The blessing of being in the presence of God is a blessing sought by men and women who love the Lord, keep his commandments, receive the First Comforter (John 14:26), and endure to the end. Doctrinally, eternal life—the same eternal life Eve said the obedient receive (see Moses 5:11)—means living in God's presence. Eternal life, or life in the celestial kingdom, is explained in latter-day revelation as follows:

> These [heirs of the celestial kingdom] shall dwell in the presence of God and his Christ forever and ever....
>
> And thus we saw the glory of the celestial, which excels in all things—where God, even the Father, reigns upon his throne forever and ever....
>
> They who dwell in his presence...see as they are seen, and know as they are known, having received of his fulness and of his grace. (D&C 76:62, 92, 94)

It would be a great blessing to be in God's presence in this life. Judging from Adam's affirmation of faith, of all the blessings lost as a result of his fall into mortality, regaining God's presence would be the most desirable to regain. Why must Adam have longed for the joy that accompanies the "quickening" by the Spirit (D&C 67:11),[23] the transfiguring a mortal must undergo to withstand the glory of the Lord? Because he had tasted of it once, in the Garden of Eden. "*Again in the flesh,*" Adam said, "I shall see God."

Moses understood this longing. After experiencing the presence and glory of God and returning unto himself, he had never felt so mortal. Of this encounter Moses said, "Now, for this cause I know that man is nothing, which thing I never had supposed" (Moses 1:10). Adam, unlike Moses, had enjoyed life in the presence of God and had that life taken away lawfully because of his transgression. This removal from God's presence has been defined as spiritual death. President Joseph Fielding Smith said: "Because of Adam's transgression, a spiritual death—banishment from the presence of the Lord—as well as the temporal death, were pronounced upon him. The spiritual death came at the time of the fall and banishment."[24]

All in mortality are subject to this spiritual death, yet through faithfulness it can be overcome, even while we dwell on earth in the flesh. LDS theology teaches the doctrine of the Second Comforter. The First Comforter we know to be the Holy Ghost. In the final days of Jesus' ministry, he taught the disciples that "the Comforter...is the Holy Ghost" (John 14:26). In the same discourse, the Savior told the disciples: "And I will pray the Father, and he shall give you *another Comforter,* that he may abide with you for ever" (John 14:16–17; emphasis added). This other Comforter is "no more nor less than the Lord Jesus Christ Himself; and this is the sum and substance of the whole matter; that when any man obtains this last Comforter [the promise of eternal life], he will have the personage of Jesus Christ to attend him."[25]

Through the prophetic eyes of Joseph Smith we can view the fulfillment of Adam's affirmation that he (Adam) would again be in the Lord's presence while in the flesh. Over an entire lifetime—930 years according to the *Lectures on Faith*[26]—Adam was faithful. He led righteously and administered his priesthood with diligence. Section 107 of the Doctrine and Covenants, known as the "Revelation on Priesthood," mentions Adam's administration (see D&C 107:41–57).

Speaking in relation to these verses Joseph Smith said, "I saw Adam in the valley of Ah-dam-ondi-Ahman [sic]—he called together his children & blessed them with a Patriarchal blessing."[27] Then Joseph said: "He (Adam) blessed them all, & foretold what should befall them to the latest generation." Why did Adam bless his posterity? "He wanted to bring them into the presence of God."[28]

Adam's faithful affirmation was fulfilled in that day he called his posterity together. He had given many the priesthood himself, emphasizing the careful shepherding of those chosen to be confirmed (D&C 107:41–50). The meeting was held in the valley of Adam-ondi-Ahman, which modern revelation places near Spring Hill, Daviess County, Missouri (D&C 116). Though we may not be certain that the following scriptural account was Adam's first manifestation of the Second Comforter, it is the one on record:

> Three years previous to the death of Adam, he called Seth, Enos, Cainan, Mahalaleel, Jared, Enoch, and Methuselah, who were all high priests, with the residue of his posterity

> who were righteous, into the valley of Adam-ondi-Ahman, and there bestowed upon them his last blessing.
>
> And the Lord appeared unto them, and they rose up and blessed Adam, and called him Michael, the prince, the archangel.
>
> And the Lord administered comfort unto Adam, and said unto him: I have set thee to be at the head; a multitude of nations shall come of thee, and thou art a prince over them forever.
>
> And Adam stood up in the midst of the congregation; and, notwithstanding he was bowed down with age, being full of the Holy Ghost, predicted whatsoever should befall his posterity unto the latest generation. (D&C 107:53–56)

The Lord *appeared* unto Adam and his posterity—thus directly fulfilling Adam's affirmation of "again in the flesh I shall see God" (Moses 5:10). Contained in the above five verses is one of the greatest meetings ever conducted upon the earth. In the presence of Christ, Adam's children extolled him as "the prince, the archangel" (D&C 107:54), thus underscoring father Adam's premortal majesty. When the Lord personally "administered comfort unto Adam" (D&C 107:55), Jesus Christ, the great Jehovah, was acting in his role as the Second Comforter, ministering peace and comfort as only a Savior can (see John 14:26). Thus, one of the crowning experiences to which mortals aspire was granted to our father Adam because of his perseverance, worthiness, and obedience in keeping the commandments and thus overcoming the world. By faith, Adam was truly born of God, having entered his presence while still a mortal.

Conclusion

The charge to overcome and be victorious applies to us all. If we develop the virtue of faith in our lives—as Adam did—and exhibit it as action, the way will be opened and the path made clear so that we may overcome the world. Though all may not receive the blessing of the Second Comforter in this life, all who conquer the world will have that blessing in the next. As resurrected beings, they will "again in the flesh" see God.

This truth was conveyed in vision to Elder David O. McKay while on board a ship near Apia, Samoa. Elder McKay had just retired to his cabin and was pondering the beautiful sunset he had witnessed when he experienced the following:

> I lay in my berth at ten o'clock that night and thought to myself: Charming as it is, it doesn't stir my soul with emotion as do the innocent lives of children, and the sublime characters of loved ones and friends. Their beauty, unselfishness, and heroism are after all the most glorious!
>
> I then fell asleep, and beheld in vision something infinitely sublime. In the distance I beheld a beautiful white city. Though it was far away, yet I seemed to realize that trees with luscious fruit, shrubbery with gorgeously tinted leaves, and flowers in perfect bloom abounded everywhere. The clear sky above seemed to reflect these beautiful shades of color. I then saw a great concourse of people approaching the city. Each one wore a white flowing robe and a white headdress. Instantly my attention seemed centered upon their leader, and though I could only see the profile of his features and his body, I recognized him at once as my Savior! The tint and radiance of his countenance were glorious to behold. There was a peace about him which seemed sublime—it was divine!
>
> The city, I understood, was his. It was the City Eternal; and the people following him were to abide there in peace and eternal happiness.
>
> But who were they?
>
> As if the Savior read my thoughts, he answered by pointing to a semicircle that then appeared above them, and on which were written in gold the words:
>
> *These Are They Who Have Overcome the World—*
> *Who Have Truly Been Born Again!*
>
> When I awoke, it was breaking day over Apia harbor.[29]

It is this beautiful doctrine—overcoming the world by our faith—that is one of the stirring lessons we can learn from the life of Adam. The Lord our God loves all of his children and desires that they should all return to him. All may come and dwell in the "City Eternal" if they utilize the power which keeping the commandments, putting the kingdom first, and developing a godlike character will bring. This power, in part, comes from our increased faith—the faith needed to overcome the world. Perhaps Elder Hugh B. Brown said it best: "History rests on the shoulders of those who accepted the challenge of difficulties and drove through to the victory in spite of everything."[30] This Adam did, and thus became both victor and champion for all to look upon as an exemplar.

Notes

1. Andrew F. Ehat and Lyndon W. Cook, comps., *The Words of Joseph Smith* (Provo, Utah: Religious Studies Center, 1981), 39; hereafter *Words.*

2. Adam is one of the few individuals whose premortal, paradisiacal, mortal, postmortal, and resurrected states are viewable in scripture. For comment on this theme, see Robert L. Millet, *Ensign*, January 1994, 8–15; and Hugh W. Nibley, *Old Testament and Related Studies*, vol. 1 of *The Collected Works of Hugh Nibley* (Salt Lake City: Deseret Book, 1986), 77.

3. Truman G. Madsen, in *The Temple in Antiquity*, Truman G. Madsen, ed. (Provo, Utah: Religious Studies Center, 1984), 13–16.

4. Ibid., 15–16.

5. *Words*, 8.

6. Ibid., 8–9.

7. Bruce R. McConkie, *Doctrinal New Testament Commentary*, 3 vols. (Salt Lake City: Bookcraft, 1973), 3:445.

8. Ezra Taft Benson, *Ensign*, November 1986, 45.

9. Joseph Smith, *Teachings of the Prophet Joseph Smith*, comp. Joseph Fielding Smith (Salt Lake City: Deseret Book, 1977), 181; hereafter *TPJS.*

10. George Q. Morris, in *Conference Report*, April 1958, 38.

11. J. Reuben Clark, Jr., *Improvement Era*, December 1955, 915.

12. Marden J. Clark, *Liberating Form* (Salt Lake City: Aspen Books, 1992), 136.

13. Joseph Fielding McConkie, in *The Man Adam*, Joseph Fielding McConkie and Robert L. Millet, eds. (Salt Lake City: Bookcraft, 1990), 27.

14. *TPJS*, 12.

15. Orson F. Whitney, in *Cowley and Whitney on Doctrine*, Forace Green, comp. (Salt Lake City: Bookcraft, 1963), 287.

16. *Words*, 33. See also p. 46, notes 1–6. Their porter evidently was Mathew Livingston Davis (1773–1850) who wrote for the *New York Enquirer.* See *Words*, 46, note 4.

17. *Liberating Form*, 135.

18. George Q. Morris, in *Conference Report,* April 1958, 40.

19. As further evidence of the spiritual death that befell Adam and Eve, the scriptures illustrate that before the Fall, the Father (Elohim) known as the "Lord God" conversed with "the man" and dealt with him in the Garden (Moses 4:28). After the Fall and driving from Eden, the Lord (Jehovah) dealt with Adam and Eve, and they only heard his voice at that, for "they were shut out from his presence" (Moses 5:4). A very careful reading of Moses chapter four, verses 14–30, and then Moses chapter five, verses 1–4, highlights this point. Verse 28 of chapter four demonstrates this relationship by stating: "And I, the Lord God, said unto mine Only Begotten: Behold, the man is become as one of us." After the Fall, it is the "Lord" who deals with Adam, Eve, and even Cain (see Moses 5:4 for Adam, and Moses 5:22 for Cain); whereas the "Lord God" used the Holy Ghost to call upon men, thus reinforcing spiritual death (Moses 5:14). Elder Bruce R. McConkie has also pointed out "that since the Fall of Adam all the dealings of God with man have been through the Son rather than coming directly from the Father (*Doctrinal New Testament Commentary*, 3 vols. (Salt Lake City: Bookcraft 1965) 1:467.

20. Robert J. Matthews, in McConkie and Millet, *The Man Adam*, 74.

21. Ibid.

22. It is interesting that the powerful spiritual outpouring recorded in chapter two of Acts, often referred to as the Day of Pentecost, was a Hebrew feast day. On this day the offering of "the first-fruits of thy labors" was given. See for example Ex. 23:16; Deut. 16:10; and Acts 2. Adam and Eve were most likely offering a "firstling" sacrifice when their manifestation occurred (see Moses 5:4–6).

23. Of note, a synonym of *quicken* is *enlighten*. A passage in the Doctrine and Covenants highlights this process:

> And if your eye be single to my glory, your whole bodies shall be filled with light, and there shall be no darkness in you; and that body which is filled with light comprehendeth all things.
>
> Therefore, sanctify yourselves that your minds become single to God, and the days will come that you shall see him; for he will unveil his face unto you, and it shall be in his own time, and in his own way, and according to his own will. (88:67–68)

It appears that part of the "quickening" is the light-filling gift which accompanies the righteous living and eternally focused nature of the sanctified.

24. Joseph Fielding Smith, *Doctrines of Salvation*, comp., Bruce R. McConkie, 3 vols. (Salt Lake City: Bookcraft, 1955), 1:111.

25. Joseph Smith, *History of The Church of Jesus Christ of Latter-day Saints*, 7 vols. (Salt Lake City: Deseret Book, 1965–68), 3:381.

26. Larry E. Dahl and Charles D. Tate, Jr., eds. *The Lectures on Faith in Historical Perspective* (Provo, Utah: Religious Studies Center, 1990), 46.

27. *Words*, 9.

28. The text dated, "Before 8 August 1839," (1), mentions "Abraham" where I have used Adam, *Words*, 9. Ehat and Cook say, "it seems probable that Joseph Smith said 'Adam,' but the recorder of this sermon wrote 'Abraham'" (*Words*, 23, note 10). Doctrine and Covenants 107: 53–57 fits the context of the Prophet's words, and Adam did bring many of his posterity into God's presence

29. David O. McKay, *Cherished Experiences from the Writings of David O. McKay*, comp. Clare Middlemiss (Salt Lake City: Deseret Book, 1976), 59–60.

30. Hugh B. Brown, as cited in *LDS Speaker's Sourcebook*, Stan Zenk and Curtis Taylor, eds. (Salt Lake City: Aspen Books, 1991), 318.

CHAPTER TWO

ABRAHAM: FATHER OF THE FAITHFUL

PHILIP WIGHTMAN

ELDER JAMES E. TALMAGE defines faith as "full confidence and trust in the being, purposes, and words of God."[1] The life of the great patriarch Abraham demonstrates how we can come to this level of assurance in our knowledge of and relationship with God. It also shows the results of such faith. His life of faith illustrates the pattern established by the Son of God that all must follow to obtain eternal life.

Abraham's is not the story of a lowly shepherd who wandered the deserts as an exile from his native land without plan or purpose. He was not, as some suppose, living under some lesser form of God's law, but enjoyed a fulness of the gospel with all its inherent blessings. Through the eyes of inspired writers we see in Abraham a noble spirit who sat in council with the Gods before coming to the earth. He was foreordained, called, and elected to come to earth and render great service to God's children. His birth came through a chosen lineage, though from a line that was in apostasy. He overcame by faith his apostate surroundings, and through the covenant process took up and fulfilled his premortal calling. He then went on to make his calling and election sure. He died, and we know through modern revelation that he has now entered into the rest of the Lord, to rule and reign with his posterity forever (D&C 132:37).

As we consider the pattern exemplified by the life of the man regarded as the "'father of the faithful,'"[2] let us remember that it played out over a long period of time. Abraham lived to be 175 years old. His faith did not spring up overnight. We need to understand that Abraham had a lifetime to nourish and develop the faith necessary to make the profound sacrifice that God would ultimately require of him. Lorenzo Snow illuminates this point:

> And if we could read in detail the life of Abraham, or the lives of other great and holy men, we would doubtless find that their efforts to be righteous were not always crowned with success. Hence we should not be discouraged if we should be overcome in a weak moment;...
>
> It can hardly be supposed that Abraham inherited such a state of mind from his idolatrous parents; but it is consistent to believe that under the blessings of God he was enabled to acquire it, after going through a similar warfare with the flesh as we are, and doubtless being overcome at times and then overcoming until he was enabled to stand so severe a test.[3]

Abraham's journey of faith began with the word of God. Paul tells us that faith comes by hearing the word of God (Rom. 10:17). The word of God came to Abraham in at least two ways: He had access to scripture (Abr. 1:28), and he was taught by priesthood leaders of the day.

Abraham had in his possession "the records of the fathers," which contained "a knowledge of the...creation" (Abr. 1:31). We have available today the Book of Moses, a record presumably similar to the records accessible to Abraham. These writings teach of the first man, Adam, and his wife, Eve. They knew God as their father. In the Garden of Eden they walked and talked with him and received his instruction. We then read of the Fall which separated Adam and Eve from their Father's presence. Through faith in their Heavenly Father's continued existence, the man and wife called on God in prayer to learn of his will for them. They were taught the gospel, the plan whereby they could come back into his presence through faith in Jesus Christ. By following God's will, they eventually walked with him once more.

Thus, the pattern was established. Others would follow it, such as Enoch and the Saints of his day. By doing so, they too overcame the effects of the Fall and once again walked with God.

By word of mouth, through the written word, and by continuing revelation, humankind retained the knowledge of God's existence and plan and were able to lay hold on all the blessings of their father Adam. As Abraham read and learned of these things, he had faith that he too could have the blessings enjoyed by those that preceded him. He trusted that, like the prophets of old, he could come to know God for himself by living the gospel as they had.

Abraham also learned of God through at least one great man of faith that was his contemporary. Melchizedek was the king of Salem and was known as the Prince of peace (JST Gen. 14:33). He administered ordinances to Abraham and ordained him to the priesthood (Gen. 14:18–20; D&C 84:14). We are told that Melchizedek and his people were translated and taken to the city of Enoch (JST Gen. 14:32–34).[4] What lessons Abraham must have learned from his associations with this great high priest.

The gospel law that Abraham learned is known to us today as the *new and everlasting covenant.* The very name of this composite of gospel laws teaches us that covenants are central to the plan for our salvation. Abraham, like each of us who seeks exaltation, was required to willingly enter into sacred agreements to do God's will. Such covenants are keys that access eternal truth. As we make and keep covenants, God can then teach us of the mysteries of godliness. Through covenants we, like Abraham, learn of God's will and the blessings that result through faithful observance of the same.

God administers his covenants through ordinances. Baptism is the first of these ordinances. We think of it as a gateway to the path that leads back to God, and it is only the beginning in our covenant relationship with God. When baptized, we covenant to take upon ourselves the name of Christ. In doing so, we demonstrate our willingness to be recognized as members of his church. We profess our belief in him and commit to do the work of his kingdom. In addition, we must be willing to receive more ordinances with their attending covenants. Elder Dallin Oaks has taught:

> Willingness to take upon us the name of Jesus Christ can therefore be understood as willingness to take upon us the

> authority of Jesus Christ. According to this meaning, by partaking of the sacrament we witness our willingness to participate in the sacred ordinances of the temple and to receive the highest blessings available through the name and by the authority of the Savior when he chooses to confer them upon us.[5]

The Lord tells us that we may know the righteous based on their willingness to come unto him to be relieved of the bondage of their sins:

> For whoso cometh not unto me is under the bondage of sin.
>
> And whoso receiveth not my voice is not acquainted with my voice, and is not of me.
>
> And by this you may know the righteous from the wicked, and that the whole world groaneth under sin and darkness even now. (D&C 84: 51–53)

Bondage is lifted as sins are remitted through the waters of baptism.

Though we have no record of Abraham's baptism, as it is required of all God's faithful, we can assume that he received the ordinance. He seems to tell us as much when he says that he was a follower of righteousness:

> And, finding there was greater happiness and peace and rest for me, I sought for the blessings of the fathers, and the right whereunto I should be ordained to administer the same; having been myself a follower of righteousness, desiring also to be one who possessed great knowledge, and to be a greater follower of righteousness, and to possess a greater knowledge, and to be a father of many nations, a prince of peace, and desiring to receive instructions, and to keep the commandments of God, I became a rightful heir, a High Priest, holding the right belonging to the fathers. (Abr. 1:2)

If indeed he was baptized, then as Elder Oaks has said, Abraham would have been under covenant to seek the greater blessings found only in the temple. This may help explain Abraham's statement that he sought greater knowledge and greater righteousness.

This would necessitate that he continue to repent and be worthy of the Holy Ghost to lead him in the sanctification process.

President Ezra Taft Benson confirms that the blessings of the priesthood Abraham sought included the blessings of temple ordinances.[6] As indicated by Abraham, even though he was righteous and had knowledge, his faith moved him to pursue greater levels of righteousness. He was not content to be good, but sought to be godly. He was not content to have knowledge, but sought for greater knowledge. What he sought could only be given to him after he received the sacred ordinances of the House of the Lord. These ordinances would not only led to further covenants, but they would also teach him the purposes of life and the process to be followed to obtain God's presence. For in the temple and through its ordinances, as described by David O. McKay, we take a "symbolic journey through eternity, a symbolic return, step by step, into the presence of the divine."[7]

The scriptures indicate that Abraham received the blessings he sought. As Abraham walks uprightly before God, on numerous occasions God promises Abraham blessings—blessings that we understand to be covenant blessings (Gen. 12:2–3; 13:14–17; 15:18; 17:1–8). Let us look at one as an example:

> And when Abram was ninety years old and nine, the LORD appeared to Abram, and said unto him, I am the Almighty God; walk before me, and be thou perfect.
>
> And I will make my covenant between me and thee, and will multiply thee exceedingly.
>
> And Abram fell on his face and God talked with him, saying,
>
> As for me, behold, my covenant is with thee, and thou shalt be a father of many nations.
>
> Neither shall thy name any more be called Abram, but thy name shall be Abraham; for a father of many nations have I made thee.
>
> And I will make thee exceeding fruitful, and I will make nations of thee, and kings shall come out of thee.
>
> And I will establish my covenant between me and thee and thy seed after thee in their generations for an everlasting covenant, to be a God unto thee, and to thy seed after thee.

> And I will give unto thee, and to thy seed after thee, the land wherein thou art a stranger, all the land of Canaan, for an everlasting possession; and I will be their God. (Gen. 17:1–8)

These words were not merely intended to make Abraham feel good. They have serious implications. God expected Abraham to be perfect, to worship, or emulate, only him. Abraham's faith could not stop short of this. God promised Abraham that if he would worship him, he would make Abraham the father of many nations, and his posterity would be eternal. Abraham would receive an eternal inheritance on earth, where he and his descendants could dwell throughout the eternities. This would be accompanied by a promised priesthood whereby he and his posterity would be kings. They would be given eternal dominion, or the right to rule and reign forever.

Simply stated, these are covenant promises. These blessings would only be realized if Abraham obeyed God's will. The stories preserved about Abraham show that he did. They seem to have been purposefully selected to present a life governed by covenants entered into and obeyed. The stories of Abraham show in at least five ways how Abraham, through faith, remained true to his covenants with God.

Obedience

Abraham learned by experience, as well as by revelation, that we are here on earth to be proven in all things, to see if we will be obedient to the will of God (Abr. 3:25). The obedience required would be based on knowing God's will and having enough faith to do it even without knowing the exact outcome. One of the first examples of such faithful obedience on Abraham's part is found in Genesis 12:1. Abraham was commanded by the Lord to leave the land of his fathers and go to a land that he knew not. The Apostle Paul tells us:

> By faith Abraham, when he was called to go out into a place which he should after receive for an inheritance, obeyed; and he went out, not knowing whither he went.

> By faith he sojourned in the land of promise, as in a strange country, dwelling in tabernacles with Isaac and Jacob, the heirs with him of the same promise:
>
> For he looked for a city which hath foundations, whose builder and maker is God. (Heb. 11:8–10)

Paul implies that Abraham left the city of his fathers and spent his life as something of a nomad. His ties were not to the earth or to earthly things. Instead, he trusted that God would provide him with an inheritance in the city of God, or the celestial kingdom.

There is another way to look at this passage of scripture as well. Our time on earth is not to be spent merely in anticipation of a better life to come. We are told to seek for the establishment of Zion (D&C 6:6–7). God expects us to establish heaven on earth. Abraham was commanded to "remember the days of Enoch thy father" (JST Gen. 13:13). It seems likely that God wanted Abraham to seek for Zion like Enoch or Melchizedek had done before him. Without knowing where or when, Abraham acted with the assurance that God would provide him with such a city, a place of peace and refuge, where he too could walk with God. Though Abraham may never have found the promised place of refuge during his lifetime, he continued to be a minister for the name of God in a strange land until he died, seeking the perfection of the saints and winning souls for Christ (Abr. 2:6, 15).

Another great test of Abraham's faith and his willingness to obey the Lord would come when he went to Egypt. As Abraham drew near to Egypt, he was commanded by God to tell the Pharaoh that Sarah was his sister so that Pharaoh would not kill Abraham and take his wife because of her beauty. After Abraham did so, Sarah was taken from him and placed in the harem of the king. Abraham now had to trust that God would protect her. According to an account found in the *Genesis Apocryphon,* Abraham's faith led him to turn to God in prayer:

> And I, Abram, wept aloud that night, I and my nephew Lot, because Sarai had been taken from me by force. I prayed that night. I begged and implored and I said in my sorrow, while my tears ran down: Blessed art Thou, O God Most High, Master of all the worlds. Thou are Lord and King of all

> things and Thou rulest over all the kings of the earth and Thou judgest them all. I cry now before Thee my Lord, against Pharaoh of Zoan the king of Egypt, because of my wife who is taken from me by force. Judge him for me, and I shall see Thy mighty hand lifted against him and against all his household, that he may not defile my wife this night (separating her) from me. And they shall know Thee, my Lord, that Thou art the Lord of all the kings of the earth. I wept and was sorrowful.[8]

The Lord heard Abraham's prayers and intervened, protecting Sarah until she could be returned to her husband. They were then sent from Egypt with great riches. Sarah was given a handmaid, Hagar, who would later play an important role in the fulfilling of Abraham's promised blessings.[9] These blessings of obedience came, though, as all such blessings do according to scripture—after the trial of his faith.

The Law of the Gospel

As previously indicated, Abraham had the records of the fathers, the scriptures of his day. Much of what he knew of God and his ways most certainly came from his study of these sacred records. How else could he really understand what principles required his obedience? He would need to search them, for the words of eternal life were found there. God will not reveal new truth if we ignore what we have already been given. The law of the gospel required Abraham, as it does us, to seek the principles of salvation as found in the scriptures. Elder McConkie taught the importance of the scriptures in this way:

> However talented men may be in administrative matters; however eloquent they may be in expressing their views: however learned they may be in worldly things—they will be denied the sweet whisperings of the Spirit that might have been theirs unless they pay the price of studying, pondering, and praying about the scriptures. [10]

It is through careful, meditative contemplation of such scripture that the Lord makes his will known to his children. There can be little question that Abraham was influenced by what he read. In his own words we read:

> But the records of the fathers, even the patriarchs, concerning the right of Priesthood, the Lord my God preserved in mine own hands; therefore a knowledge of the beginning of the creation, and also of the planets, and of the stars, as they were made known unto the fathers, have I kept even unto this day, and I shall endeavor to write some of these things upon this record, for the benefit of my posterity that shall come after me. (Abr. 1:31)

As Abraham learned through the written word of the ultimate blessings of the priesthood, his faith led him to seek them for himself. He also taught what he learned to others and was successful in bringing souls to Christ (Abr. 2:15). Abraham understood that knowing and living the law of the gospel requires diligent scripture study.

Chastity

We may ask, as did Joseph Smith, how God could justify Abraham in having more than one wife. Joseph Smith learned, through revelation, that whatever God requires is right.[11] Though he had more than one wife, Abraham was true to his commitment of chastity because he did nothing but that which God commanded him to do. He took Hagar as a wife as well as other concubines only after he received instruction from the Lord to do so (D&C 132:29–37). As Jacob tells us in the Book of Mormon, God gives such commands at times in order to raise up a righteous posterity (Jacob 2:30). This, of course, is at the heart of God's promises to Abraham (Gen. 17:4; Abr. 3:12–14). Once again, these blessings were possible because of his willingness to fully trust God's direction.

Consecration

If we expect to receive all that God possesses, we must be willing to consecrate all that we have to that end. Abraham was required, as we are, to put the kingdom of God first in his life. Obtaining the great blessing of godhood would demand his total dedication, and he would have to consecrate the things of this world to obtain those of a higher. In doing so, he would show God where the desires of his heart truly lay.

When Abraham and Lot entered the promised land, Abraham allowed Lot to choose first as to where he would settle. Abraham had God's promise that all the land he could see would be for his eternal inheritance. Abraham had the faith that he could return to God's presence as a king and a priest and receive a fulness of his glory. He trusted in the promise of eternal posterity. He knew, as we should, that the world has little to offer in comparison to such grand eternal rewards. Where Lot chose to live would be at best just temporary, and his choice provides us with excellent contrast in the choices available to all of us. His choosing the rich, fertile plains of Sodom and Gomorrah proved to be shortsighted. It was not long before God destroyed the wicked people in those cities along with all that they held dear. As Elder Neal A. Maxwell quoted English clergyman William Law as saying: "If you have not chosen the Kingdom of God, it will make in the end no difference what you have chosen instead."[12] This is true of all that this world has to offer. The day will come when it ends, for it is all temporary. On the other hand, the blessings Abraham sought will never end. They are as eternal as the God that promised them.

Perhaps the best example we have of Abraham's consecrated life is found in the account of his relationship with the King of Salem. We are told that Melchizedek, as the high priest, was the keeper of the storehouse of God and received tithes for the poor.

> Wherefore, Abram paid unto him tithes of all that he had, of all the riches which he possessed, which God had given him more than that which he had need. (JST Gen. 14:39)

To those familiar with the law of consecration as revealed to Joseph Smith, this sounds very similar (D&C 42:30–34; 119:5). Abraham was committing his excess to the building up of God's kingdom.

Sacrifice

In spite of the fact that Abraham had been obedient, had lived the law of the gospel, had been chaste, and had consecrated his life to the kingdom of God, the Lord required one more test of his faith before all the blessings of the fathers could be his. We read in a revelation given to Joseph Smith:

> Verily I say unto you, all among them who know their hearts are honest, and are broken, and their spirits contrite, and are willing to observe their covenants by sacrifice—yea, every sacrifice which I, the Lord, shall command—they are accepted of me. (D&C 97:8)

Abraham's God required that he keep his covenants at any cost. Exaltation would require a willingness to sacrifice all things, even life itself. In Abraham's case, he was asked to go beyond the sacrifice of his own life and sacrifice the life of his long awaited son. He had learned early in his life of the evils of human sacrifice. His own life had been endangered by such wicked and idolatrous practices (Abr. 1:7, 12, 15). Abraham had been God's spokesman against such things. Now he was being asked to go against everything he had been taught and every tender feeling he possessed as a father. He would also be jeopardizing the promise from God he most desired, that of posterity through Sarah. John Taylor explains just how difficult this sacrifice must have been:

> I speak of these things to show how men are to be tried. I heard Joseph Smith say—and I presume Brother Snow heard him also—in preaching to the Twelve in Nauvoo, that the Lord would get hold of their heart strings and wrench them, and that they would have to be tried as Abraham was tried. Well, some of the Twelve could not stand it. They faltered and fell by the way. It was not everybody that could stand what Abraham stood. And Joseph said that if God had known any other way whereby he could have touched Abraham's feelings more acutely and more keenly he would have done so. It was not only his parental feelings that were touched. There was something else besides. He had the promise that in him and in his seed all the nations of the earth should be blessed; that his seed should be multiplied as the stars of the heaven and as the sand upon the sea shore. He had looked forward through the vista of future ages and seen, by the

> spirit of revelation, myriads of his people rise up through whom God would convey intelligence, light and salvation to a world. But in being called upon to sacrifice his son it seemed as though all his prospects pertaining to posterity were to come to naught. But he had faith in God, and he fulfilled the thing that was required of him. Yet we cannot conceive of anything that could be more trying and more perplexing than the position in which he was placed.[13]

Conclusion

Having kept his covenants by sacrifice, even through this ultimate test, God swore an oath that Abraham would indeed receive the eternal rewards he had sought for over one hundred years:

> And the angel of the LORD called unto Abraham out of heaven the second time,
>
> And said, By myself have I sworn, saith the LORD, for because thou hast done this thing, and hast not withheld thy son, thine only son:
>
> That in blessing I will bless thee, and in multiplying I will multiply thy seed as the stars of the heaven, and as the sand which is upon the sea shore. (Gen. 22:15–17)

Abraham was now worthy to have his calling and election made sure, having sought the blessings of the fathers before him and obtained them by faith. We know, through revelation, that he was among the faithful that met the Savior in the spirit world (D&C 138:16, 41). We know he was given power to come forth in the first resurrection and that he rules today as a god (D&C 132:29). Now as his sons and daughters we must seek those same blessings. God, being no respecter of persons and a God that cannot lie, will reward our faith even as he did the faith of Abraham. Joseph Smith had such faith and encouraged us to seek the same:

> Most assuredly it is, however, that the ancients, though persecuted and afflicted by men, obtained from God promises of such weight and glory, that our hearts are often filled with gratitude that we are even permitted to look upon them

while we contemplate that there is no respect of persons in His sight, and that in every nation, he that feareth God and worketh righteousness, is acceptable with Him.... And though we cannot claim these promises which were made to the ancients for they are not our property, merely because they were made to the ancient Saints, yet if we are the children of the Most High, and are called with the same calling with which they were called, and embrace the same covenant that they embraced, and are faithful to the testimony of our Lord as they were, we can approach the Father in the name of Christ as they approached Him, and for ourselves obtain the same promises. These promises, when obtained, if ever by us, will not be because Peter, John, and the other Apostles, with the churches at Sardis, Pergamos, Philadelphia, and elsewhere, walked in the fear of God, and had power and faith to reveal and obtain them; but it will be because we, ourselves, have faith and approach God in the name of His Son Jesus Christ, even as they did; and when these promises are obtained, they will be promises directly to us, or they will do us no good. They will be communicated for our benefit, being our own property (through the gift of God), earned by our own diligence in keeping His commandments and walking uprightly before Him. If not, to what end serves the Gospel of our Lord Jesus Christ, and why was it ever communicated to us?[14]

NOTES

1. James E. Talmage, *Articles of Faith* (Salt Lake City: The Church of Jesus Christ of Latter-day Saints, 1925), 96.

2. See *Bible Dictionary:* Abraham.

3. Lorenzo Snow, "Blessings of the Gospel Only Obtained by Compliance to the Law," reprint, *Ensign*, October 1971, 19, 20.

4. See also Bruce R. McConkie, *Mormon Doctrine,* 2d ed. (Salt Lake City: Bookcraft, 1966), 804–5.

5. Dallin H. Oaks, *Ensign*, May 1985, 81.

6. Ezra Taft Benson, *Ensign*, August 1985, 9.

7. Marion D. Hanks (devotional address delivered at Ricks College in Rexburg, Idaho, 27 November, 1990).

8. *The Genesis Apocryphon,* cited by Thomas W. Mackay, in "Abraham in Egypt," *BYU Studies*, Summer 1970, 445–46.

9. Ibid., 450–51.

10. Bruce R. McConkie, as quoted by Ezra Taft Benson, *Ensign,* May 1986, 81.

11. Joseph Smith, *Teachings of the Prophet Joseph Smith,* comp. Joseph Fielding Smith (Salt Lake City: Deseret Book, 1976), 256; hereafter *TPJS.*

12. Neal A. Maxwell, *The Smallest Part* (Salt Lake City: Deseret Book, 1973), 1.

13. John Taylor, in *Journal of Discourses* (Liverpool, England: Latter-Day Saints' Book Depot 1855–86), 24:264.

14. *TPJS,* 65–66.

CHAPTER THREE

IS ANYTHING TOO HARD FOR THE LORD? THE FAITH OF SARAH

AUDREY M. GODFREY

Introduction

PAUL, ENCOURAGING THE Roman Saints to remain faithful, used as exemplars the great steadfast individuals of religious history known to them. As their feminine example he chose Sarah, a woman of faith chosen to be the mother of a posterity "so many as the stars of the sky in multitude, and as the sand which is by the sea shore innumerable" (Heb. 11:12).

Like Sarah, all who come to earth have a mission to perform. Our patriarchal blessings, our understanding of the plan of salvation, and personal revelation help us learn what our specific purpose is. Mordecai informed his niece, Esther, that she had been chosen "for such a time as this" to deliver the Jews from bondage (Esth. 4:14). An angel announced to Mary her role as the mother of Jesus (Luke 1:31). And an amazing message to Sarah in her old age informed her that she would be "a mother of nations; kings of people shall be of her" (Gen. 17:16).

The reactions of these three women exemplify how we ought to receive guidance from the Lord. Esther simply created a setting wherein she could fulfill her calling. Mary accepted her mission by saying, "be it unto me according to thy word" (Luke 1:38). Abraham and Sarah's laughter indicated both their joy and astonishment. But all faithfully accepted God's direction. Today, even though our roles more likely involve temple work, missionary service, parenting, service to others, or callings in the Church, our reactions can be as positive as those of our biblical exemplars and as faithfully carried out.

Peter's first epistle to the Romans instructed both women and men in their behavior as Saints (1 Pet. 3:6–7). His directive reminds women they are the daughters of Sarah as long as they live righteous lives. The fact that this and other scriptures cite Sarah as a faithful exemplar suggests that closer scrutiny of her life will enable latter-day women and men to be more diligent in their faith as well.

A Lesson in Personal Progress

After leaving Ur, Abraham and Sarah spent two years in Haran, where the promise of being the progenitors of the chosen people was given. Upon being told of her mission in life, Sarah might easily have assumed she and Abraham would settle down and she would bear many children. But the fruition of this blessing was long in coming, and in the meantime Sarah wisely went on with her life.

A recent book about Chinese women in Chungking during World War II tells of their efforts to create joy out of catastrophe: "What was worse, we asked among ourselves, to sit and wait for our own deaths with proper somber faces? or to choose our own happiness?"[1] Often, we miss wonderful experiences and thwart our personal growth by looking backward or forward instead of gaining all we can from present opportunities. Sarah's example is a lesson in individual progress while waiting for promised blessings. In Haran she assisted Abraham in teaching the gospel and winning many converts. She practiced her religion.

One writer posits that Sarah functioned as a priestess in her ancient culture. She argues that Sarah was initially childless, not barren, in keeping with her exalted religious role. "The recurring mention of the barrenness of the matriarchs is especially significant in view of the fact that the primary purpose of marriage in a patriarchal world is to provide a husband's family with male heirs."[2] She thinks that Abraham did not take another wife when

Sarah failed to produce an heir because of his respect for her divine calling. With the insight we have from and into the gospel plan we might also argue that Abraham and Sarah loved each other and were waiting faithfully for God to send them children. However, it is unusual that at no time did Abraham exercise his patriarchal powers in his interaction with Sarah, even requesting that she tell Pharaoh she was his sister rather than commanding her to do so. This deference from him in a male dominated culture indicates something unique about their relationship which may well have had religious significance.

Other references also support a special religious calling. The *Aggadah,* which is part of the literature of the Oral Law in rabbinic teaching, labeled Sarah as one of the seven prophetesses able to "discern…by means of the Holy Spirit." Her prophetic gifts were considered superior even to those of Abraham, according to these early narratives.[3] Hugh Nibley alludes to her elevated status in his article "The Sacrifice of Sarah." He writes that prior to her marriage Sarah "was well-known as Jisa, 'the Seeress,' either because she had the gift of prophecy or because of her shining beauty, or both."[4] The meanings given Sarah's names in various translations also assign her an elevated status. The usual interpretation is "princess," but other connotations include "chieftainess" and "ruler."

As Sarah waited for the fulfillment of the promise she supported Abraham in his endeavors and followed him in his travels. Already Sarah had left all that was familiar—her friends and family, her culture and traditions—in Ur. Now as famine again threatened, the couple left Haran for Egypt, a journey which would further test Sarah's trust in the Lord.

A Trial of Faith in Egypt

As Abraham and Sarah journeyed they built altars and sacrificed to Jehovah, who gave them strength and guidance (Gen. 12:7). This guidance included Abraham's being instructed to have Sarah identify herself as his sister to protect his life from an Egyptian ruler who would desire Sarah for his harem because of her great beauty. The *Encyclopedia Judaica* says that ancient custom permitted a man to adopt a woman as his sister upon marriage to give her greater legal and social status, so Abraham had a precedent for referring to her as his sister. Furthermore, most biblical experts concur that Sarah was Abraham's half sister; the scriptures indicate that they had the same father (see Gen. 20:12) but different mothers.[5]

By agreeing to Abraham's request Sarah was taken into Pharaoh's household and thus risked losing her chance to be the wife through whom Abraham would bring forth his chosen posterity. As S. Kent Brown says, "Egypt represented...a haven from the famine...[but also] a place of testing for Sarah."[6] Apocryphal sources suggest a scenario of what occurred during this trial in Sarah's life. After Abraham related the warning to Sarah and made his entreaty, the account says, "Sarai wept that night because of my words."[7] When Pharaoh took Sarah into his harem, Abraham spent the night in prayer and weeping. He begged the Lord to protect Sarah that she might not be defiled. Sarah, too, prayed. She reminded Jehovah that he had commanded Abraham to go to Canaan—"a strange land"—to people they did not know. This they had done. Now she beseeched God to remember their faithfulness and asked for deliverance and mercy. God hearkened to their prayers and protected Sarah. But it may have been as long as two years before Pharaoh returned Sarah to Abraham undefiled, along with gifts of sheep, oxen, asses, servants, and camels (see Gen. 12:11–20). It is probable that Sarah received Hagar as a servant at this time.[8]

When we live righteously, as Sarah did, God hears our prayers and gives us strength to bear our burdens and survive the challenges we encounter. For the last year of her life, my mother—widowed and alone—lived with daily pain from bone cancer. She often could not sleep because of the pain. She said God was her companion and her only comfort during the long, dark hours of the night. Her story parallels those of many people who endure physical or emotional pain, whose strength to bear their burdens comes from God's love. Surely the Lord comforted Sarah in her separation from Abraham, even while He tried her patience and her faith (Mosiah 23:21).

Sarah in Hebron

Having escaped from Pharaoh's harem, perhaps Sarah and Abraham heaved sighs of relief as they distanced themselves from Egypt. We know they again offered sacrifices as they journeyed to Hebron (Gen. 13:1–4), the place which would become Sarah's home for the rest of her life—except for a period of time when King Abimelech desired Sarah for a wife. But before any of this took place, a momentous event occurred—an event which made Sarah's third great act of faith even more impressive.

The Promise of Posterity Reaffirmed

The Lord repeated his marvelous promise of innumerable seed before the couple arrived in Hebron, and again after Abraham paid his tithes to Melchizedek. At this time, Abraham questioned the Lord about the promised seed. After all, much time had passed with no offspring forthcoming. Surely Sarah, too, wondered when the time would come. She most likely expected the lifting of the constraints of childlessness when she received the promise of her role as the covenant mother.

Ten years passed. We don't know what occurred during this time, but if Sarah was true to form she probably filled her days with good works, entertaining travelers, and caring for Abraham and her household. Apocryphal sources call her a hospitable woman: "her dough increased and a light burned" from Sabbath to Sabbath.[9]

Finally Sarah determined to help the covenant be fulfilled by giving her servant, Hagar, to Abraham as his wife to produce a child for Sarah, a practice which conformed to Mesopotamian rules governing the conduct of women. Surely, this sacrifice was difficult for a woman who yearned for her own promised children.

Hagar conceived, but instead of rejoicing, Sarah found it difficult to accept Hagar's good fortune. Her faith wavered and she banished Hagar. But God was in control and admonished Hagar to return and submit herself to Sarah (Gen. 16).

As a sign that a covenant still existed, God established the law of circumcision and the noble couple's names were changed.

Until then they had been known as Abram and Sarai, meaning "exalted father" and "a princess to her own people," respectively, but now they became Abraham and Sarah, meaning "father of a multitude" and "a princess for all mankind," names which reflected their expanded roles. The Lord sensed Sarah's wavering faith and through her husband reassured her: "And I will bless her, and give thee a son also of her: yea, I will bless her, and she shall be a mother of nations; kings of people shall be of her" (Gen. 17:16). What comfort this must have given Sarah to realize God had not forgotten her and that if she would remain faithful her womb would be fruitful. Still, much time had passed, and such a promise at first seemed incredible.

Is Anything too Hard for the Lord?

Abraham laughed at the impossibility of such a child coming to a man of one hundred and a woman of ninety. The Lord repeated the promise and later sent three angels to reinforce his words. During this second visit, Sarah also laughed, whereupon the Lord asked a question in response to her doubt: "Is any thing too hard for the Lord?" (Gen. 18:14).

A contemporary Christian writer counsels us that faith requires a decision from those who are tested, and perhaps we need to think deeply before we are called upon to make those decisions. While a member of the Council of the Twelve, President Spencer W. Kimball told Church members to build "reservoirs of faith" to meet the challenges of life.[10] If we are so prepared we will realize that nothing is impossible to the Lord. The scriptures remind us of this again and again. In Exodus 15, Miriam's song of exultation after the Israelites are safely across the Red Sea reads, "Who is like unto thee, O Lord, among the gods? Who is like thee, glorious in holiness, fearful in praises, *doing wonders?*" (Ex. 15:11; emphasis added).

When an angel visits Mary to announce her pregnancy, he answers her queries as to how an unmarried woman can become the mother of the Son of God by telling her that an aging Elizabeth is also expecting a child. Then he says, "For with God nothing shall be impossible" (Luke 1:37). Jesus personally taught this truth to his disciples when he said, "If ye have faith, nothing shall be impossible unto you" (Matt. 17:20).

The Nephites are reminded that God will work wonders "among the children of men according to their faith" (2 Ne. 26:13). I saw this promise fulfilled in the 1970s in a little branch in West Virginia. The small congregation had a piano but no one who could play it. Then a missionary couple arrived. Though the sister could not play the piano she was so moved by their plight that she prayed for a solution to their problem. Thinking, no doubt, that someone would be converted or move into the branch who could play, she was disappointed. But one Sunday she sat at the piano and began to play. For the remainder of her service in the branch she possessed the gift of piano playing. Her faith resulted in a wondrous demonstration of God's love for his Saints. This blessing occurs repeatedly in diverse ways throughout the Church among faithful members. Indeed, there is nothing too hard for the Lord.

Isaac's Birth: a Blessing of Faith

In the April 1988 general conference of the Church, Elder Russell M. Nelson promised that if we "foster [our] faith and "fuse [our] focus" we will "be given power and protection from on high."[11] This principle of faith was tested once more before Sarah's promised child could be conceived. She again found herself the object of desire, this time by King Abimelech. But Sarah's love for Abraham and desire to protect him caused her to rely on her faith and submit to God's will. The scriptures tell us her steadfastness was rewarded. The Lord told Abimelech in a dream that Sarah was not Abraham's sister but his wife. Fearing the wrath of God, he restored Sarah to Abraham, chastising her in the process—perhaps to save face (see Gen. 20).

Now, after all the years of waiting, Sarah finally bore her only child, Isaac. The scriptures record her joy: "And Sarah said, God hath made me to laugh, so that all that hear will laugh with me. And she said, Who would have said unto Abraham, that Sarah should have given children suck? for I have born him a son in his old age" (Gen. 21:6–7).

On the day Isaac was weaned, Abraham threw a party. But during the festivities Sarah observed something which disturbed her. She saw Hagar's son, Ishmael, mocking Isaac. Because of Sarah's harsh reaction, we can assume this was not just an act of teasing, but one which endangered Isaac's upbringing (Gen. 21:9–13). Some have suggested that Ishmael was disrespectful of things Sarah held sacred. In any case, Sarah felt threatened by the idolatrous practices of Hagar and so she banished Hagar and Ishmael. This is more understandable when we consider that Sarah and Abraham had left their home in Ur to escape the wickedness there and that her foremost concern was Isaac's religious upbringing.

Sarah as Exemplar

That Sarah's motherly teachings and love for Isaac were successful and reciprocated is revealed after her death when Isaac brings Rebekah to his mother's tent. The scriptures tell us that this marriage and the arrival of his new wife "comforted" Isaac "after his mother's death" (Gen. 24:67). The fulfillment of the Lord's promise that Sarah would be the mother of many nations and a covenant people would come to pass through her son, Isaac, and through her grandsons Esau and, in particular, Jacob.

Through the ages, prophets have cited Sarah as an example of faith and righteousness. Paul encouraged the Saints at Corinth by using Abraham and Sarah as examples to demonstrate that blessings come "through the righteousness of faith" (Rom. 4:13). Peter admonished Christian women that as long as they "do well" and show respect for their husbands, they are daughters of Sarah (1 Pet. 3:5–6). In a beautiful passage written to give hope to Israel in Babylon, Isaiah declared,

> Hearken to me, ye that follow after righteousness, ye that seek the Lord: look unto the rock whence ye are hewn, and to the hole of the pit whence ye are digged.
>
> Look unto Abraham your father, and unto Sarah that bare you. (Isa. 51:1–2)

Isaiah "spoke to laughing young women and to heartbroken old men," priests, sages, children playing in the streets, mothers and merchants. He spoke to parents, grandchildren, those who remembered life in Jerusalem and those who did not. All longed to return to Jerusalem with a descendant of David as their king. Isaiah urged them to emulate Sarah and Abraham and have courage.[12]

Modern-day Israel would do well to look to these ancient parents also. Isaiah speaks to us as well—to women torn between children and career, to men of the priesthood who have exercised unrighteous dominion over these women, to children struggling to find their way through drugs, to those who live good lives and still are discouraged. We should remember that when we add our faith to God's power all things are possible to do and to bear.

In the years following Adam and Eve's expulsion from Eden, as their descendants multiplied, so too did wickedness. The Lord sent the Flood to destroy the wicked and saved Noah and his family of righteous people. When wickedness returned and people built the Tower of Babel, the Lord scattered them upon the earth. Each event brought about the opportunity for a new beginning of righteousness. Katheryn Pfisterer Darr suggests that "the singling-out of Abram and Sarai appears as still another attempt by God to set things right."[13] The Lord told Abraham and Sarah to leave their native land and kindred, and go to a land that he would show them. He promised to make of them a great nation, to bless them and all the families of the earth by them (Gen. 12:1–3).

As descendants of these covenant people we too must make new beginnings. We can institute righteous homes as we marry. We can stand with courage against wickedness. At times we must make sacrifices as needed to perfect ourselves and help God's kingdom move forward. While we do so, we should look for the wondrous power of God and develop and exercise our faith. As we are obedient and righteous we can be as Sarah—"full of years, great with child, great with hope, laughing at the impossibility of it all."[14]

NOTES

1. Amy Tan, *The Joy Luck Club* (New York: Ivy Books, 1989), 12.

2. Savina J. Teubal, *Sarah the Priestess, the First Matriarch of Genesis* (Athens, Ohio: Swallow Press, 1984), 102.

3. *Encyclopedia Judaica* (Jerusalem: Keter Publishing House Jerusalem Ltd., 1972), 14:869.

4. Hugh Nibley, "The Sacrifice of Sarah," *Improvement Era,* April 1970, 88.

5. *Judaica,* 14:868.

6. S. Kent Brown, "Biblical Egypt: Land of Refuge, Land of Bondage," *Ensign,* September 1980, 46.

7. Cited in Thomas W. Mackay, "Abraham in Egypt: a Collation of Evidence for the Case of the Missing Wife," *BYU Studies* 10, no. 4, 442.

8. Ibid., 446–47.

9. *Judaica,* 14:869

10. Spencer W. Kimball, *Faith Precedes the Miracle* (Salt Lake City: Deseret Book, 1972), 110.

11. Russell M. Nelson, *Ensign,* May 1988, 35.

12. See Katheryn Pfisterer Darr, *Far More Precious Than Jewels, Perspectives on Biblical Women,* (Louisville: Westminister/John Knox Press, 1991), 87–88.

13. Ibid., 92–93.

14. Ibid., 123.

Chapter Four

The Faith of Isaac

James A. Carver

Introduction

Probably the most recognized trinity of prophets in ancient scripture is Abraham, Isaac, and Jacob. A billion people in the Islamic world, fourteen million Jews, and almost one and one-half billion Christians recognize these three as great Hebrew prophets and patriarchs. Of the three, Isaac is perhaps the least known and written about. He is undoubtedly best remembered for his role in the Abrahamic test, when God commanded Abraham to offer his son, his "only Isaac,"[1] as a sacrifice.

A considerable number of the two billion people who revere Isaac as a prophet fail to understand his great significance as a type of Christ through the unusual commandment of sacrificial offering. In the actions of a father offering up a son, the greatest event in the history of all of God's creations—the atonement of Jesus Christ—is beautifully foreshadowed. Many who do not understand or recognize this typology continue to search for a Messiah who has already come.

This seemingly contradictory commandment given to Abraham also draws our attention to a war that often rages between faith and reason. However, as we can learn from the life of Isaac, faith and reason are not really opponents but work in tandem as great driving forces for good. Reason without faith can be spiritually hazardous to the natural man, just as a pseudo faith may hamper reason. Faith encompasses reason, but is much more than empirical or scientific thought. As Paul said, it is "the substance of things hoped for, the evidence of things not seen" (Heb. 11:1). Faith is based on physical evidence *and* spiritual substance. This faith, the kind Paul speaks of, played a dominant role in the decisions made by Isaac, as it did for his father Abraham.

It is this faith, too, which helps prophets become oracles and mighty servants of God. Sometimes we get the notion that things are automatic for prophets. We take it for granted that they will make the right decision, prove faithful when tested, and never doubt themselves, simply because they are prophets. But they, like us, are human. Prophets have feelings and emotions and, like us, sometimes make mistakes. However, they manage to overcome the weaknesses of mortality and rise above the failings of the natural man because of their exceeding faith in God and their Redeemer, Jesus Christ. This faith allows them to surpass natural weaknesses and doubts and reach high enough to overcome the obstacles that block their advancement and the progress of their people. The humanity of the ancient patriarchs is evident in their recorded histories, but from these histories one learns that it is faith which enabled them to put off the natural man (1 Cor. 2:14) and comply with God's will. The story of Isaac and his family is such a story of faith, a story of human weakness overcome by faith in God and a willingness to keep the commandments regardless of the price.

The Birth and Naming of Isaac

Our treatment of Isaac really needs to begin with Sarah, Abraham's wife. The scriptures indicate that Sarah was unable to bear children, and the days of possible childbearing were thought to have passed her by without fulfillment. As a result, Sarah consented to give her Egyptian handmaid Hagar to Abraham, so that perchance through her he could be blessed with the posterity God had promised. However, a problem developed when Hagar conceived a child. Sarah complained to Abraham that she was now despised in the eyes of Hagar. There may indeed have been more to Sarah's complaint than mere jealousy. According to the Jewish Rashi commentary,[2] Hagar accused Sarah of hypocritical righteousness, feeling that a righteous person would have been able to bear a child. Since Hagar had conceived quickly and Sarah had not conceived at all, Hagar thought that it must have been Sarah's unworthiness that stalled conception. In essence, Hagar considered herself to be more righteous in God's eyes than Sarah.[3]

Abraham, perceiving the conflict, allowed Sarah to deal with Hagar as she felt best. Genesis says that Sarah "dealt hardly with her" (Gen. 16:6). The word *hardly* is translated from the Hebrew word in the piel form meaning "to oppress" or "to afflict."[4] In the end, Sarah's treatment of Hagar caused her to flee into the wilderness. The fact that an angel of the Lord was sent to comfort and help Hagar may also be an indication that Sarah had indeed dealt "hardly" with her (see Gen. 16:7–11).

The angel instructed Hagar to return to Sarah and Abraham and foretold the birth of a son who would be blessed with a large posterity (JST Gen. 16:11–12). The Rashi commentary suggests that Hagar had conceived but had suffered a miscarriage, and when she fled into the wilderness the angel informed her she was again pregnant. This may explain the language of the angel when he said, "Behold, thou *art* with child, and shalt bear a son" (Gen. 16:11; emphasis added). The angel then counseled Hagar to return to the tents of Sarah and Abraham—which she did.[5] Hagar returned and delivered to Abraham a son whom they named Ishmael.

At eighty-six years of age, Abraham now had a son, Ishmael, to whom he could give his inheritance. However, the Lord was not finished with Abraham. He and Sarah would yet have a child in spite of the fact that they were both elderly, and this birth would be preceded by the annunciation of angels to Abraham and Sarah, in a type of the Savior's birth.

When the Lord told Abraham that Sarah would conceive and bear a son, the King James Bible says that Abraham "fell upon his face, and laughed" (Gen. 17:17). The Joseph Smith Translation corrects this by stating that "Abraham fell on his face and rejoiced" (JST Gen. 17:23). The problem in translation arises from the ancient text's use of the Hebrew word *yitschaq*, which translates either "to laugh" or "to rejoice," depending on context. In this case either translation could be defended based on the context of the passage. The Lord through the Joseph Smith Translation gives us the correct interpretation, which is "to rejoice." This was the emotion that Abraham displayed when he heard the Lord's promise.

On the other hand, when Sarah heard the angel informing Abraham of this miraculous birth, she "*laughed* within herself" (Gen. 18:12; emphasis added). When the angel confronts Sarah, she denies this, but the angel corrects Sarah, saying, "Nay; but thou didst laugh" (Gen. 18:15). Perhaps Sarah can be excused for her reaction to a certain extent. To Sarah the suggestion that she would conceive at ninety years of age and after a lifetime of being barren must have seemed outrageous. In any case, considering the dual translations of the Hebrew *yitschaq,* it was fitting that their child should be named Isaac, a name which comes from this same Hebrew word—to laugh, or to rejoice.

Isaac as a Type of Christ

Even the commandment of the Lord that the child be named Isaac has far reaching significance and symbolism (Gen. 17:19). Today, many educated people "laugh" at the atonement of Jesus, saying it is an impossibility, and even many Christians have lost faith in its significance and reality. But as we begin to understand and comprehend the Atonement, even slightly, we too rejoice at the possibilities Christ's sacrifice brings to each of us. Eventually, all the world will rejoice, even those who have lived a telestial law. This rejoicing will extend beyond our earth to all the worlds created through the Lord Jesus Christ (see Moses 1:35). As Abraham and Sarah would rejoice at the miraculous birth of their child, so would heaven and earth rejoice at the birth of Christ, for whom young Isaac would be a type or shadow.

However, while the annunciation of Isaac's birth by angels and some implications of his name can point to Christ, the greatest type we see in Isaac's life is in God's commandment to offer him as a sacrifice. One could ask why God chose to teach the Atonement in such a dramatic and unusual manner—one which on the surface involved violation of his laws. A possible answer is found in the Joseph Smith Translation of Genesis chapter 17.

The Nature of Apostasy in Abraham's Day

The JST indicates that Abraham lived in a time of widespread apostasy, even among the children of Shem, or children of the covenant. Unfortunately, Abraham's father, Terah, had also been swept into it. According to JST Genesis 17, a key element of Terah's apostasy was the rejection and misunderstanding of the real atonement to be made by Jesus Christ:

> And God talked with [Abraham], saying, My people have gone astray from my precepts, and have not kept mine ordinances, which I gave unto their fathers;
>
> And they have not observed mine anointing, and the burial, or baptism wherewith I commanded them;
>
> But have turned from the commandment, and taken unto themselves the washing of children, and the blood of sprinkling;
>
> And have said that the blood of the righteous Abel was shed for sins; and have not known wherein they are accountable before me. (JST Gen. 17:4–7)

As the Lord talked to Abraham, he outlined the extent of his covenant people's apostasy. They had gone astray from God's precepts and ordinances, in addition to forgetting the anointing and baptism, all of which were given as commandments (JST Gen. 17:4–5). The people of Shem had supplanted these commandments with "the washing of children, and the blood of sprinkling" (JST Gen. 17:4–6). The washing of children referred to may be an allusion to infant baptism, for when the Lord instructed Abraham further he said that "children are not accountable before me until they are eight years old" (JST Gen. 17:11). Thus, it would seem that children younger than eight years old were being baptized.

Along with this, and perhaps the most serious heresy, the shedding of Abel's blood was being accepted by many as an atoning sacrifice for sins rather than the blood that would be shed by the yet-to-come Son of God. Abel was believed to be the redeemer of the world. This was a mockery not only of the death of a righteous servant who "hearkened to the voice of the Lord" (Moses 5:17) but also a mockery of the one true atonement.

Faith in the atonement of Jesus Christ had to be reestablished among the patriarchs. At a time of such apostasy it was necessary to find a patriarch, such as Abraham, who could preside over the Lord's covenant people and be a living testimony of the Atonement.

Thus it was essential to establish a righteous patriarchal line. This would require both a testing and a strengthening process. Tests not only *try* one's faith, but when successfully passed, they also *strengthen* one's faith.

Abraham and Isaac were chosen to be tested in a most difficult and perplexing way—a father sacrificing a son. Their test would, in a small way, mimic the supreme test to which the Savior would be placed. Abraham would become a type of the Father and Isaac a type of the Christ. In this way, Noah's posterity would learn of the redemptive power of God's Only Begotten Son, as they came to understand that the experience of Abraham and Isaac foreshadowed, in a mortal way, the sacrifice to be made by Jesus for all God's children. That Abraham and Isaac were worthy to be chosen for this tremendous test and atoning symbol is a credit in itself to their faith and trust in God.

The Sacrifice of Isaac

When the time arrived to reestablish faith in the Lord's sacrifice, God spoke to Abraham saying, "Take now thy son, *thine only Isaac,* whom thou lovest, and get thee into the land of Moriah; and offer him there for a burnt offering, upon one of the mountains of which I will tell thee" (JST Gen. 22: 2; emphasis added).

It is interesting that Abraham and Isaac were instructed to make their offering "upon one of the mountains of which I will tell thee." They were to ascend to a holy place, the top of a mountain, and the holy place would be revealed by God. Therefore, there should be no surprise when Abraham recognized the mountain of sacrifice by sight (see JST Genesis 22:5).

In verse 6 of this same chapter, Abraham calls Isaac a "lad" (Hebrew *na'ar*). This has led to a variety of conclusions as to Isaac's age at this time. The meaning of the Hebrew word has a wide range of use. It occurs over 200 times in the Old Testament and can refer to an infant of a few months (Ex. 2:6; 2 Sam. 12:16) on up to a mature adult (2 Sam. 14:21, 18:5). It is the same word used for the two young men of verse 3 that accompanied Abraham and Isaac (JST Gen. 22:3). It would seem, in this case, that Isaac was an adult rather than a young child. Why would Abraham take two more "children" with him to offer Isaac? It is much more probable that Isaac was a mature man and thus equally responsible as Abraham was in fulfilling this unparalleled event.[6] This concern about the age of Isaac pales, however, in significance to the lesson that Abraham and Isaac would learn. Who else could now teach the meaning and principle of the Atonement better than they? Who else would know better the doctrine of Christ than these two great prophets and patriarchs?

The extent and depth of both Abraham and Isaac's faith is hard to fathom, but it must have been considerable. Isaac may have believed that if he was offered as a burnt offering he could again be raised up.[7] Additionally, he must have been aware of the promise made to Abraham of a large posterity through him, Isaac. Therefore, when Isaac was placed on the altar he must have had considerable trust in his father's judgment. Similarly, Isaac must have known that if they did God's will, God would make all things right.

After traveling for three days (Gen. 22:4), the party arrived at the appointed location, ascended the mount, and prepared the sacrifice. The scripture states:

> And they came to the place which God had told him of; and Abraham built an altar there, and laid the wood in order, and bound Isaac his son, and laid him on the altar upon the wood. (Gen. 22:9)

When the fateful moment arrived for Abraham to plunge the knife it must have taken all the faith Abraham and Isaac could produce to carry out the sacrificial commandment.[8] It could have been a rational deduction for either Abraham or Isaac to conclude that the commandment was improper, or not from God—that something was wrong. Human sacrifice had in all instances been forbidden by the Lord. Here, then, was the great moment of faith.[9] Here, all earthly reasoning fell short. This was the moment of stepping from the edge of the light into darkness, the moment when one has to let go and "[rely] wholly upon the merits of him who is mighty to save" (2 Ne. 31:19).

Of course God's contradictory commandment to Abraham and Isaac wasn't meant to be fulfilled by them; they were only to provide a type of the Atonement and to "prove [themselves] in all things" (D&C 98:14). The actual sacrifice would come at a later time when God's "only" Son would voluntarily give his life to save humankind. This test, no doubt, was given so that this earthly father and son would have a deep and expansive understanding of this infinite atonement that would save the world from sin. Abraham and Isaac would now be in a powerful position to teach this principle to a people who had rejected the Atonement and had replaced this sacred principle with false teachings of men. They learned that redemption can only come through the sacrifice of the Son of God. Only after the Christ would sweat his blood at Gethsemane and shed his blood at Calvary could it be said "that the blood of the righteous...was shed for sins" (JST Gen. 17:7). And the blood shed was not Abel's but the Holy One of Israel's. Faith in this atonement and its Mediator would be the first principle of the gospel which would lead humankind to repent and apply the power of this sacrifice in their own lives and withstand their own Abrahamic tests and trials as did Isaac and his father.

Isaac and Rebekah

Sarah died when she was 127 years old. She was 90 years of age when Isaac was born. This means that Isaac must have been in his thirty-seventh year or younger when he was offered as a sacrifice. Apostasy was still so great in the land that Abraham sent his servant Eliezer to Haran to find Isaac a wife among his kinsfolk. Rebekah was the daughter of Bethuel, the son of Milcah, who was the wife of Abraham's brother, Nahor. She is described as being "very fair to look upon,...neither had any man known the like unto her" (JST Gen. 24:16). Whether or not she was a devout believer in Jehovah is not mentioned, but the fact that she was willing to marry Isaac without having ever seen him would indicate that much of her motivation to consent to the marriage and to move from her family may have had religious considerations. As beautiful as she is described to be, she surely would have had no difficulty finding powerful and wealthy suitors in Haran.

Rebekah first saw Isaac as Eliezer's caravan came near the well Laharoi. Isaac had gone into the field to meditate when the caravan came upon him, and here the cousins met for the first time. Isaac brought Rebekah to the tent of Sarah and she became his wife. Isaac was forty years old. Then the scriptures record, "he loved her: and Isaac was comforted after his mother's death" (Gen. 24:67).

Although this account of Isaac and Rebekah coming together in marriage is brief, it demonstrates first, a bond of affection and trust in the families of Abraham and his brothers. It is possible that Bethuel and his family had been affected by the apostasy and succumbed to the false religious practices and idolatry so prevalent in their environment. But it is nonetheless evident that an essential belief in the God of Abraham and Isaac was familiar to Rebekah. The Rashi commentary declares that Rebekah was a righteous person but her family had turned to wickedness. That seems likely from the account in Genesis. At least it is certain that in her later life she had great concern for the faith of her children.

Isaac and His Sons

Like Sarah, Rebekah was also barren. The scriptures tell us that "Isaac entreated the Lord for his wife, because she was barren" (Gen. 25:21). Once again, the faith of a patriarch would be tested. For even promised blessings are not automatically obtained, and "without faith it is impossible to please him" (Heb. 11:6).

The Lord heard Isaac's plea and Rebekah conceived and gave birth to twins. The Lord had told Rebekah that she would deliver "two nations" and "two manner of people" (Gen. 25:23). The elder, by only a few minutes, would serve the younger. The Rashi commentary rationalizes this order by suggesting that Jacob was conceived before Esau but Esau was born before Jacob, so technically, Jacob was the firstborn.[10] Regardless, God made it clear that Jacob would receive the birthright with the accompanying blessing and rights of primogeniture.

Esau, described by the Bible as red and hairy, was born first. (The name Esau means hairy.) Jacob was born second, but he had his hand on Esau's heel, as if he were indeed trying to be born first. Although this makes an interesting story, and without a doubt depicts the forthcoming struggle for the birthright and blessing, it is the Lord's will that determines the right of blessing and that Esau would serve Jacob.

The birthright story is briefly interrupted by another famine which forces Isaac and his family to move to Gerar. Here Isaac's story duplicates that of his father, Abraham. Rebekah, like Sarah, was a beautiful woman, and Isaac calls his wife his sister for fear of the Philistine king Abimelech. Abimelech only discovers they are husband and wife after he sees Isaac "sporting" with Rebekah (Gen. 26:7–8). Both the name *Isaac* and the word *sporting* come from the same Hebrew word, *Yitschaq*. As mentioned before, it can mean to laugh, to rejoice, and also, as in this case, to sport or to cohabit. Contrary to Isaac's fears, upon discovering this, Abimelech gave them protection.

Eventually, Abimelech sent Isaac and his wife away because Rebekah's husband was "much mightier" than himself. Although Isaac displays the weaknesses and fears of his mortality at times, it is apparent he was a man of a great faith because the Philistine king saw that the Lord was with Isaac (Gen. 26:28). Further evidence from this same time period which illustrates the faithfulness of Isaac and Rebekah comes when Esau marries two Hittite women, Judith and Bashemah. This act was a "grief of mind" to his parents (Gen. 26:35), underscoring the love Isaac and Rebekah had for Esau and their love and respect for the Lord and his covenants: their grief resulted from Esau's marrying outside of the Covenant.

The Blessing of Jacob

Genesis says that "Esau was a cunning hunter, a man of the field; and Jacob was a plain man, dwelling in tents" (25:27). The word translated "plain man" in Hebrew can mean "simple," "perfect," or "complete." At this point in Jacob's life it would seem that he was a more well-rounded or well-balanced individual than was his brother Esau. Regardless of Jacob's "more complete" nature, Isaac favored Esau because Esau was a hunter and Isaac enjoyed the venison his son brought to him. However, Rebekah loved Jacob best.[11] This becomes an important fact in the birthright battle.

It appears that Isaac had determined to bless Esau rather than Jacob with the birthright, in spite of the fact that the Lord had told Rebekah that the "elder shall serve the younger" (Gen. 25:23). When Isaac sent Esau to hunt for venison in celebration of the blessing that he intended to bestow upon Esau, Rebekah heard Isaac's plans. Being fearful that he would indeed give the birthright blessing to Esau, she called Jacob to her to plot how they might obtain the blessing for Jacob. Jacob agreed to follow Rebekah's plan, and she took the responsibility for their intended deception of Isaac upon herself, saying, "Upon me be thy curse," if their plan should go awry (Gen. 27:13). How motivated Jacob was to deceive his father is difficult to determine. He may have felt justified in receiving the blessing since Esau had married outside the covenant made to Abraham and seemed little concerned about spiritual matters. However, the temporal aspects of the blessing would be considerable, and naturally the loss would disturb Esau when he was betrayed by Jacob.

Following his mother's instructions, Jacob deceived Isaac into thinking he was Esau and thus received the birthright blessing from his father. When Esau returned from hunting for venison, to both his and Isaac's dismay, Jacob had already obtained the blessing.

At this point Isaac reacts in a very unusual manner. He affirms the blessing he bestowed upon Jacob as being both effectual and binding, and he refuses to cancel the blessing because of the deceit. It would have been appropriate in such a situation to declare the blessing given to Jacob null and void and to place it upon Esau. However, in spite of Esau's pleadings to the contrary, Isaac declares the blessing upon Jacob as valid and binding. Isaac does not explain his reasoning but he is firm in his decision.

There is little question that Jacob was preferred of the Lord, and, setting the deceit aside, he was far more worthy and prepared for the blessing than Esau. One must remember that Esau had sold his birthright to Jacob for a "mess of pottage" because he was hungry coming from the field. To Esau, his birthright was not worth the temporary hunger his physical body was suffering, so he bartered his birthright to Jacob. As Esau said, "What profit shall this birthright do to me?" (Gen. 25:32).

Because God was displeased with Esau for selling his birthright for some pottage (the Hebrew Bible calls the pottage *edom,* which means red), God changed his name from Esau to Edom to memorialize his rejection of the birthright for Jacob's "red stuff." So Esau becomes known as Red, and Jacob would soon be known as Israel, or "wrestler" for God, after his willingness to wrestle with an angel for a blessing. Today the children of Israel are called to fight for the kingdom of God while the children of Esau, figuratively speaking, continue to sell their birthrights for that which has no greater value than the red pottage.

It is also clear that Esau realized he could not obtain the blessing. The Bible says:

> And when Esau heard the words of his father [i.e., that Jacob should be blessed], he cried with a great and exceeding bitter cry, and said unto his father, Bless me, even me also, O my father.
>
> And he said, Thy brother came with subtilty, and hath taken away thy blessing.
>
> And he said, Is not he rightly named Jacob? for he hath supplanted me these two times: he took away my birthright; and, behold, now he hath taken away my blessing. And he said, Hast thou not reserved a blessing for me?
>
> And Isaac answered and said unto Esau, Behold I have made him thy lord, and all his brethren have I given to him for servants. (Gen. 27:34–37)

At this point, Isaac blesses Esau with some temporal blessings, and the scriptures announce Esau's hatred toward Jacob and his intent to kill his supplanting brother.

Esau's actions indicate the wisdom of Isaac in refraining from nullifying the blessing given to Jacob. In the end, Isaac's commitment to his God overcame his natural desire to favor Esau. Isaac reflected the human feelings of a parent who more easily identified with Esau, but when the crisis arrived was willing to abide by the promptings of the Spirit. Faith in God and a sensitivity to his Spirit brought Isaac, eventually, to the correct decision.

The record of Isaac now comes to an end. There is no further record of his works other than the mention of his death:

> And the days of Isaac were an hundred and fourscore years.
>
> And Isaac gave up the ghost, and died, and was gathered unto his people, being old and full of days: and his sons Esau and Jacob buried him. (Gen. 35:28–29)

Another great patriarch ended his days filled with faith and good works.

Conclusion

Prior to his death, the Book of Mormon prophet Helaman told his sons:

> And now, my sons, remember, remember that it is upon the rock of our Redeemer, who is Christ, the Son of God, that ye must build your foundation; that when the devil shall send forth his mighty winds, yea, his shafts in the whirlwind, yea, when all his hail and his mighty storm shall beat upon you, it shall have no power over you to drag you down to the gulf of misery and endless wo, because of the rock upon which ye are built, which is a sure foundation, a foundation whereon if men build they cannot fall. (Hel. 5:12)

These could well have been the words of Abraham to Isaac or Isaac to his son Jacob, for a knowledge of the atonement of Jesus Christ was as important and central to the patriarch Isaac and his family as it is to Church members in our day. Even the little we know of his life reveals that the ancients were taught and trained by the Lord, as people have been in all dispensations, to rely wholly on the atonement of Jesus Christ.

NOTES

1. See Genesis 22:2, 15, 20 of the Joseph Smith Translation; hereafter JST. Apparently, Isaac was called an "only" child by the angel because Isaac was born to Sarah, Abraham's first wife, thus illustrating the right of primogeniture and the prophetic calling by the Lord.

2. Rashi is an acronym for Rabbi Shlomo ben Isaac, who lived from 1040–1105 A.D. in France. He wrote a commentary on the Talmud that now appears in the *Steinsaltz Edition* of the Talmud.

3. Abraham ben Isaiah, Benjamin Sharfman, Harry Orlinski, Morris Charmer, *The Pentateuch and Rashi's Commentary* (Brooklyn: S.S.& R Publishing Company, Inc., 1949), 134–35; hereafter *Rashi.*

4. *Gesenius' Hebrew and Chaldee Lexicon* (Grand Rapids, Michigan: Baker Book House, 1979), 642.

5. *Rashi*, 134–35.

6. See Hugh Nibley, *Nibley on the Timely and the Timeless* (Provo, Utah: Religious Studies Center, 1978), 136.

7. See Spencer W. Kimball, in *Conference Report,* October 1952, 49. See also Bruce R. McConkie, *Doctrinal New Testament Commentary* 3 vols. (Salt Lake City: Bookcraft, 1973), 3:208.

8. See Joseph Fielding Smith, *The Way to Perfection* (Salt Lake City: Genealogical Society of The Church of Jesus Christ of Latter- day Saints, 1958), 87.

9. See Joseph Smith, *Teachings of the Prophet Joseph Smith,* comp. Joseph Fielding Smith (Salt Lake City: Deseret Book, 1977), 256, 322.

10. *Rashi,* 243.

11. Genesis 25:28 says that Isaac loved Esau because he ate of his venison. This kind of reasoning might indicate that Isaac was suffering from the effects of age. However, it could just be an oversimplification.

CHAPTER FIVE

JACOB: TRIAL AND TRIUMPH

STEPHEN D. RICKS

Introduction[1]

IN DOCTRINE AND COVENANTS section 132, the great revelation to Joseph Smith on marriage, we learn that Abraham, Isaac, and Jacob "have entered into their exaltation, according to the promises, and sit upon thrones, and are not angels but are gods" (D&C 132:37). This is the final reward of the life of faith, as noted by the prophet Nephi in the book of Helaman: "as many as should look upon the Son of God with faith, having a contrite spirit, might live, even unto that life eternal" (8:15). As was the case with his father and grandfather, Jacob's life was filled with challenge, conflict, hardship, and promise, but was ultimately crowned with triumph and peace. The lives of few biblical figures are recounted in greater detail than is Jacob's—only the stories of David and Moses (whose life parallels that of Jacob in remarkable ways[2]) cover more chapters in the Old Testament. While I focus on the biblical account of Jacob, I will occasionally refer to later Jewish traditions concerning his life, which sometimes broaden the contours of the story or sharpen its focus on a particular issue.

Conflict and Resolution as the Leitmotif of Jacob's Life

The central conflict in Jacob's life is his struggle with his brother Esau. The birth of Jacob and Esau came in answer to Isaac's prayer to remove Rebekah's barrenness. But even in her womb "the children struggled together" (Gen. 25:22). In answer to her query as to why this was so, she was informed: "Two nations are in thy womb, and two manner of people shall be separated from thy bowels; and the one people shall be stronger than the other people; and the elder shall serve the younger" (Gen. 25:23). Esau was born first, but Jacob followed closely thereafter, with his hand on Esau's heel. As a consequence, Jacob received his name, which means "heel."[5] Unexpectedly, the Lord's word to Rebekah created a dilemma. The elder son in a family generally received the birthright. Esau was the elder son, but it was Jacob who was to receive the birthright. How was this to be accomplished? The remainder of Genesis 25 and Genesis 27 provides the answer. First, Jacob exploited a seemingly desperate situation for Esau—ravenous hunger after a hunting trip—to secure the birthright from him. Then Jacob and Rebekah engaged in a ploy in order to convince Isaac, who was then old and blind but still expected to pass on the birthright to his son Esau, that Jacob was Esau.

Were Rebekah and Jacob justified in their actions? Before answering this question negatively, we should bear in mind that Abraham engaged in duplicity—acting with the intent to deceive, even if what he said was at some level true—when claiming to the Egyptian king's men that Sarai was his sister and not his wife (Gen. 12:10–13). This passage, which so vexed the ancient rabbis, is given a very different turn in the book of Abraham in the Pearl of Great Price:

> And it came to pass when I was come near to enter into Egypt, the Lord said unto me: Behold, Sarai, thy wife, is a very fair woman to look upon;
>
> Therefore it shall come to pass, when the Egyptians shall see her, they will say—She is his wife; and they will kill you, but they will save her alive; therefore see that ye do on this wise:
>
> Let her say unto the Egyptians, she is thy sister, and thy soul shall live.
>
> And it came to pass that I, Abraham, told Sarai, my wife, all that the Lord had said unto me—Therefore say unto them, I pray thee, thou art my sister. (Abr. 2:22–25)

There, God told Abraham to claim that Sarai was his sister, not his wife. The issue becomes one of obedience to God, not of acting deceptively. Obedience to God is man's paramount duty, as Joseph Smith makes clear in a letter to Nancy Rigdon:

> That which is wrong under one circumstance, may be and often is, right under another. God said thou shalt not kill,—at another time he said thou shalt utterly destroy. This is the principle on which the government of heaven is conducted—by revelation adapted to the circumstances in which the children of the kingdom are placed. What God requires is right, no matter what it is, although we may not see the reason thereof till long after the events transpire.[6]

What is required of us is the faith to discern and then act upon what God requires. Perhaps Rebekah was instructed by God, in a detail that is not in our current versions of Genesis, to say the things that she did. In any event, she had faith in the answer to her prayer that said Jacob would receive the birthright, and there is no blame attached to her in the text for attempting to fulfill God's command. It is a principle of free agency that God sometimes gives individuals a general charge without necessarily providing all of the details on how that charge is to be fulfilled. For example, two bishops may be given the same assignment without being told precisely how to carry it out. They may fulfill it in very different ways, but with equal diligence and sincerity. We might not be equally well disposed to each way, but the Lord may equally justify both ways of going about it.

Like Rebekah, Sarah knew that her child, Isaac, was the heir of the covenant promises made to Abraham. In order to protect him against any competing claims made by Ishmael, Sarah ordered Ishmael and his mother Hagar expelled. Abraham, very displeased with the arrangement, at first demurred. Then, however, he was told by the Lord: "Let it not be grievous in thy sight because of the lad, and because of thy bondwoman; in all that Sarah hath said unto thee, hearken unto her voice; for in Isaac shall thy seed be called" (Gen. 21:12).

Hagar appears to be insignificant in God's plan—a mere throw-away figure—but there are no throw-away characters in God's plan. She alone among the matriarchs received an angelic visitation not once, but twice in the biblical record. Her life was spared in a miraculous manner through angelic intervention. She became the matriarch of a great people, just as Abraham had been promised: "And also of the son of the bondwoman will I make a nation, because he is thy seed" (Gen. 21:13). In a similar manner, Esau was denied the prime blessing that Isaac had to bestow on his sons, but he was still richly blessed during his own lifetime, so much so that he felt no need to receive any gifts from his brother Jacob (Gen. 34:1–4).

Esau is described as a rough-hewn hunter, while Jacob was a "plain man" who preferred life around the tents (Gen. 25:27). But the differences between these twins go far deeper than that. Esau was a precipitate, reactive creature of the moment. He willingly gave up his birthright because of temporary hunger. He spoke to Jacob as though he were starving, but real starvation would scarcely have allowed him to act so vigorously. Thereafter, he assumed no responsibility for the loss of his birthright, but laid the blame solely on the shoulders of Jacob: "Is not he rightly named Jacob? for he hath supplanted me these two times: he took away my birthright; and, behold, now he hath taken away my blessing" (Gen. 27:36). The way in which Esau's statement is phrased suggests the possibility that there was some physical token associated with the transfer of the birthright from Esau to Jacob—such as a garment, as later Jewish traditions suggest (about which more will be said below).

Always inclined to think only in terms of the present—while faith requires living with an eye to the future and "things not seen" (Heb. 11:1; Alma 32:21)—Esau interpreted the loss of the birthright as the forfeiture of his own creature comforts. There is never an indication that Esau understood that it included the covenant promises made to Abraham and his father. Sensing the loss of personal advantages and creature comforts, Esau's anger bordered on the murderous, and his threatening behavior convinced Rebekah to tell Jacob to leave for his own safety. When Esau later discovered that the loss of the birthright and the receipt of the lesser blessing had no noticeable impact on his affluence, he forgot his wrath—and it scarcely seemed to bother him that this loss would affect his posterity for generations to come. When Jacob returned from Padanaram, unaware that Esau was no longer angry with him, Jacob made rich gifts to him, but Esau returned them, saying: "I have enough, my brother; keep that thou hast unto thyself" (Gen. 33:9). It appears that Esau's concerns were with the here and now.

By contrast, Jacob seems to have lived by foresight and calculation. He certainly determined the best time to strike a bargain with Esau for the birthright. Jacob worked together with his mother in order to gain the birthright blessing from his father Isaac. He accepted a long-term arrangement with his future father-in-law, Laban, in order to gain the hand of Rachel, but was so focused on the goal and absorbed by his love for her that the time "seemed unto him but a few days" (Gen. 29:20). When returning home from Padanaram, unsure of how Esau might respond to him, Jacob calculated how best to assuage his anger.

Jacob's sojourn in Padanaram provided a vital training ground for his own maturation. He learned by his own experience the pain that can be caused by duplicity, even when that duplicity can be rationalized or defended. Jacob worked seven years for Rachel, but received Leah as wife instead. Laban rationalized this act by informing Jacob: "It must not be so done in our country, to give the younger before the firstborn" (Gen. 29:26). Following the marriage celebration for Jacob and Leah, Jacob received Rachel as well, but was obliged to work for Laban another seven years. Laban's deceptions continued thereafter. When Jacob finally determined to leave, he complained to Laban of his own fair dealings and of Laban's unjustified sharpness:

> These twenty years have I been with thee; thy ewes and thy she goats have not cast their young, and the rams of thy flock have I not eaten.
>
> That which was torn of beasts I brought not unto thee; I bare the loss of it; of my hand didst thou require it, whether stolen by day, or stolen by night.
>
> Thus I was; in the day the drought consumed me, and the frost by night; and my sleep departed from mine eyes.
>
> Thus have I been twenty years in thy house; I served thee fourteen years for thy two daughters, and six years for thy cattle: and thou hast changed my wages ten times.

> Except the God of my father, the God of Abraham, and the fear of Isaac, had been with me, surely thou hadst sent me away now empty (Gen. 31:38–42).

Jacob was further chastened by his domestic difficulties; indeed, it is Jacob's problems at home that consistently represent his greatest challenges during his lifetime. Try though he might to be fair, his preference for Rachel must have been clear for all to see: in the absolutizing and polarizing Hebrew, Leah was "hated" by him. Yet, can Jacob be fully blamed for preferring Rachel? He never bargained for Leah in the first place, had no expectation of marrying her, and only found himself wed to her because of a ruse.

Jacob found himself in the middle of other domestic squabbles not of his own making. The family competition and conflict continued to the next generation, and he lost Joseph—permanently, so he thought, but only temporarily, as it turned out—through the anger and jealousy of Joseph's brothers. Jacob had caused his brother Esau distress and his father confusion and anguish. On his return to Canaan, he felt fear and distress when it was reported to him that Esau was advancing in his direction with four hundred men, a fear that must have reached nearly a fever pitch when Esau met him face to face.

Perhaps the most important event that Jacob experienced was his encounter at Penuel (with a man? an angel? God himself? Jewish tradition preferred an angel or a man, while early Christian tradition preferred the interpretation of God or of Christ[7]). However this passage might best be interpreted at a literal level, at a symbolic level it reflects Jacob's struggle with his own fears, weaknesses, and personal demons, and of his triumph over them.

The story of Jacob is preeminently one of domestic difficulties and triumph. But through all of this the Lord, "the God of Abraham and the fear of Isaac," blessed and enlarged him, as he matured to fill his role as the father, not merely of a family, but of a people.

Genesis 28–32: a Temple Text?

The temple stands as the pinnacle of Latter-day Saint worship and the great symbol of our faith and commitment. Here, the faithful can symbolically complete their journey back to the presence of God. The central chapters that deal with Jacob contain a remarkable number of features that are characteristic of temples and coronations in the ancient Near East. But why would characteristics of the temple and of kingship figure so prominently in the story of Jacob? Both the temple and coronations may represent rites of passage from one stage or level of existence to another. The story of Jacob may also be viewed as a rite of passage from youthful trickster to mature and reverent worshiper of God, from deceptive son and brother to benevolent and loving father.

Of the eighteen elements in John Lundquist's temple typology,[8] several can be found in the story of Jacob, which I will list in the order in which they occur in the Genesis text (the numbers in parentheses refer to their order in Lundquist's typology).

1. "Inside the temple, images of deities as well as living kings, temple priests, and worshippers are washed, anointed, clothed, fed, enthroned, and symbolically initiated into the presence of the deity, and thus into eternal life" (10).

While nothing is said in Genesis about a sacred garment in connection with the transfer of the birthright from Esau to Jacob, it is an important part of later Jewish traditions, where it is linked to the birthright. But to understand fully the importance of Jacob's sacred garment in these stories, one must go back generations before Jacob and Esau. The garment was one of the items that Noah saved and carried with him in the ark. It was thought to have power that might be misused by those into whose hands it fell. It was stolen by Ham, who handed it down to his son Cush, who later gave it to Nimrod. Nimrod used this garment to obtain power and glory among men, and as a means of deceiving them and gaining unconquerable strength.[9] Nimrod would also use the garment while hunting, which caused all the birds and other animals to fall down in honor and respect before him. As a result, the people made him king over them.[10] He first became king of Babylon, and "was soon able through skillful and subtle speeches to bring the whole of mankind to the point of accepting him as the absolute ruler of the earth."[11] Appropriately, it was the garment that finally cost Nimrod his life. According to one account, he went forth with his people on a great hunt; at that time he was jealous of the great hunter Esau. As Nimrod approached with two attendants, Esau hid, then cut off Nimrod's head and killed the two attendants.[12]

Having obtained the garment, Esau either buried it[13] or sold it to Jacob along with his birthright. *Numbers Rabbah* relates that Jacob desired to offer sacrifice but could not because he was not the firstborn and did not have the birthright, part of which consisted of Adam's garment. It was for this reason that Jacob bought the birthright from Esau, who said, "There is no afterlife, death ends everything, and the inheritance will do me no good," and willingly let Jacob have the garment, along with his birthright. Immediately Jacob built an altar and offered sacrifice.[14] Similarly, the early church Father Hippolytus says that when Isaac laid his hands on Jacob, at the same time feeling Esau's skin garment, he knew that this son was the legitimate heir to the blessing. The garment proved that, for Esau would hardly have parted with the garment if he had been worthy of it.[15] It was this same garment—referred to as the "coat of many colors"—that was passed on to Joseph, both as a sign of his father's favor and as a token of his priesthood authority.

2. "God's word is revealed in the temple, usually in the holy of holies, to priests or prophets attached to the temple or to the religious system that it represents" (14); and "The temple is built on separate, sacral, set apart space" (5).

After being advised by his parents not to take a wife "of the daughters of Canaan," Jacob departed from Beersheba toward Haran. On the way

> he lighted upon a certain place, and tarried there all night, because the sun was set; and he took of the stones of that place, and put them for his pillows, and lay down in that place to sleep.
>
> And he dreamed, and behold a ladder [Hebrew "ramp, staircase"] set up on the earth, and the top of it reached to heaven: and behold the angels of God ascending and descending on it.
>
> And, behold, the Lord stood above it, and said, I am the Lord God of Abraham thy father, and the God of Isaac. (Gen. 28:11–13)

This story is an outstanding example of "dream incubation," which typically occurred in temples or other sacred spaces in the ancient Near East.[16] When a king, priest, or other person wished to receive a communication from his God/god, he entered a temple or shrine. He would sleep near the altar, where he might expect to receive a message in the form of a dream. The Hebrew word translated "place" in Genesis 28:11, 16, 19—*ma¯qom*—frequently has the meaning of "shrine," and may be understood in that sense here.[17] Further, the form of this entire section in Genesis 28 follows, as Robert Karl Gnuse shows, the dream revelation pattern, of which he provides several other examples from the Old Testament (e.g., Gen. 15:16; 20:118; 46:17; Num. 22:8–13, 19–21): (1) the reference to a dream (Gen. 28:12); (2) the appearance of the Lord ("and the Lord stood above it," Gen. 28:13); the "self-identification of the deity" (Gen. 28:13); (4) the message, a promise of blessing (Gen. 28:15–16); and (5) the formal end of the dream revelation ("and Jacob awoke" Gen. 28:16).[18]

Sacred space, including the sacred space of temples, is discovered by man, never chosen by him.[19] Jacob's vision assured him of the holiness of the place where he had received the vision. He exclaimed: "Surely the Lord is in this place [Heb. "shrine"].... And he was afraid, and said, How dreadful [Heb. "awesome"] is this place [Heb. "shrine"].... And he called the name of that place [Heb. "shrine"] Bethel [Heb. "Abode of God"] (Gen. 28:16–17, 19). After Jacob got up the following morning, he "took the stone that he had put for his pillow, and set it up for a pillar, and poured oil on top of it" (Gen. 28:18). Such stone pillars mark off "a sacred area or geographical threshold" in the ancient world.[20] Pouring oil on the stone marks that site as particularly significant.[21] Jacob further vows that if the Lord will protect him, the stone set up for a pillar "shall be God's house" [Heb. "BethEl"] (Gen. 28:22). The "Bethel," according to the historian of religions Mircea Eliade, "is the place where the heavenly and earthly realms meet; it is an *axis mundi*, a place of the incursion of the sacred in the profane world,"[22] precisely the characteristics of the temple.

In the postbiblical period, the stone that Jacob slept on assumed a life of its own in legend. It was identified with the Stone of Scone, or the Stone of Destiny, or King Edward's Stone, and was brought by Edward I from the Abbey of Scone in Scotland to Westminster Abbey in 1296. It now forms the base of the throne in Westminster Abbey where the English monarch is crowned.[23]

3. "Temples, in their architectonic orientation, express the idea of a successive ascension toward heaven. The Mesopotamian ziggurat or staged temple tower is the best example of this architectural principle. It was constructed of three, five, or seven levels or stages. Monumental staircases led to the upper levels, where smaller temples stood" (7).

In the dream-vision that Jacob received, he saw "a ladder [Hebrew "ramp, staircase"] set up on the earth, and the top of it reached to heaven; and behold the angels of God ascending and descending on it. And, behold, the Lord stood above it" (Gen. 28:12–13). The notion of the temple is patent in this picture and, according to Walter Brueggemann, "it refers to something like the Mesopotamian ziggurat, a land mass formed as a temple through which earth touches heaven."[24]

4. "Sacral, communal meals are carried out in connection with temple ritual, often at the conclusion of or during a covenant ceremony" (12); and "The temple is a place of sacrifice" (16).

After pursuing Jacob and his company for several days, Laban and his sons finally overtook them on a mountain (a feature also regularly connected with temples).[25] Following a series of recriminations and countercharges, Jacob and Laban finally made peace together, symbolized by a covenant, and built a stone altar, named by Laban in Aramaic Jegar-Sahadutha and by Jacob in Hebrew Galeed—suggesting a difference in language between these two, as among many other speakers in the Bible.[26] They offered sacrifice, ate a ritual meal,[27] and "tarried the night in the mount" (Gen. 31:54)—an interesting detail in the light of dream incubation practices mentioned above.

During Jacob's revelatory dream in Genesis 28 he was blessed with the same covenant and promise of posterity as Abraham had been in Genesis 17:18: "The land whereon thou liest, to thee will I give it, and to thy seed; And thy seed shall be as the dust of the earth, and thou shalt spread abroad to the west, and to the east, and to the north, and to the south: and in thee and in thy seed shall all the families of the earth be blessed" (Gen. 28:13–15).

Covenant-making is also closely connected with the temple in the ancient Near East.

In addition to these elements of the story that correspond to the temple typology, there is one, the name change, that is also characteristic of kingship and coronation ceremonies, as well as of initiation rites, when an individual attains a new, and generally higher, stage of life. According to Arthur M. Hocart, the king at his coronation "usually acquires a new name, either a title or the name of a predecessor; so do priests very frequently."[28] In ancient Egypt, the king, who had at least five names, received one of them, the praenomen, or throne name, at the time of his accession to rule.[29] The Mesopotamian king, who had borne the "name of smallness" before his coronation, was given a new name when he became king. Several Israelite kings had two different names, the "birth name" and the "regnal name," which had led Roland de Vaux to surmise that the kings of Judah received a new name when they were enthroned.[30] Besides the kings of ancient Israel, the Bible provides several other examples of individuals who received new or changed names, frequently connected with an important transition (usually of a spiritual nature) in their lives: Abram becomes Abraham (Gen. 17:5); Sarai becomes Sarah (Gen. 17:15); Joseph becomes Zaphnathpaaneah (Gen. 41:45); Jesus gave Simon the name Cephas (whose Greek reflex is Peter; Matt. 16:17–18; John 1:42); and Saul took on the Latin name Paul, probably indicating his role as missionary to the Gentiles. (Acts 13:9 gives the first mention of the name Paul, at the beginning of his missionary labors among the Gentiles.) Jacob's name change presents an interesting conjunction of kingship and coronation practices and initiation rites. As is the case with initiation rites, Jacob's name change to Israel is connected with his changed status. Jacob, a "wandering Aramaean" without a permanent home, as Israel becomes the head of a family—and, by extension, the ruler of a kingdom as well.[31]

Conclusion

Jacob's life began in conflict, and conflict continued to define it throughout. He engaged in duplicity, and suffered from the deceptions of others. He labored seven years for a love match, but was given instead one whom he had not bargained for and did not have the same feelings for. But the Lord says he will try two things in particular in his people: their patience and their faith (Mosiah 23:21). The successful trial of one seems to contribute to the growth of the other. Through the chastening resulting from the conflict with his brother, father-in-law, wives, and children, Jacob, who became Israel, matured in faith to the point that he could properly stand at the head of a nation named for him.

Excursus:
Folkloric Elements in the Story of Jacob

There are a number of puzzling folkloric features in the story of Jacob, including the use of mandrakes and the "ringed and straked" sheep and goats. Each of these will be discussed in the light of their folkloric content and significance for understanding the story of Jacob.

1. Mandrakes (Gen. 30:14–16). During the wheat harvest, Jacob and Leah's son Reuben found mandrakes in the field. He brought them to his mother. Rachel asked for some of them, which she received from Leah in return for allowing Jacob to spend the night with Leah. As a result, Leah became pregnant and gave birth to her fifth son, Issachar (Gen. 30:14–18). But why did Rachel want the mandrakes in the first place? In the view of the ancient Israelites, mandrakes were believed to be an aphrodisiac, as well as a powerful remedy against infertility. In Song of Solomon 7:14, when the woman invites her lover to enjoy her charms, she also gives as one of her inducements a store of "fragrant mandrakes" for him. According to Jewish folklorist Raphael Patai, the mandrake has long been thought to prevent barrenness.[32] Indeed, the Hebrew word for mandrake, *du¯day,* comes from the root for "to love." It is in this sense that the word is used in Genesis. Rachel wished to eat them in order to induce pregnancy.

2. The rods and the "speckled" and "spotted" cattle (Gen. 30:28–43). Genesis provides a fascinating example of what might be termed "folk eugenics." It also demonstrates how Jacob was able to take a situation that was seemingly disadvantageous to himself and turn it to his own purposes. Sheep with light coats and goats with dark coats were preferred in the ancient Near East. Jacob, however, arranged to take striped and spotted goats and sheep. He took branches of poplar (Hebrew *libneh,* a probable play

on the name Laban), almond, and plane trees whose bark had been peeled, thereby exposing the inner wood, and placed them by the watering troughs where the sheep and goats would be mating. Jacob's expectation was that this would result in a larger than normal percentage of speckled and spotted sheep and goats being born. In fact, this is precisely what happened. As a result, Jacob's flocks grew at an unprecedented rate, while those of Laban languished. While we may smile at such quaint genetic concepts, Jacob ultimately sees God as the cause of his eminent good fortune (Gen. 31:9).

3. Teraphim (Gen. 31:19–42). Before their hasty departure from Padanaram, Rachel took the *teraphim*—generally understood to be the "images" or "household gods" or "household idols"—from her father, Laban (Gen. 31:19). The loss of the *teraphim* was a source of great consternation to Laban and his sons. Why did they care so much? It appears that the *teraphim* may not have been associated merely with the family's worship practices, but were also a sign of inheritance rights. A document dating from 1400 B.C. from Nuzi, an ancient city of northern Mesopotamia, indicates that the family member who wishes to take "the prime portion of an estate" must be in possession of the household gods, or actually hold them in his hands.[33] Thus, by taking the *teraphim*, Rachel may have been making such a claim for Jacob.[34] Others believe that they were nothing more than "family talismans which were dear to her and which she was later forced by her husband to abandon at Bethel."[35] According to this reading, Laban's concern to have them returned simply indicated his greed and desire not to lose any property.[36]

Notes

1. I wish to thank my student Brian Dickman for sharing with me his unpublished paper "Did Jacob Wrestle an Angel?" which I found most helpful.

2. Ronald S. Hendel, *The Epic of the Patriarch: The Jacob Cycle and the Narrative Traditions of Canaan and Israel* (Atlanta: Scholars Press, 1987), 140, notes the following common elements in the lives of Jacob and Moses: "special

birth," "youthful (illicit/subversive) deed," "flight, as a result of youthful deed," "promise/commission by deity at sacred place," "return to land of birth at command of deity)," "dangerous encounter with deity," "meeting with brother, arrival home"; cf. 137–65.

3. By this designation I mean primarily Genesis 25–36. Needless to say, however, Jacob remains an important figure in the final chapters of the book of Genesis (37–50), but these are primarily devoted to recounting the lives of Joseph and his other sons.

4. John G. Gammie, "Theological Interpretation By Way of Literary and Tradition Analysis: Genesis 25–36," in Martin J. Buss, *Encounter with the Text: Form and History in the Hebrew Bible* (Philadelphia: Fortress Press, 1979), 121–22; cf. idem, "Jacob," in Paul J. Achtemeier, *Harper's Bible Dictionary* (San Francisco: Harper and Row, 1985), 444; Michael Fishbane, *Text and Texture: Close Readings of Selected Biblical Texts* (New York: Schocken, 1979), 40–62; but see also Hendel, *The Epic of the Patriarch*, 141, who is more cautious on this point.

5. Others have suggested that his name comes from the Hebrew word meaning "to struggle," while still others suggest that his name was originally "Jacobel," meaning "may God protect (him)." Gammie, "Jacob," 444.

6. "To Nancy Rigdon," in Dean Jessee, ed., *The Personal Writings of Joseph Smith* (Salt Lake City: Deseret Book, 1984), 508.; cf. Stephen D. Ricks, "The Early Ministry of Abraham (Abr. 1, 2)," in Robert L. Millet and Kent P. Jackson, *Studies in Scripture, Volume Two: The Pearl of Great Price* (Salt Lake City: Randall Book, 1985), 221–22.

7. William T. Miller, *Mysterious Encounters at Mamre and Jabbok* (Chico: Scholars Press, 1984), provides an extensive discussion of the early Jewish and Christian interpretation of Gen. 32:23–33; cf. Steven Molen, "The Identity of Jacob's Opponent: Wrestling with Ambiguity in Genesis 32:32," *Dialogue* 26/2 (Summer 1993): 187–200.

8. John Lundquist, "The Common Temple Ideology of the Ancient Near East," in Truman G. Madsen, ed., *The Temple in Antiquity* (Provo: Religious Studies Center, 1984), 57–59.

9. Louis Ginzberg, *Legends of the Jews*, 7 vols. (Philadelphia: Jewish Publication Society, 1969), 1:177; Micha Joseph bin Gorion, *Die Sagen der Juden*, 5 vols. (Frankfurt: Rütten & Loening, 1913–27), 2:19. The supernatural power of the garment can be seen in the *Testament of Job* 46:7–53:8. The garment protects Job and enables his daughters to speak in tongues and to proclaim the glory of God when they put it on.

10. *Pirqe de Rabbi Eliezer* 24; cf. Ginzberg, *Legends of the Jews* 1:177; M. Sel, "Nimrod," in *The Jewish Encyclopedia*, 12 vols. (New York: Funk and Wagnalls, 1905), 9:309. According to another source, recounted in bin Gorion, *Sagen der Juden*, 2:19–20, Cush loved Nimrod, the child, "and gave him a skin

garment, which God had made for Adam as he went out of the Garden of Eden." From Adam the garment passed by descent to Enoch, Methusaleh, and Noah, from whom Ham stole it as they were coming out of the Ark. Ham gave it to his firstborn, Cush, who gave it to Nimrod. According to *Jasher* 7:29, "Cush was concealed then from his sons and brothers and when Cush had begotten Nimrod, he gave him those garments through his love for him, and Nimrod grew up, and when he was twenty years old he put on those garments, and Nimrod became strong when he put on the garments...and he hunted the animals and he built altars, and he offered the animals before the Lord."

11. Bernhard Beer, *Das Leben Abraham's nach Auffassung der jüdischen Sage* (Leipzig: Leiner, 1859), 7.

12. Bin Gorion, *Sagen der Juden*, 2:365–66; cf. *Pirqe de Rabbi Eliezer* 24; *Jasher* 27:7. In the *Apocalypse of Abraham* 13, the garment is passed on to Abraham: when Satan was rebuked for taunting Adam and Eve after their transgression, God tells him that the garment that had belonged to him in heaven would be given to Abraham.

13. *Pirqe de Rabbi Eliezer*, 24.

14. *Numbers Rabbah* 4:8; cf. bin Gorion, *Sagen der Juden*, 2:371. In other sources, Jacob is said to have stolen the garment from Esau, *Pirqe de Rabbi Eliezer* 24. However, as *Jasher* 26:17 indicates, Esau deserved to lose the garment: "Esau was a designing and a deceitful man, and an expert hunter in the field, and Jacob was a man perfect and wise." When Nimrod, king of Babel, "went to hunt in the field...Nimrod was watching Esau all the days, for a jealousy was formed in the heart of Nimrod against Esau" (*Jasher* 27:23). But Esau lay in ambush, cut off Nimrod's head, and "took the garments of Nimrod...with which Nimrod prevailed over the whole land, and he ran and concealed them in his house." This was the birthright he sold to Jacob (*Jasher* 27:7, 10).

15. Hippolytus, *Fragmenta in Genesin* 3, in *PG* 10:604.

16. I have been greatly aided in my discussion of "dream incubation," both in content and bibliography, by my student Brian Dickman's unpublished paper "Did Jacob Wrestle a Man?"

17. Robert Karl Gnuse, *The Dream Theophany of Samuel: Its Structure in Relation to Ancient Near Eastern Dreams and Its Theological Significance* (Lanham: University Press of America, 1984); Bruce Vawter, *On Genesis: A New Reading* (Garden City: Doubleday, 1977), 313. On the function of dreams in the Bible and in the Christian tradition, see John A. Sanford, *Dreams: God's Forgotten Language* (Philadelphia: Lippincott, 1968); idem, *Dreams and Healing* (New York: Paulist Press, 1978); idem, *The Man Who Wrestled with God*, 23–28; Morton T. Kelsey, *God, Dreams, and Revelation: A Christian Interpretation of Dreams* (Minneapolis: Augsburg, 1974).

18. Gnuse, *The Dream Theophany of Samuel*, 64–73.

19. Mircea Eliade, *Patterns in Comparative Religion* (New York: New American Library, 1974), 369.

20. Hendel, *The Epic of the Patriarch*, 66, where he cites examples from ancient Mesopotamia and Greece.

21. Walter Burkert, *Structure and History in Greek Mythology and Ritual* (Berkeley: University of California, 1979), 42.

22. Idem, *The Myth of the Eternal Return*, W. R. Trask, trans. (Princeton: Princeton University Press, 1954), 12–17; quotation from Hendel, *The Epic of the Patriarch*, 65.

23. Bruce Vawter, *On Genesis: A New Reading* (Garden City: Doubleday, 1977), 313.

24. Walter Brueggemann, *Genesis* (Atlanta: John Knox Press, 1973), 243.

25. Lundquist, "Common Temple Typology," 157.

26. Henry Snyder Gehman, *The Interpreters of Foreign Languages Among the Ancients* (Lancaster, PA: Intelligencer Printing, 1914), 30–33; Alfred Hermann, "Dolmetschen im Altertum," in Karl Thieme, Alfred Hermann, and Edgar Glässer, *Beiträge zur Geschichte des Dolmetschens* (Munich: Isar Verlag, 1956), 25–59. This certainly is not like much of science fiction, which seems to have no difficulty in having creatures from opposite ends of the universe speak American English—Midwestern dialect, no less—with complete ease and no sense of irony.

27. On ritual meals in connection with covenant making in the Old Testament, see Walter T. McCree, "The Covenant Meal in the Old Testament," *Journal of Biblical Literature* 45 (1926): 120–28; Hans-Josef Klauck, *Herrenmahl und hellenistischer Kult: eine religionsgeschichtliche Untersuchung zum ersten Korintherbrief* (Münster: Aschendorff, 1982), 48–51; cf. also Ruth E. Thomas, *The Sacred Meal in the Older Roman Religion* (Chicago: University of Chicago Libraries, 1937).

28. Arthur M. Hocart, "Initiation," *Folklore* 35 (1924): 312; cf. Bruce H. Porter and Stephen D. Ricks, "Names in Antiquity: Old New, and Hidden," in John M. Lundquist and Stephen D. Ricks, eds., *By Study and Also by Faith: Essays in Honor of Hugh W. Nibley*, 2 vols. (Salt Lake City: F.A.R.M.S./Deseret Book, 1990), 1:501–22; Stephen D. Ricks and John Sroka, "King, Coronation, and Temple: Enthronement Ceremonies in History," in Donald W. Parry, ed., *The Temple in History* (Salt Lake City: F.A.R.M.S./Deseret Book, forthcoming).

29. Henri Frankfort, *Kingship and the Gods* (Chicago: University of Chicago Press, 1978), 36; cf. also John A. Wilson, *The Culture of Ancient Egypt* (Chicago: University of Chicago Press, 1962), 102.

30. Roland de Vaux, *Ancient Israel* (New York: McGraw-Hill, 1961), 108.

31. See Miller, *Mysterious Encounters*, 119–34 for a discussion of early Christian interpretations of Jacob's new name.

32. Raphael Patai, "Folk Customs and Charms Relating to Birth," in *Talpioth* 6 (1953): 248, cited in Theodor H. Gaster, *Myth, Legend, and Custom in the Old Testament,* 2 vols. (San Francisco: Harper and Row, 1975), 1:200. Gaster, ibid., also gives other uses in the ancient world: according to Josephus, *Jewish War,* VII, 6, 3, it is used as a protection against charms; in the view of Theophrastus, *Historia Plantarum* X, 15, 7, it may be used to counteract charms; among the modern Arabs, it is sometimes used in making love potions. The late historian of religions, Mircea Eliade, has noted mythic traditions that associate the mandrake with the first man, "Gayomart et la mandragore," *Ex Orbe Religionum: Studia Geo Widengren,* J. Bergman, K. Crynjeff, H. Ringgren, ed., 2 vols. (Leiden: Brill, 1972), 2:65–74; idem, "Adam, Le Christ, et la Mandragore," in *Mélanges d'histoire des religions offerts à Henri-Charles Puech* (Paris: Presses Universitaires de France, 1974), 611–15; idem, "La Mandragore et les mythes de la 'naissance miraculeuse,'" *Zalmoxis* 3 (1940–42): 348; cf. Frederick Starr "Notes upon the Mandrake," *The American Antiquarian and Oriental Journal* 23 (1901): 259–69; Charles Brewster Randolph, "The Mandragora of the Ancients in Folklore and Medicine," *Proceedings of the American Academy of Arts and Sciences* 40 (1905): 4855 37; Alfred Schlosser, *Die Sage vom Galgenmännlein im Volksglauben und in der Literatur* (Münster: Theissing, 1912); Adolph Taylor Starck, *Der Alraun: Ein Beitrag zur Pflanzensagenkunde* (Baltimore: Furst, 1917); James George Frazer, "Jacob and the Mandrakes," *Proceedings of the British Academy* (1917–1918): 57–79.

33. Gaster, *Myth, Legend, and Custom,* 1:200–1. Gaster, ibid., cites a striking parallel to this in the *Aeneid* II, 293–94, where Hector addresses Aeneas, who is fleeing a burning Troy: "To you Troy commends her household gods / Now take them as companions of your fate."

34. In a development of this idea, Ktziah Spanier, "Rachel's Theft of the Teraphim: Her Struggle for Family Supremacy (Gen. 31)," *Vetus Testamentum* 42 (1992): 404–12, sees the theft of the teraphim as a symbol of the claim of Rachel's descendants (i.e., Joseph, Ephraim, Manasseh) to preeminence among the Israelite tribes.

35. Vawter, *On Genesis,* 339.

36. It is interesting to note that in one of the early references to the Nephite interpreters as "Urim and Thummim"—a phrase that is never used in the Book of Mormon itself—the interpreters are also identified with or described as "teraphim," i.e., also an object, like the Urim and Thummim, through which God's will may be determined.

Chapter Six

Joseph—Faithful Student of Jesus Christ

John G. Scott

Joseph of old has been revered for thousands of years, and even a casual perusal of the passages in Genesis that cover his life (37–50) leads one to the conclusion that Joseph had a deep and active faith in Jehovah.[1] This faith would allow him to be steered and instructed by his God over the course of his lifetime. "Regarding divine tutorials," Elder Neal A. Maxwell has said, "we must not overlook ancient Joseph who was sold into Egypt, though the record we have of him is far from complete. His closeness to the Lord ensured that he was tutored."[2] These divine tutorials and Joseph's faithful life placed him in a position to act as a temporal savior not only to his household but also to the entire House of Israel.

Joseph's Youth

Joseph's story is well known, but certain highlights bear repeating in an investigation of Joseph's faith. It is not difficult to imagine that Joseph was taught by his father about the reality of Jehovah. This theme of passing on knowledge of the divine permeated the culture of the early patriarchs.[3] Indeed, "the evidence which these men had of the existence of a God was the testimony of their fathers, in the first instance."[4] It was the passing of this firsthand knowledge and faith from parent to child which led Adam's posterity to "search after a knowledge of his [Jesus Christ's] character, perfections, and attributes until they became extensively acquainted with him."[5] Jacob, Joseph's father, was well acquainted with the God of his fathers, and "faith," as Mark McConkie concludes, "was Joseph's familial inheritance."[6]

The Lord often communicates to his faithful servants in dreams,[7] and this was one of the earliest manifestations of young Joseph's faith—though at the time, this privilege must have seemed to bring only trouble. In his prophetic night visions Joseph saw, symbolically, his brothers and even his parents bowing in obeisance to him (see Gen. 37:5–11). The record is plain that because of the implications of this dream Joseph's brothers "envied him" and thus "conspired against him to slay him" (Gen. 37:8, 11).[8]

This conspiracy had its fruition in the sons of Jacob selling their younger brother into servitude (see Gen. 37:28), which deprived Joseph from the comforts and familiarity of the house of Israel, but placed him into a situation where the Lord could instruct him more fully. Only through "[God's] pressing, tutorial love,"[9] as Elder Neal A. Maxwell puts it, could Joseph develop the quality of faith in Jehovah, or Jesus Christ, that he would need for his mission here upon the earth. In speaking of personal opposition and adversity, Elder Marvin J. Ashton has said that "in times of hurt and discouragement, it may be consoling…for all of us to recall that no one can do anything permanently to us that will last for eternity. Only we ourselves can affect our eternal progression."[10] Without eternal perspective, surely the unfavorable circumstances of his early life might have weakened or destroyed Joseph's faith in Christ.

Slavery, Seduction, and Strength

Apparently Joseph was well acquainted with the Lord and was worthy of his blessings, for the guiding hand of the great Jehovah prepared the way for Joseph in Egypt. He was purchased by Potiphar, a powerful man in the land, and brought into a household where young Joseph was kept relatively safe from the physical hardships which he might have endured under different circumstances. Here Joseph gained the trust of his master, and "the Lord blessed the Egyptian's house for Joseph's sake; and the blessing of the Lord was upon all that he had in the house, and in the field" (Gen. 39:5).

Joseph was in his late teens or early twenties when Potiphar's wife tried to seduce him. Evidently grounded in the foundation of the gospel which advocates complete chastity before marriage and fidelity after marriage,[11] Joseph refused the advances she made "day by day" (Gen. 39:10). The scriptural record makes it appear that this temptation was easy for Joseph to deflect; however, as Richard D. Draper has observed:

> There is a popular myth which teaches that good people know little if anything about the power of temptation. This is patently false. It is the wicked who know little of its allure, its seducing force, and its punishing power because they never resist. How do they know what it is like to have to be strong for an hour, a day, or a year.[12]

Joseph's answer to his master's wife reflects both his spiritual maturity and faith:

> But he refused, and said unto his master's wife, Behold, my master wotteth not what is with me in the house, and he hath committed all that he hath to my hand;
>
> There is none greater in this house than I; neither hath he kept back any thing from me but thee, because thou art his wife: *how then can I do this great wickedness and sin against God?* (Gen. 39:8–9; emphasis added)

For Joseph, adultery would have been tantamount to sinning against his testimony of Jesus. With his integrity at stake, Joseph chose to be the man of virtue his faith taught he should be. Marden Clark, speaking on the subject of virtue, describes the personal significance of and responsibility for such choices:

> Virtue as mere abstinence may be a way to get through crucial years toward maturity; but it can never bring genuine maturity...virtue must be conceived as a positive, creative, even healing force.... What kind of me will result if I commit fornication or adultery? What kind of society will I tend toward creating? Such questions do not leave behind the fact of God's commandments. They even intensify, especially for Mormons, the probable personal and social results of violating

> the commandments. But they also place squarely the responsibility where it has to rest anyway: on *me* as agent consciously and creatively willing the act, or the abstention.[13]

After escaping the moral danger of Potiphar's wife, Joseph faced the wrath of Potiphar himself. At the evil report of attempted rape made by his wife, Potiphar, who may even have been the head of the king's executioners,[14] "took [Joseph] and put him into the prison, a place where the king's prisoners were bound: and he was there in prison" (Gen. 39:20). It is interesting to consider that, with all his power, Potiphar exercised a minimal penalty upon Joseph for his alleged crime. Once again, it appears, the Lord blessed Joseph with his life.

The School of the Prison

Though Joseph's life may have been spared, his initial reward for his faithful obedience was prison. The Lord says he will try both the patience and the faith of his saints (Mosiah 23:21), and Joseph stood up well to the test of both. According to Josephus:

> Joseph, commending all his affairs to God, did not betake himself to make his defense, nor to give an account of the exact circumstances of the fact, but silently underwent the bonds and the distress he was in; firmly believing, that God, who knew the cause of his affliction, and the truth of the fact, would be more powerful than those that inflicted the punishments upon him; a proof of whose providence he quietly received.[15]

Joseph did not wait on the Lord in vain. For as it was in Potiphar's house, so it was in prison:

> But the Lord was with Joseph, and showed him mercy, and gave him favor in the sight of the keeper of the prison. And the keeper of the prison committed to Joseph's hand all the prisoners that were in the prison; and whatsoever they did there, he was the doer of it. (Gen. 39:23)

It is likely that Joseph understood an important principle that George A. Smith—an early apostle of this dispensation and cousin to the Prophet Joseph—taught about having a persevering faith:

> He [Joseph Smith] told me I should never get discouraged, whatever difficulties might surround me. If I were sunk into the lowest pit of Nova Scotia and all the Rocky Mountains piled on top of me, I ought not to be discouraged, but hang on, exercise faith, and keep up good courage, and I should come out on top of the heap.[16]

With his faith placed firmly in his God, Joseph rose to the top of the heap and continued his journey toward a fascinating destiny of fate, power, prestige, and honor.

The Dreams of Pharaoh and His Servants

While in prison, Joseph became acquainted with two of the king's former servants, the chief butler and the chief baker, who fell under his charge (see Gen. 40:1–4). During their stay, Joseph would interpret troubling dreams for each of the king's former servants. Joseph's bold offer to interpret the night visions—"Do not interpretations belong to God? tell me them, I pray you" (Gen. 40:8)— is a convincing indication that he had faith that he would be able to do so. From the chief butler Joseph exacted a promise in return for his inspired interpretation: "But think on me when it shall be well with thee,...and make mention of me unto Pharaoh, and bring me out of this house" (Gen. 40:14). Unfortunately, the butler failed to mention Joseph for a full two years (see Gen. 41:1). This failure, or ingratitude, must have begun another test for Jacob's son.

It took a perplexing dream by Pharaoh to jar the memory of his butler. Again, according to the Lord's designs and Joseph's faith, a bad situation was turned for good, and "Pharaoh sent and called Joseph, and they brought him hastily out of the dungeon" (Gen. 41:14). To be sure, Joseph had been guided by the hand of the Lord, for nowhere else in all of Egypt was there a man who could interpret the king's dreams.

Joseph was not bashful in telling Pharaoh that God, not man, had showed this dream to the Pharaoh. The young seer instructed Pharaoh as to what he must do to save his kingdom from destruction, and it is reasonable to suggest that Pharaoh recognized the hand of the Lord in Joseph's interpretation of seven years each of plenty and famine and his proffered solution:

> And Pharaoh said unto his servants, Can we find such a one as this is, a man in whom the Spirit of God is?
>
> And Pharaoh said unto Joseph, Forasmuch as God hath showed thee all this, there is none so discreet and wise as thou art:
>
> Thou shalt be over my house, and according unto thy word shall all my people be ruled: only in the throne will I be greater than thou....
>
> And he made him to ride in the second chariot which he had; and they cried before him, Bow the knee: and he made him ruler over all the land of Egypt. (Gen. 41:37–39, 43)

Joseph rose from prisoner to Governor of Egypt, as God blessed the humble life of a man who placed his faith and confidence in Jehovah. As Joseph Smith said: "In a word, there was nothing impossible for them who had faith."[17] On his part, Pharaoh must have believed that Joseph was inspired of God.[18] Why else would he allow his young protégé to make large investments in the purchasing of corn and other edible items during years when there was a plentiful harvest? Joseph, on the other hand, had faith enough to stake everything on this prophecy. If, at the appointed time, the famine did not occur, Joseph stood to lose Pharaoh's trust, his position, and quite possibly his life.

The Temporal Salvation of the House of Israel

This famine affected a major part of the Middle East, eliciting the comment that "the famine was over all the face of the earth" (Gen. 41:56). The famine directly affected the House of Israel, as well; it would be the means whereby the Lord would bring Joseph's brothers to him, thus fulfilling the prophecy that Joseph's family would one day bow in obeisance to him (see Gen. 37:5–11; 42:6). In the face of this famine, the venerable prophet Jacob said, "Behold, I have heard that there is corn in Egypt: get you down thither, and buy for us from thence; that we may live, and not die" (Gen. 42:2).

It was during their second such visit to Egypt that Joseph's brothers "bowed down their heads, and made obeisance" to their as yet incognito brother (Gen. 43:28). As the brothers departed this second time, Joseph commanded his steward to fill their sacks with food, return their money, and hide Joseph's own silver cup in the sack of Benjamin, the youngest. Through this test Joseph undoubtedly wanted to measure his brothers' loyalty to Benjamin. Would they do to Benjamin as they had done with him over two decades before? This test was designed by a man who knew all too well the importance of tests in one's life.

The next morning, Joseph's steward stopped the caravan and accused the brothers of stealing Joseph's silver cup. Jacob's sons protested, offering the life of the offender and the servitude of the rest should the cup be found among them. As the sacks were searched, from the eldest to the youngest, the cup was found in Benjamin's sack. With clothes rent in anguish, the brothers returned to Joseph for judgment.

As the brothers stood before Joseph, Judah, who had once betrayed Joseph, offered himself a slave in the stead of Benjamin. This stretched Joseph's heart to the breaking point, and the Grand Vizier of Egypt informed his brothers who he was, proclaiming his deep faith in God at the same time:

> Now therefore be not grieved, nor angry with yourselves, that ye sold me hither: for God did send me before you to preserve life.
>
> For these two years hath the famine been in the land: and yet there are five years, in the which there shall neither be earing nor harvest.
>
> And God sent me before you to preserve you a posterity in the earth, and to save your lives by a great deliverance.
>
> So now it was not you that sent me hither, but God: and he hath made me a father to Pharaoh, and lord of all his house, and a ruler throughout all the land of Egypt. (Gen. 45:5–8)

Once the brothers returned to Beersheba, where Israel dwelt, they shared with him the good news that Joseph was alive and a great ruler in Egypt. "It is enough," Israel said, "Joseph my son is yet alive: I will go and see him before I die" (Gen. 45:28). The record indicates that upon reuniting with his father, Joseph "fell on his [Jacob's] neck, and wept on his neck a good while" (Gen. 46:29). Nearly two and one half decades had passed since he had seen his father. After all of these years, filled with trial and testing, the fruition of Joseph's faith in God was a glorious reunion with his family and the preservation of the House of Israel, enabling covenants made generations earlier to be kept.

Faith and Forgiveness

After Jacob's death the brothers of Joseph feared for their safety. They thought, "Joseph will preadventure hate us, and will certainly requite us all the evil which we did unto him" (Gen. 50:15). Because of this fear Joseph's brothers sent an emissary to their esteemed brother to beg his forgiveness. His reaction is one filled with tender forgiveness:

> And Joseph said unto them, Fear not: for am I in the place of God?
>
> But as for you, ye thought evil against me; but God meant it unto good, to bring to pass, as it is this day, to save much people alive.
>
> Now therefore fear ye not: I will nourish you, and your little ones. And he comforted them, and spake kindly unto them. (Gen. 50:19–21)

Once again we see Joseph practicing his faith in God, this time unto forgiveness. He did not seek retribution for past mistakes; instead, Joseph forgave his brothers their trespass against him, as God commands his servants to do.

Joseph, Seer of the Lord: a Legacy of Faith

The story of Joseph in Genesis does not end with chapter fifty; Joseph Smith's inspired translation of that chapter contains significant visions and revelations given to Joseph the seer for all of the House of Israel. As a seer, Joseph obtained a view of his posterity which vividly detailed the important part they would play in the fulfillment of the Abrahamic covenant. Why was this gift of seership given to Joseph, and what would be the "great benefit to his fellow beings" which would flow from this gift? Ammon, in teaching King Lamoni about the gift of being a seer, records: "Thus God has provided a means that man, *through faith*, might work mighty miracles; therefore he becometh a *great benefit to his fellow beings*" (Mosiah 8:18; emphasis added).[19]

Harold B. Lee said, at the passing of another great seer of the Lord, David O. McKay: "As a special witness of our Lord and Master, he lighted the lamps of faith of many by the intensity of the fire within his own soul. His was the sure word of prophecy that Jesus Christ was indeed our Savior and our Redeemer and literal Son of God, our Heavenly Father."[20] Through his own prophecies, Joseph became a lamp for all Israel. Through his faith-filled visions, our fires of conviction can be kindled, as surely as those of ancient Israel were. In speaking of the light which would emanate to the world through Joseph's lineage, his father, Jacob, stated: "For thou shalt be a light unto my people, to deliver them in the days of their captivity, from bondage; and to bring salvation unto them, when they are altogether bowed down under sin" (JST Gen. 48:11).

Joseph's prophecies revealed that: (1) a seer called Moses would be given to deliver Israel out of Egyptian bondage; (2) Israel, once free from bondage, would be scattered, and a remnant of Joseph's posterity would be preserved; (3) descendants of Judah and Joseph would keep sacred records; and (4) a choice seer would be raised up in the last days to bring about the restoration, with the same name as Joseph of old. Each of these prophecies, in its time, offered sustaining faith to the children of Israel yet unborn.

A Seer Called Moses

Ever concerned for his family, Joseph obtained knowledge from the Lord respecting the generations beyond his. He saw, through the eyes of faith, that Israel would find itself in bondage to Egypt (see JST Gen. 50:24). Just prior to his death he revealed that:

> I go down to my grave with joy. The God of my father Jacob be with you, to deliver you out of affliction in the days of your bondage; for the Lord hath visited me, and I have obtained a promise of the Lord, that out of the fruit of my loins, the Lord God will raise up a righteous branch out of my loins; and unto thee, whom my father Jacob hath named Israel, a prophet; (not the Messiah who is called Shilo); and this prophet shall deliver my people out of Egypt in the days of thy bondage....

> And I will make him great in mine eyes, for he shall do my work;...for a seer will I raise up to deliver my people out of the land of Egypt; and he shall be called Moses. And by this name he shall know that he is of thy house; for he shall be nursed by the king's daughter, and shall be called her son. (JST Gen. 50:24, 29; emphasis added)

Since Israel's records are not complete we can only presume what effect this prophecy had on the tribes of Israel during their long bondage. Assuming that the Israelites had access to this prophecy, this vision most likely gave hope and faith in the delivering power of Jehovah to the posterity of Jacob during their long confinement in Egypt. The Israelites knew the name of their deliverer, Moses, and the record seems to imply that Moses himself may have come to an understanding of his lineage through this prophecy as he learned of the significance of his name. Therefore, Joseph's faith in Christ that led to visions resulted in a powerful witness of Israel's great lawgiver, Moses—himself a type of Christ.

Israel Scattered and a Remnant Preserved

Joseph blessed countless lives by foretelling the scattering of Israel after their Egyptian bondage. Perhaps his vision was enlarged by his father, Jacob, during the blessings which Jacob gave to his sons prior to Jacob's death. Jacob specified that this final blessing given to his household concerned "that which shall befall you in the *last days*" (Gen. 49:1; emphasis added). Jacob blessed Joseph that his posterity would be "a fruitful bough, even a fruitful bough by a well; whose branches run over the wall" (Gen. 49:22). From this we conclude that there would never be a barrier, even the great ocean, that would stop Joseph's posterity from inhabiting the land beyond.

Apparently these prophesies about Joseph's seed, as well as prophesies made by Joseph himself, were on the brass plates obtained by Nephi (see 2 Ne. 3:5; Alma 46:24). One of the first things Lehi learned from the plates of brass was that he was a descendant of Joseph. In fact, Lehi and his family constituted part of the "remnant" spoken of by Joseph in one of his prophesies:

> And it shall come to pass that they shall be scattered again; and a branch shall be broken off, and shall be carried into a far country; nevertheless they shall be remembered in the covenants of the Lord, when the Messiah cometh; for he shall be made manifest unto them in the latter days, in the spirit of power; and shall bring them out of darkness into light; out of hidden darkness, and out of captivity unto freedom. (JST Gen. 50:25)

Perhaps Lehi took these prophesies into account as he and his family journeyed into the wilderness, considering that he, a descendant of Joseph, was meant to fulfill the promises made to his forefather in ancient Egypt. These promises must have acted as a guiding light, a glowing torch which strengthened the faith of the Nephites along their path to destiny in a new world. It is apparent from the words of Nephi that the revelations of Joseph were prized and that he understood their implication for his own people. In speaking of Joseph of old, he exclaimed:

> For behold, he truly prophesied concerning all his seed. And the prophecies which he wrote, *there are not many greater.* And he prophesied concerning *us*, and our future generations; and they are written upon the plates of brass. (2 Ne. 4:2; emphasis added)

These prophesies did not dim with time. In an obvious reference to the plates of brass, Moroni, the great Nephite military leader, stated:

> Yea, let us preserve our liberty as a remnant of Joseph; yea, let us remember the words of Jacob, before his death, for behold, he saw that a part of the remnant of the coat of Joseph was preserved and had not decayed. And he said—Even as this remnant of garment of my son hath been preserved, so shall a remnant of the seed of thy son be preserved by the hand of God, and be taken unto himself, while the remainder of the seed of Joseph shall perish, even as the remnant of his garment. (Alma 46:24)

Obviously, the prophecies of Joseph had a great impact on the Nephite civilization for generations. In this case Moroni quoted them as a rallying point to his people, teaching them that they should remain faithful in the liberty of Christ, that they not turn out to be that remnant which should perish. Truly, even down to the time of Moroni in 73 B.C.[21] the prophecies of Joseph were acting as "a great benefit to his [Joseph's] fellow beings" (Mosiah 8:18). These prophecies produced faith and gave hope and direction to an entire civilization.

Judah and Joseph Keep Sacred Records

Joseph prophesied that the tribes of both Judah and Joseph would keep sacred records and indicated what benefit these records would have for us in the latter days. The Lord revealed through Joseph:

> Wherefore the fruit of thy loins shall write, and the fruit of the loins of Judah shall write; and that which shall be written by the fruit of thy loins, and also that which shall be written by the fruit of the loins of Judah, shall grow together unto the confounding of false doctrines, and laying down of contentions, and establishing peace among the fruit of thy loins, and bringing them to a knowledge of their fathers in the latter days; and also to the knowledge of my covenants, saith the Lord. (JST Gen. 50:31; emphasis added; see also 2 Ne. 3:12)

The Latter-day Saints are the recipients of this record. Like the ancients before, we have the opportunity to exercise faith in the prophecies given. A faithful study of the sticks of Judah and Joseph should be the goal of every Latter-day Saint (see Ezek. 37). Through that study we, like those who studied the brass plates and the prophecies of Joseph, can gain the faith necessary to overcome the world and move mountains (Jacob 4:6 and Alma 31:15).

A Choice Seer in the Latter Days

The Saints of the latter-days are the beneficiaries also of the revelations given to the ancient Joseph about Joseph Smith. We can look to those prophecies to increase faith in the greatness of the prophet who stands at the head of this dispensation. The son of Jacob saw this great latter-day seer. Indeed, he identifies him and his work very specifically:

> And that seer will I bless, and they that seek to destroy him shall be confounded; for this promise I give unto you; for I will remember you from generation to generation; and his name shall be called *Joseph*, and it shall be after the name of his father; and he shall be *like unto you*; for the thing which the Lord shall bring forth by his hand shall bring my people unto salvation. (JST Gen. 50:33; emphasis added)

Additionally, the Lord specified through Joseph of old that:

> Thus saith the Lord God of my fathers unto me, a choice seer will I raise up out of the fruit of thy loins, and he shall be esteemed highly among the fruit of thy loins; and unto him will I give commandment that he shall do a work for the fruit of thy loins, his brethren.
>
> And he shall bring them to the knowledge of the covenants which I have made with thy fathers; and he shall do whatsoever work I shall command him.
>
> And I will make him great in mine eyes, for he shall *do my work*; and he shall be great like unto him whom I have said I would raise up unto you, to deliver my people, O house of Israel... (JST Gen. 50:27–29; emphasis added)

The Name

The name of the future seer is remarkably specific. Joseph testifies that this prophet would be "called Joseph, and it shall be after the name of his father" (JST Gen. 50:33.) Why this particular name? Some conclusions can be drawn when we look at the etymology of the name. Joseph Fielding McConkie has noted that

> the name [Joseph] is usually given as "the Lord addeth" or "increaser." Though appropriate, such renderings have veiled a richer meaning. In the Bible account wherein Rachel names her infant son Joseph the Hebrew text reads Asaph, which means "he who gathers," "he who causes to return," or perhaps most appropriately "God gathereth" (Gen. 30:24; see also the footnote to the LDS edition). No more appropriate name could be given to the prophet of the restoration or to the tribe destined to do the work of the gathering than the name of their ancient father who gathered his family in Egypt.[22]

It is important to note that not only did God know the names of his prophets before they came into mortality, but he also watched the bloodlines which would eventually produce the latter-day prophet of God. That prophet was not born into the house of Joseph Smith Sr. by mere chance.[23] Wilford Woodruff summed up this fact when he stated that

> I believe that God Almighty reserved a certain class of men to carry on his work. They have been born into the world in this generation. I believe this was the case with Joseph Smith. I believe he was ordained to this work before he was tabernacled in the flesh. He was a literal descendant of Joseph who was sold into Egypt, and the Lord called him and ordained him. He gave unto him the keys of the kingdom. He received the record of the stick of Joseph from the hands of Ephraim, to stand with the Bible, the stick of Judah, in the last days as a power to gather the twelve tribes of Israel, before the coming of Shiloh, their king.[24]

We are blessed in having seen this prophecy fulfilled in the latter-days. The prophesies of Joseph of old provide faith-confirming evidence of the divine calling of the Prophet Joseph Smith.

Joseph of old prophesied that this choice seer would accomplish a great work as a seer of the Lord. His first and greatest work would be to bring the Lord's people unto salvation through the re-establishment of the covenants of the Lord. In large part, this prophecy was fulfilled through the translation and publication of the Book of Mormon to all the world. The command to bring forth this record is presently being fulfilled in great measure. In 1992 there were more than three million copies printed.[25] Also, in 1992 "the Book of Mormon was rated the eighth most influential book in America."[26]

The bringing forth of the Book of Mormon was only one part of the great work Joseph's namesake was to accomplish. In summation of Joseph Smith's works, John Taylor states that:

> Joseph Smith, the Prophet and Seer of the Lord, has done more, save Jesus only, for the salvation of men in this world, than any other man that ever lived in it. In the short space of

> twenty years, he has brought forth the Book of Mormon, which he translated by the gift and power of God, and has been the means of publishing it on two continents; has sent the fullness of the everlasting gospel, which it contained, to the four quarters of the earth; has brought forth the revelations and commandments which compose this book of Doctrine and Covenants, and many other wise documents and instructions for the benefit of the children of men; gathered many thousands of the Latter-day Saints, founded a great city, and left a fame and name that cannot be slain. He lived great, and he died great in the eyes of God and his people; and like most of the Lord's anointed in ancient times, has sealed his mission and his works with his own blood. (D&C 135:3)

Robert L. Millet, Dean of Religious Education at Brigham Young University, also summarized up the ministry of Joseph Smith, using these words:

> Joseph Smith, like Adam, Enoch, Noah, Abraham, Moses and Jesus stands as a dispensation head. The dispensation head becomes the means by which the knowledge and power of God are channeled to men and women on earth. They become the means by which the gospel of Jesus Christ–the plan of salvation and exaltation–are revealed anew, the means by which divine transforming powers, including saving covenants and ordinances, are extended to people during an age of time we call a dispensation. The dispensation head is the preeminent witness of Christ; he knows firsthand because of what he has seen and heard and felt and experienced. Because of his central place in the plan and because it is by means of the power of his testimony that men and women come to know the Lord and bask in the light of the spirit, the calling and position of the dispensation head thus becomes something about which his followers feel to bear witness. Indeed, and appropriately so, men and women of a particular dispensation who stand to express the witness which burns in their bosoms, find themselves bearing testimony of Christ and of the dispensation head–the revealer of Christ–in almost the same breath. This is just as it should be.[27]

The work of Joseph Smith was to bear testimony of the reality and divinity of Jesus Christ, and thus create faith in the reality of the Savior. As Brother Millet says, the dispensation head is "the revealer of Christ." Thus it was with Joseph. His human testimony (see JS—H 1:15-20, D&C 76:22-23) of a divine being is calculated to produce within us the most solemn and reverent faith about the reality of Christ.

Conclusion

Thirty percent of the book of Genesis is used to cover the life of Joseph, whose life only occupies five percent of the time recorded in Genesis.[28] Evidently, the Lord inspired Moses to include this lengthy rendition of Joseph's life for a reason. As this chapter has pointed out, one reason was to describe for the reader how Joseph worked by faith throughout his life and how he helped others along the pathway of time by faith. His use of the gift of seership for example, benefitted the entire House of Israel.

Although the writings of Joseph are not complete, we can see that his great concern for his posterity has reached beyond the span of death and time and has indeed had an effect on the faith of key players who have had such a mighty influence on the House of Israel. One example of his tender concern is given to us through Joseph Smith's patriarchal blessing. As his father, Joseph Smith Sr., placed his hands upon the head of his seeric son, he said:

> I bless thee with the blessings of thy father Abraham, Isaac and Jacob; and even the blessings of thy father Joseph, the son of Jacob. Behold he looked after his posterity in the last days, when they should be scattered and driven by the Gentiles, and wept before the Lord; he sought diligently to know from whence the son should come who should bring forth the word of the Lord, by which they might be enlightened and brought back to the true fold, *and his eyes beheld thee, my son*; his heart rejoiced and his soul was satisfied...[29]

Surely, this blessing touched the life of the young prophet. It is likely that through this knowledge Joseph was able to take faith and courage and endure severe trials. In countless ways, like this example, the prophecies of Joseph have been a blessing and a benefit to those who would look after his posterity.

Ancient Joseph's posterity must have looked to his revelations for faith, hope, inspiration, and peace. The very fact that the Church is restored testifies that his posterity found what they were looking for. As modern descendents of Joseph, we also have the responsibility and privilege to look to these revelations for the same comforts.

Seers do not operate as a genie in a lamp, for us to rub the brass and suddenly have a view of things which will come to pass. Seers are given to men so that they might see the past as it really existed and the future as it will actually be, which will hopefully have a profound positive effect on the present. Once we have this reality in view of the present and how it is connected to the past and the future, we will have cause to exercise faith and correctly evaluate our performance in the present. The Director of the Center for the Study of American Religion at Princeton University has summed up this idea by saying:

> We miss the whole point of the future when we approach it as something to predict. Then we become forecasters, trying to guess tomorrow's weather so we can carry umbrellas or sunglasses. The real reason we reflect on the future, I suspect, is not to control it, but to give ourselves room in the present to think about what we are doing.[30]

A sense of gratitude distills upon the mind when the prophecies of Joseph are reviewed. His life is an example of one who was a faithful student of Jesus Christ. His life is a testimony that God honors the faith of his servants. We as Latter-day Saints in the present would do well to act like the ancients, to have the faith to follow the directions, counsels, and commandments given to us by our own prophets, seers, and revelators, and thereby become ourselves, students of Jesus Christ.

Notes

1. As Latter-day Saints we believe that the God of the Old Testament is Jesus Christ. For a treatment on this subject see David R. Seely, "Jehovah, Jesus Christ," in *Encyclopedia Of Mormonism* (New York: Macmillan Publishing Co., 1992), 2:720–21.

2. Neal A. Maxwell, *Meek and Lowly,* (Salt Lake City: Deseret Book, 1987), 117–18.

3. *The Lectures on Faith in Historical Perspective,* ed. Larry E. Dahl and Charles D. Tate, Jr. (Provo, Utah: BYU Religious Studies Center, 1990), 45.

4. Ibid, 45.

5. Ibid, 46.

6. Mark L. McConkie, *The Father of the Prophet: Stories and Insights from the Life of Joseph Smith, Sr.* (Salt Lake City: Bookcraft, 1993), 31.

7. Bruce R. McConkie, *Mormon Doctrine* (Salt Lake City: Bookcraft, 1979), 208.

8. For a historical treatment of Joseph and his brothers see: *The Complete Works of Josephus: Antiquities of the Jews,* 10 vols (New York: The World Syndicate Publishing Co.), 77–81. See also Paul L. Maier, *Josephus, The Essential Writings* (Grand Rapids, Michigan: Kregel Publications, 1988), 37–38.

9. As quoted in *Riches of Eternity,* ed. John K. Challis and John G. Scott (Salt Lake City: Aspen Books, 1993), 62.

10. Marvin J. Ashton, *Ensign,* May 1984, 10.

11. Bryce J. Christensen, "Chastity, Law Of", *Encyclopedia Of Mormonism* (New York: Macmillan Publishing Co., 1992), 1:265–66

12. Richard D. Draper, *Journal of Book of Mormon Studies* (Provo, Utah: Foundation for Ancient Research and Mormon Studies, Spring 1993), 88.

13. Marden Clark, *Liberating Form* (Salt Lake City: Aspen Books, 1992), 43–44.

14. *Old Testament Institute Manual,* 95.

15. *Josephus,* 86.

16. George A. Smith, as quoted by Ezra Taft Benson in *Teachings of Ezra Taft Benson* (Salt Lake City: Bookcraft, 1988), 396.

17. N.B. Lundwall, comp., *Lectures on Faith* (Salt Lake City: Bookcraft, n.d.), 67.

18. Certainly Pharaoh's dreams were given to him by the Lord, for Joseph issued an inspired interpretation of them (see Gen. 41:25, 28, 32). This *might* indicate that Pharaoh was a righteous man, or at the very least not a wicked man. Bruce R. McConkie said that "[i]nspired dreams are the fruit of faith; they are not given to apostate peoples. (See McConkie, *Mormon Doctrine,* 208.) We speculate that at this time the Pharaohs of Egypt were not the native seed of Ham to whom the Priesthood was denied because of apostasy and disobedience (see Abr. 1:21–27). Rather they were the Hyksos, or "Shepherd

kings," (J.R. Dummelow, *A Commentary on the Holy Bible* [New York: Macmillian Publishing Co., 1936], 40.) These were a Semitic people "who had conquered Egypt and ruled it for many years" (George A. Horton, Jr., *Studies in Scripture, Volume Three,* 70). From what is known, this Semitic speaking people conquered Egypt sometime prior to Joseph's arrival. Then, sometime after Joseph's death the native Egyptians asserted dominion over the Hyksos and recaptured control of the empire. Apparently, as was the custom, all evidence of the Hyksos rule was erased. For a treatment of the Hyksos reign see *Civilization, Past and Present, Sixth Edition,* comp. T. Walter Wallbank, Alastair M. Taylor, Nels M. Bailkey, George F. Jewsbury, Clyde J. Lewis, and Neil J. Hackett (Glenview, Illinois: Scott, Foresman and Co., 1987), 16, 18. In any case, God's purposes were not completely hidden from Pharaoh.

19. James R. Clark, "Writings of Joseph." For an enlightening treatment of Joseph, and the possible effects which he has had on others see Arthur R. Bassett, "Joseph, Model of Excellence," *Ensign,* September 1980, 9–13.

20. Harold B. Lee, *Stand Ye in Holy Places* (Salt Lake City: Deseret Book, 1975), 77.

21. See data reference, *The Book of Mormon, Another Testament of Jesus Christ* (Salt Lake City: The Church of Jesus Christ of Latter-day Saints, 1981), 322.

22. Joseph Fielding McConkie, *Gospel Symbolism* (Salt Lake City: Bookcraft, 1985), 38.

23. Truman G. Madsen, *Joseph Smith the Prophet* (Salt Lake City: Bookcraft, 1989), 107–8. See also Kenneth Godfrey, "More Treasures Than One: Section 111," in *Hearken, O Ye People* (Sandy, Utah: Randall Books, 1984), 195–96.

24. Wilford Woodruff, in *Journal of Discourses* (Liverpool, England: Latter-Day Saints' Book Depot, 1854–86), 22:206.

25. Gordon B. Hinckley, "As One Who Loves the Prophet," in *Joseph Smith, the Prophet, the Man* (Provo, Utah: BYU Religious Studies Center, 1993), 4.

26. Ibid, 5.

27. Robert L. Millet, "Joseph Among the Prophets," in *Joseph Smith, the Prophet, the Man* (Provo, Utah: BYU Religious Studies Center, 1993), 22.

28. Robert J. Matthews, "Our Heritage from Joseph" (Remarks made at the 22nd Annual Sidney B. Sperry Symposium: Provo, Utah, Brigham Young University), 2.

29. Joseph Fielding McConkie, *Encyclopedia of Mormonism,* 2:761.

30. Robert Within, *Christianity in the 21st Century* (New York: Oxford University Press, 1993), 4.

Chapter Seven

Moses: Spiritual Preparation of A Mighty Man of Faith

Robert J. Matthews

Introduction

In Paul's great discourse on faith in Hebrews chapter 11, he spends seven verses citing examples of faith in the life of Moses—Abraham is the only other person given such attention. According to Paul, "by faith" Moses was saved by his parents, chose to suffer with the people of God rather than enjoy the pleasures of Egypt, endured the perils of leaving Egypt, kept the Passover, and passed through the Red Sea (Heb 11:23–29). His life was such that hundreds of years later and a continent away, a young Nephi would cite Moses as an example as he tried to arouse in his wavering brothers the faith necessary to try once again to obtain the plates of brass from Laban (1 Ne. 4:1–4).

We cannot, in one chapter, cover all the interesting and significant items pertaining to Moses, but I will highlight some topics in order to show his spiritual greatness and the results of a life of faith. The views and interpretations expressed here are my own, but I believe that what I have written is true. I am sobered by the awareness that we are discussing an actual person, a prophet and seer who is alive and is real and whom we shall see in the eternities. I want to be certain that Moses would approve of what I say about him.

Elder Bruce R. McConkie has written of Moses:

> In prophetic power, spiritual insight, and leadership qualifications, *Moses* ranks with the mightiest men who have ever lived. All succeeding generations have classed him as the great law-giver of Israel. The miracles and majesty attending his ministry can scarcely be duplicated. Indeed, his life and ministry stand as a prototype of the mortal life and ministry of our Lord himself. So great was Moses that even Christ is described as a Prophet like unto this ancient leader of Israel's hosts. (Deut. 18:15–19; Acts 3:22–23; 3 Ne. 20:23.)
>
> ...But the importance of the ministry of Moses to men now living lies primarily in his return to earth in modern times to carry out his part in the great restitution of all things. (Acts 3:19.) On the 3rd of April in 1836 he appeared to Joseph Smith and Oliver Cowdery in the Kirtland Temple and committed unto them the keys of the gathering of Israel and the leading of the Ten Tribes from the land of the north. (D&C 110:11.) These were the special powers and endowments that rested with the kingdom in his day, and by virtue of their restoration men are now authorized to use the priesthood for these great purposes.[1]

With this great eulogy ringing in our ears we will proceed to examine what the historical and scriptural records say concerning Moses.

There are many things about the ancient world that we do not know. This is especially true of precise dates. There is much about the culture of ancient Israel that we do not know, but as we learn to use latter-day revelation as our key, we are able to see God's purposes as they were unfolded among the ancient Israelites under the leadership of Moses. We do not have the date of the exodus of Israel from Egypt—probably not within a century. Nor do we know which Pharaoh enslaved and oppressed Israel, or which Pharaoh ruled at the time of the Exodus. Unfortunately, Egypt's records make no viable mention of Jacob, Joseph, or Moses, and therefore give no hint about Israel being led out of Egypt by a prophet of God. Four hundred years of our ancestral history, the mighty works of God—such as the ten plagues, the destroying angel at the Passover, the dividing of the Red Sea—and the records of Egypt are as silent about it as the great stone sphinx.

For sources, then, we will draw upon the King James Version of the Bible, the Joseph Smith Translation of the Bible, the Latin Vulgate translation, the writings of Josephus, the Book of Mormon, the Doctrine and Covenants, and the Pearl of Great Price. And where faith is not overtly spoken of in the record, it is certainly implied, or manifested, in the works and life of God's lawgiver.

Moses Is Prominent in Three Great Religions Today

Moses is prominent in the literature and belief of millions of people. He is revered by three large segments of the religious world: Judaism, Islam, and Christianity. James observed at the Jerusalem Conference that the writings of Moses were "read in the synagogues every sabbath day" (Acts 15:21). In fact, in the synagogue service it was the custom not to read anything from the prophets, such as Isaiah or Ezekiel, or from the writings, such as Psalms, until after there had been a reading from the law that was written by Moses.

Moses is mentioned by name in the Old Testament 657 times, the New Testament 65 times, the Book of Mormon 26 times, the Doctrine and Covenants 21 times, and in the Pearl of Great Price 29 times, for a total of 798. As an illustration of how important he is to Latter-day Saints, in the Pearl of Great Price we find the Book of Moses, revealed through Joseph Smith, which contains significant information about the prophet. The *Catholic Encyclopedia,* Volume X, gives two large pages in small print to Moses; and the *Jewish Encyclopedia,* Volume 9, spends fourteen large pages in small print on Moses. *The Encyclopedia of Religion,* Volume 10, devotes six pages to Moses.

Birth and Early Life of Moses

The first mention of the name Moses in the Bible occurs in Exodus 2:10, the story of his birth. But in the Joseph Smith Translation, the patriarch Joseph mentions Moses by name in prophecy at least 300 years before his birth. In Joseph's prophecy, Moses's mission in life is clearly defined. Joseph was speaking to his brothers about their future condition in Egypt, and he told them that the house of Israel would come into "bondage" and "affliction," but that he (Joseph) had obtained a promise of deliverance from the Lord: "the Lord God will raise up...unto thee, whom my father Jacob hath named Israel, a prophet; (not the Messiah who is called Shilo); and this prophet shall deliver my people out of Egypt in the days of thy bondage" (JST Gen. 50:24).[2]

Joseph further prophesied:

> ....For a seer will I [the Lord] raise up to deliver my people out of the land of Egypt; and he shall be called Moses. And by this name he shall know that he is of thy house; for he shall be nursed by the king's daughter, and shall be called her son.
>
> And the Lord sware unto Joseph that he would preserve his seed forever, saying, I will raise up Moses, and a rod shall be in his hand, and he shall gather together my people, and he shall lead them as a flock, and he shall smite the waters of the Red Sea with his rod.
>
> And he shall have judgment, and shall write the word of the Lord. And he shall not speak many words, for I will write unto him my law by the finger of mine own hand. And I will make a spokesman for him, and his name shall be called Aaron. (JST Gen. 50:29, 34–35)

When the right time arrived, and in answer to promises made to the faithful that Israel would be delivered, Moses was born. He was of the tribe of Levi, a son of Amram and Jochebed. Josephus, the Jewish historian, is careful to show that Moses was a special child and was the seventh generation from Abraham.[3] This is because the ancient Jews put great credence in being the seventh son, or the seventh generation. They also put an emphasis on threes, and the scriptures speak of three forty-year periods in Moses's life: 1–40 in Egypt, 40–80 in Midian and Sinai, and 80–120 leading Israel in the wilderness.

The account in the book of Exodus about Moses's birth and first forty years of life is brief. There had arisen a Pharaoh "who knew not Joseph," and the children of Israel were made to work at hard labor: "and they made their lives bitter with hard bondage, in morter [sic], and in brick, and in all manner of service in the field: all their service, wherein they made them serve, was with rigour" (Ex. 1:14). The children of Israel were also employed in the building of two treasure cities, Pithom and Raamses (v. 11). Because the Israelites were becoming so numerous, the Pharaoh grew uneasy and commanded that "every [Israelite] son that is born ye shall cast into the river, and every daughter ye shall save alive" (Ex. 1:22).

After Moses was born, his parents kept him three months and then placed him in a basket among the cattails along the banks of the Nile, while Miriam, his older sister, watched nearby. The Pharaoh's daughter found the baby, had compassion on him, recognized him as a Hebrew child, and took him out of the basket. Miriam, standing by, offered to find a woman who would care for the baby, to which the princess agreed. Miriam ran home and got Moses's mother, who nursed her own son with the permission of the royal household and was even paid wages to do so (Ex. 2:1–9). "And the child grew, and she brought him unto Pharaoh's daughter, and he became her son" (Ex. 2:10). It is a most unusual paradox that Pharaoh's command to destroy the sons of the Israelites led to the bringing up in his own household the very man who would eventually take the Israelites away from him.

Moses a Mighty Man in Egypt

The Old Testament tells us little else about Moses's boyhood or life in Egypt until he was forty years old. At that time, he saw an Egyptian smiting an Israelite and came to the rescue. In the struggle, according to Exodus 2:12, the Egyptian was slain. The next day, Moses saw two Israelites fighting, and he "said to him that did the wrong, Wherefore smitest thou thy fellow?" (Ex. 2:13).

At this point we have the only allusion given in the Old Testament that Moses was a great man in the Egyptian government, for the Israelite said to Moses: "Who made thee a *prince* and a *judge* over us? intendest thou to kill me, as thou killedst the Egyptian?" (Ex. 2:14; emphasis added). Those words may imply that Moses may have been looked upon as a prince and a judge among the Egyptians, and perhaps even a future Pharaoh, even though the Israelites wouldn't accept him as their leader. Prince or not, "when Pharaoh heard this thing [the death of the Egyptian], he sought to slay Moses. But Moses fled...and dwelt in the land of Midian" (Ex. 2:15). Moses stayed in Midian forty years, during which time he married the daughter of Jethro and tended Jethro's flocks in the area known as the Sinai peninsula, the approximate area in which he would later lead the children of Israel.

With so little information about Moses's life during his boyhood and young manhood, we cannot help but wonder *if* he knew that he was an Israelite and not an Egyptian; and *if* he knew it, when and how did he learn it? We wonder also if during those first forty years in Egypt he knew what his mission was and if there was any significance to his name being "Moses." We do not know how much his mother could have told him. If he had been with her long enough, she certainly informed him that he was an Israelite, but we do not know if she knew what his mission was to be. There is no mention in our present Old Testament of Moses's activity and training as a prince of Egypt, and we are again left to wonder if it was a difficult thing for Moses to give up the splendor and the prestige of the palace to live in the barren, harsh desert with the sheep. We are left without any answers to these questions unless we turn to other sources.

The New Testament tells us more about Moses. Both Paul and Stephen knew things about Moses not recorded in our current Old Testament. They either had a better account of the book of Exodus than we do, or they had other sources, or both. We read from Stephen's address to the Sanhedrin recorded in Acts 7:17–25 (emphasis added):

> But when the time of the promise drew nigh, which God had sworn to Abraham, the people grew and multiplied in Egypt,
>
> Till another king arose, which knew not Joseph.
>
> The same dealt subtilly with our kindred, and evil entreated our fathers, so that they cast out their young children, to the end they might not live.
>
> In which time Moses was born, and was *exceeding fair,* and nourished up in his father's house three months:
>
> And when he was cast out, Pharaoh's daughter took him up, *and nourished him for her own son.*
>
> And Moses was *learned* in all the wisdom of the Egyp-

> tians, *and was mighty in words and in deeds.*
>
> And when he was full forty years old, it came into his heart to visit his brethren the children of Israel.
>
> And seeing one *of them* suffer wrong, he defended *him*, and avenged him that was oppressed, and smote the Egyptian:
>
> For he supposed his brethren would have understood how that God by his hand would deliver them: but they understood not.

We ascertain from this passage that Moses did know of his own identity and of his mission and also that he was learned and active in things Egyptian.

Paul says more about Moses in the book of Hebrews. Note that Moses makes a conscious choice to serve the Lord God of Israel instead of the gods of the Egyptians, a choice made "by faith":

> By faith Moses, when he was born, was hid three months of his parents, because they saw *he was* a proper child; and they were not afraid of the king's commandment.
>
> By faith Moses, when he was come to years, *refused* to be called the son of Pharaoh's daughter;
>
> *Choosing* rather to suffer affliction with the people of God, than to enjoy the pleasures of sin for a season;
>
> Esteeming the reproach of Christ greater riches than the treasures in Egypt: for he had respect unto the recompence of the reward.
>
> By faith he forsook Egypt, not fearing the wrath of the king: for he endured, as seeing him who is invisible. (Heb. 11:23–27; emphasis added)

These sources also show that Moses knew of his own identity and of his mission years before being called at the burning bush.

This brings us back to the prophecy of Joseph in the JST, which we read earlier. How did Moses learn who he was and what his mission was to be? JST Genesis 50:29 may have considerable bearing on this point, especially when read in conjunction with the words of Stephen and Paul. The Lord had spoken to Joseph in Egypt, and he then recorded:

> ...for a seer will I raise up to deliver my people out of the

> land of Egypt; and he shall be called Moses. And by this name he shall know that he is of thy house; for he shall be nursed by the king's daughter, and shall be called her son. (JST Gen. 50:29)

Since Moses was a prince of Egypt and was educated "in all the learning of the Egyptians," we might wonder if one day in the royal archives he discovered Joseph's writings and there read, even as we have just done, the prophecy telling of Moses being reared in the Pharaoh's household—and even his exact name as a key word. Furthermore, as cited earlier, the name of his brother Aaron was also given in Joseph's prophecy. This would be impressive to a bright, young future prophet and may even have been part of his spiritual education. Moses might also have read the record of Abraham in the same royal library.

Josephus, the Jewish historian, adds another dimension to Moses's life during those first forty years in Egypt: that of Moses as a military leader. Josephus says that Ethiopia conquered much of Egypt, all the way down to Memphis, and it was Moses who led an Egyptian army and freed Egypt from Ethiopian domination—even taking his army up the Nile into Nubia and Ethiopia and bringing back treasures, hostages, and even the king's daughter as a wife.[4]

The Bible is silent about Moses's spiritual activities while in Midian as Jethro's son-in-law and shepherd. In fact, it says only that Jethro was the priest of Midian. However, Doctrine and Covenants 84:6 teaches that it was Jethro (a descendant of Abraham through Abraham's wife Keturah and thus a non-Israelite) who ordained Moses to the Melchizedek Priesthood. This is from a line of priesthood outside of Israel. We are accustomed to thinking of Abraham, Isaac, Jacob, Joseph, Ephraim, etc., but from the foregoing revelation we learn that others also had the holy priesthood of God. In future years, as the gospel is taught to all the descendants of Abraham, it may be helpful for it to become known that Moses, perhaps the greatest prophet of ancient Israel, obtained the Melchizedek Priesthood within Abraham's lineage, but outside of the house of Israel.

Moses Was Trained Both in Secular and Spiritual Things

We can be certain that Moses received considerable training and experience—both in Egypt as a prince and in Midian as son-in-law to the high priest Jethro—that would prepare him for the great task of getting nearly a million Israelites out of Egypt, leading them as a prophet, and preserving them as the Lord's covenant people. During that first forty-year period, he no doubt learned reading, writing, astronomy, and architecture, and gained experience with leadership principles and military strategy; he probably also read the records of Abraham and of Joseph in the sacred Egyptian archives. During the second forty-year period, he would be baptized and ordained to the Melchizedek Priesthood, learn much from his high priest father-in-law, and no doubt have other revelations and spiritual tutoring. He also reared at least two sons. The book of Moses chapter one shows that Moses had profound spiritual depth and intellectual curiosity. The image of Moses given in Moses chapter one does not show the average mortal man; it illustrates the mark of one who is called of God and prepared not only in this life but in the premortal existence. You remember that Joseph prophesied in Egypt that Moses would be a man mighty in writing and in judgment. Likewise, Paul and Stephen spoke of these particular intellectual and spiritual accomplishments of Moses.

Moses and the Melchizedek Priesthood

It would be well to consider here an important contribution of latter-day revelation. We have already noted that Moses received the Melchizedek Priesthood from Jethro (D&C 84:6). Nothing is said in either ancient or modern scripture about Moses being baptized in water or having hands laid on his head for the gift of the Holy Ghost, yet these two things had to take place before he could receive the priesthood. Such is the order of the kingdom. The plan of salvation and the sacred ordinances are always the same. There are no bargain-days or shortcuts. Even though the scripture does not expressly so state, we know that not only Moses, but every other true and righteous prophet of God who held the priesthood was first taught faith in Jesus Christ who was to come, the plan of salvation, and the principles and ordinances of the gospel. They all had a knowledge of the plan, were personally acquainted with Jehovah, and looked forward in faith to his earthly mission as Jesus Christ. Prior to Moses's time, the priesthood was called *"the Holy Priesthood, after the Order of the Son of God"* (D&C 107:3) as a reminder of the mission of the Savior (Alma 13:14–16). The Prophet Joseph Smith taught these great concepts, which, when understood, open wide a doorway of knowledge about the ancient prophets and patriarchs. Here are some of his words:

> It was the design of the councils of heaven before the world was, that the principles and laws of the priesthood should be predicated upon the gathering of the people in every age of the world.... Ordinances instituted in the heavens before the foundation of the world, in the priesthood, for the salvation of men, are not to be altered or changed. All must be saved on the same principles....
>
> If a man gets a fullness of the priesthood of God he has to get it in the same way that Jesus Christ obtained it, and that was by keeping all the commandments and obeying all the ordinances of the house of the Lord.[5]

> [Jesus] set the ordinances to be the same forever and ever, and set Adam to watch over them, to reveal them from heaven to man, or to send angels to reveal them....
>
> These angels are under the direction of Michael or Adam, who acts under the direction of the Lord. From [Heb. 1:14] we learn that Paul perfectly understood the purposes of God in relation to His connection with man, and that glorious and perfect order which He established in Himself, whereby he sent forth power, revelations, and glory.[6]

> [W]e have sufficient grounds to go on and prove from the Bible that the gospel has always been the same; the ordinances to fulfill its requirements, the same, and the officers to officiate, the same; and the signs and fruits resulting from the promises, the same: therefore, as Noah was a preacher of righteousness he must have been baptized and ordained to the priesthood by the laying on of the hands, etc. For no man taketh this honor unto himself except he be called of God as

was Aaron, and Aaron was baptized in the cloud and in the sea, together with all Israel, as is related by the Apostle in Corinthians.[7]

When we thus learn the established order of the kingdom, we see that Moses, along with all other righteous prophets and patriarchs whom the Lord chose and tutored, was baptized, confirmed, and ordained according to the heavenly order.

Moses Is Called to Deliver Israel

The next we hear of Moses in the Old Testament is the episode of the burning bush, where God called him back to Egypt. Moses was approximately eighty years old. He was out with the sheep and saw the bush aflame, but not consumed. The Exodus account tells us that God spoke to Moses out of the bush and told him that he must go back to Egypt and get the children of Israel out of the land by "a mighty hand," which means by power and by wonders (Ex. 3:1–20). Moses is naturally hesitant and says that the Israelites will never accept him and will say, in effect: "God has not appeared unto you." Moses was reluctant for at least two reasons. First, he had tried to help his countrymen forty years earlier, but they would not receive him. Remember the words of Stephen: "For he supposed his brethren would have understood how that God by his hand would deliver them: but they understood not" (Acts 7:25). Secondly, Pharaoh would clearly object. Egypt at this time was the most powerful nation on earth, with armies, wealth, and influence. Moses, with neither army, wealth, nor influence (maybe not even supported by his own people), was being asked to take on the Egyptian establishment. No wonder Moses said, "Who am I, that I should go unto Pharaoh, and that I should bring forth the children of Israel out of Egypt?" (Ex. 3:11).

This is an example of the way the Lord works—not by physical or worldly force but by divine power and miracles—so that the children of Israel would know that it was not themselves but God who got them out of the land of Egypt. Their faith was to be in God, not in their armaments or their own strength. This is one meaning of the scriptures that teach that God hath chosen the weak things of the world to confound the things which are mighty (1 Cor. 1:27–29; D&C 1:19). We see it again with David and Goliath (1 Sam. 17), and in Gideon with his 300 men (Judg. 7). This is the way the Lord still works with his people today.

It took ten grievous plagues before Pharaoh was willing to let the Israelites go. These plagues are presented in Exodus as: (1) turning the waters into blood; (2) frogs in the houses, in the ovens, the beds, the granaries; (3) lice; (4) flies; (5) hail; (6) fire; (7) sickness among the cattle and boils on the people; (8) locusts; (9) darkness; and (10) the death of the firstborn in whatever house did not have the lamb's blood on the doorpost (Ex. 7–12).

Though a mighty struggle, Moses eventually got a large population (Exodus 12:37 says 600,000 men, besides women and children) out of Egypt and into the wilderness and the desert. When they came to the Red Sea, the prophet Moses commanded the waters and they obeyed and parted, allowing the Israelites to pass through as if on dry ground; whereas 600 chariots of the Egyptians in hot pursuit, when they got into the center of the opening, the wheels came off the chariots, "they drave heavily," and the water came in upon them and most, if not all, were drowned (Ex. 14). This great event was later memorialized in the Psalms (78:13, 53; 106:9–12).

Continued Spiritual Education of Moses

The biblical record says little about any of Moses's spiritual preparation between the time of his call at the burning bush and the encounters with Pharaoh. It briefly tells of Moses leaving Midian, meeting his brother Aaron, and returning to Egypt. Here again, latter-day revelation adds much to our understanding of Moses and his spiritual preparation to become a prophet, a seer, and a witness for the Messiah.

Before Moses embarked on his mission back to Egypt, the Lord gave him a series of visions to prepare him. We find a record of this in the Book of Moses, chapter one. This special revelation given to the Prophet Joseph Smith provides a perspective of Moses not available from any other source. It contains knowledge entirely lost to all other records, and we are fortunate to have it in the Pearl of Great Price, to which it came as an extract from the Joseph Smith Translation of the Bible. From this revelation we learn that Moses was shown the heavens and worlds without number. He saw inhabitants thereon. He talked with God face to face. He beheld the brightness, glory, and majesty of God and discovered that he could not stand in God's presence unless he was transfigured, for he would have "withered and died." This can all be read in Moses 1:1–11.

Even for a man who might have been a prince of Egypt, a great military leader, and mighty as to the strength of men, being compared with even a small portion of the works and glories of God made him seem insignificantly small and weak, something he had never before imagined.

Next, Satan came to him. This can be read in Moses 1:12–23. Moses could distinctly see the difference between God's brightness and Satan's darkness. Moses had been told that he, Moses, was in the similitude of the Only Begotten. This pleased Moses, and he referred to it several times. When Satan sought Moses's allegiance, Moses told Satan that he would not worship him—he would worship God in the name of the Only Begotten, and he wanted to commune again with the God of glory and knowledge. When Satan challenged him, Moses resisted, and Satan threw a tantrum. Finally, after a confrontation in which Satan claimed that he himself was the Only Begotten and demanded that Moses worship him, Moses commanded Satan in the name of the Only Begotten to depart. Satan very reluctantly left, with "weeping, and wailing, and gnashing of teeth." Thus ended Moses's fierce and emotional encounter with the very devil himself. The Lord then reappeared and said that he, Moses, would deliver chosen Israel from bondage and that he would command the waters and they would obey him—an allusion to his future experience with the Red Sea (Moses 1:24–26).

The Lord then showed Moses a vision of many lands and many peoples, even all the people of this earth and of many earths. It is at this point that we sense the great spiritual capacity and mind of Moses, for he asks the Lord two fundamental questions about the earth and about mankind. There are many things a person might ask about the earth: How long did it take to create it? How long has it been since the creation? But Moses asked two more basic questions (see v. 30): first, "*Why* did you create worlds and people?" and second, "*How* did you do it?" The answers to these questions are fundamental aspects of man's existence, and we have the Lord's reply right here in the book of Moses. To the first, the Lord says, "This is my work and my glory—to bring to pass the immortality and eternal life of man" (Moses 1:39). Such are the things that gods do—they create worlds and put their children on them so that they can become gods also.

As to *how* it was done, we have the answer in the Lord's account of the six-day creation process (Moses chapters 2 and 3). This great revelation was given to Moses *after* the burning bush and *before* he parted the Red Sea (see Moses 1:17, 26). The Bible is entirely silent on this whole episode. Moses included a record of all this when he wrote the book of Genesis, but because wicked persons tampered with the scriptures the material has been removed from all known manuscripts, so that today no Bible or ancient manuscript contains the account of Moses' conversations with God about the creation, nor his encounter with Lucifer. Since Lucifer lost in his battle with Moses, and was dispatched by the power of the Only Begotten, it is certain that it was he who influenced wicked persons to take this part of the record out of the biblical manuscripts (see Moses 1:17–25, 40–41).

Why would the Lord have put Moses through all these experiences? He was molding this prince of Egypt (great as that position was) into a prophet and a seer (which is even greater). It was necessary that Moses understand the plan of salvation and be a personal witness of Christ. He would also have to know of the great power that the devil has. Moses would not have been able to endure all the opposition of the next forty years had he not been spiritually prepared, which included a proper concept of his mission and a correct knowledge of his relationship to the Lord.

When the Lord wants to change things on the earth, he has a baby born—a baby such as Noah or Moses or Paul or Joseph Smith or Howard W. Hunter or Jesus. As these babies grow to maturity the Lord trains and tutors them. He teaches them of the great work of God, the great plan of redemption, and the cunning craftiness of the devil. He then commands them to do his will and helps them to bring about certain events that change the destiny of nations. The faith to obey increases with obedience and enables such servants to become mighty instruments of God.

Dramatic Events at Sinai

It was a mighty struggle to get Israel out of Egypt, but it was an even greater struggle to get Egypt out of the Israelites. The geographical change was not as difficult as the cultural and personal change needed in the peoples' thinking and habits. Three months after crossing the Red Sea, the Israelites were camped in the area of Mount Sinai (which is probably the same mountain on which Moses had seen the burning bush), and the Lord gave Moses instructions relative to receiving the Ten Commandments and giving the people the fullness of the gospel.

The events on Mt. Sinai are surely among the most dramatic in the scriptures and of all time. The people were to remain at the foot of the mount, a respectable distance back, while Moses ascended into the mountain. The Lord would descend, appear to Moses, and write upon the tablets of stone with his own finger. The people would hear a loud trumpet, then the voice of God, and see fire and smoke, hear thunder, and feel the quaking of the earth. All of this can be found in Exodus 19:5–9, 16–20, and Exodus 20:18–25.

At this time the Lord gave Moses and Israel the Ten Commandments, and the scriptures say they literally heard God speak the words (Deut. 5:1–4, 22–25). Since this was just three or four months out of Egypt, the memory of the stone statues of the pharaohs and Egyptian gods, the bulls, the falcons, the crocodiles, and the great pyramids, etc., were fresh on the Israelites' minds. Remembering this gives a clear context to the first two commandments—"Thou shalt have none other Gods before me," no "graven image...*of any thing*" on earth or in heaven, and "Thou shalt not bow down thyself unto them, nor serve them" (Deut. 5:7–9; emphasis added).

The Lord Gives the Law of Moses as a Lesser Law

The people were troubled at the thought of being in God's presence, and they said to Moses: You deal with God, we'll deal with you—"but let not God speak with us, lest we die" (Ex. 20:19). Israel's resistance to God was a symptom of a spiritual malady and deficiency that soon led them to reject the gospel, and as a consequence the Lord gave them the law of Moses and the lesser Aaronic Priesthood instead of the gospel and the greater Melchizedek Priesthood. This concept has been greatly misunderstood by biblical scholars and even by some of our own Church members because it is not clearly explained in the Bible. However, it has been made clear in the Joseph Smith Translation and in the Doctrine and Covenants.

When Moses came down from the Mount after forty days, the people had built a golden calf like they had known in Egypt to worship. Forty days proved too long for their weak faith. They said they were not sure Moses was ever coming down from that awful smoking, trembling mountain. When Moses and Joshua saw the Israelites' revelry and the golden image, Moses threw down the tablets of stone and broke them. These contained the fullness of the gospel—the Ten Commandments and the ordinances of the Melchizedek Priesthood, i.e., the temple covenants.

The Lord told Moses to make a new set of tablets and come up again to the Mount. Moses did so and received the Ten Commandments again, but in place of the higher ordinances, the new tablets contained the law of carnal commandments, which functioned under the Aaronic Priesthood. One of the major differences in these two laws is that the gospel and Melchizedek Priesthood will prepare a person to enter into God's presence, whereas the law of Moses and Aaronic Priesthood will not. The Melchizedek Priesthood deals with the ministry of Jesus Christ and beholding the face of God. The Aaronic Priesthood deals with the "preparatory gospel" and ministry of angels. An explanation of these two laws can be found in the following comparison of the JST and the KJV:

JST Exodus 34:1–2	KJV Exodus 34: 1–2
And the Lord said unto Moses, Hew thee two *other* tables of stone, like unto the first, and I will write upon *them* also, the words *of the law, according as they were written* at the first on the tables which thou brakest;	And the Lord said unto Moses, Hew thee two tables of stone like unto the first: and I will write upon these tables the words that were in the first tables, which thou brakest.

but it shall not be according to the first, for I will take away the priesthood out of their midst; therefore my holy order, and the ordinances thereof, shall not go before them; for my presence shall not go up in their midst, lest I destroy them.

But I will give unto them the law as at the first, but it shall be after the law of a carnal commandment; for I have sworn in my wrath, that they shall not enter into my presence, into my rest, in the days of their pilgrimage. Therefore do as I have commanded thee, and be ready in the morning, and come up in the morning unto mount Sinai, and present thyself there to me, in the top of the mount.

And be ready in the morning, and come up in the morning unto mount Sinai, and present thyself there to me in the top of the mount.

And again:

Deuteronomy 10:1–2:

At that time the Lord said unto me, Hew thee two *other* tables of stone like unto the first, and come up unto me upon the mount, and make thee an ark of wood.

And I will write on the tables the words that were in the first tables, which thou brakest, *save the words of the everlasting covenant of the holy priesthood,* and thou shalt put them in the ark.

Deuteronomy 10:1–2

At that time the Lord said unto me, Hew thee two tables of stone like unto the first, and come up unto me into the mount, and make thee an ark of wood.

And I will write on the tables the words that were in the first tables which thou brakest, and thou shalt put them in the ark.

This clarification by the JST makes all the difference in understanding what happened in the wilderness and what the difference was between the first and second set of tablets. No one can understand this matter properly without the help of the revelations given to the Prophet Joseph Smith. This subject is also clarified in Doctrine and Covenants 84:19–27.

Moses Was Blessed in Not Entering the Promised Land

Because of Israel's lack of desire and their cultural attachment to Egypt, the Lord kept them in the wilderness for forty years, until all who had come out of Egypt had died and a new generation (born in the wilderness) began growing up. Only Joshua and Caleb were permitted to make the complete trip (Num. 26:64–65; 32:11–12; Deut. 1:34–39). Israel's wandering is symbolic: Come out of Egypt, be tested in the wilderness, cross over Jordan and enter into the rest of the Lord in the promised land. It is just like our lives: We come out of the "world," endure the wilderness of trial and affliction, and eventually "cross over" through the veil into the celestial kingdom where there is rest from the toils and troubles of mortality.

But why was Moses not permitted to enter the promised land—that "goodly land," as it is called? The scriptures suggest that the Lord was angry with Moses because he took the credit for getting water from the rock (Num. 20). However, there is a more fundamental reason. I suppose the event at the rock actually happened, but I do not think that was the reason why Moses did not go into the promised land. Moses held the keys of the Melchizedek Priesthood and the sealing power, and was a man who could stand in the presence of God. As I read the explanation given by the Lord in Doctrine and Covenants 84:20–24, I get the feeling that the Lord was indeed angry—not with Moses, but with the children of Israel. They did not deserve Moses any longer, so Moses was translated and taken from the earth.

I have been to Israel several times. It is a remarkable place. But being translated would seem to be even better. If the Lord was too angry with Moses to let him go into the promised land, why would he be pleased enough with him to take him into heaven? I suppose that under such circumstances Moses may have felt properly repaid for missing out. It was also necessary that Moses be translated so that he and Elijah could later lay on hands to confer the keys of the holy priesthood on Peter, James, and John at the Mount of Transfiguration (Matt. 17). Since Moses was translated, and hence not buried, the account of his burial in Deuteronomy (34:5–6) is obviously an error.

Moses, Israel's Greatest Prophet

The scripture says of Moses: "And there arose not a prophet since in Israel like unto Moses, whom the Lord knew face to face" (Deut. 34:10). Moses was a leader, a prophet, and a lawgiver. But more significantly, he was personally acquainted with the Lord Jesus Christ through several visions and the workings of the Holy Ghost. He was a military man, a pioneer, and a man versed in moral, civil, and religious law. Through him the Lord accomplished one of the greatest migrations in history, preserved the covenant people, and established a written legal code that laid a foundation and pattern for many millions of people. He was a prophet, seer, revelator, and special witness for the Savior. Through it all, Moses was something of a reluctant and humble leader and was said to be the meekest of all men (Num. 12:3).

Moses not only ministered in his own time, but also to Peter, James, and John in New Testament times (Matt. 17) and to Joseph Smith at Kirtland, Ohio (D&C 110). The worldwide mission of the Church today, to gather Israel, is conducted under the keys of gathering which Moses conferred upon Joseph Smith and Oliver Cowdery in the Kirtland Temple. The Doctrine and Covenants extols the greatness of Moses in 28:2; 84:6, 17–25; 103:16–20; 107:91–92, and declares the Prophet Joseph Smith to be a man "like unto Moses," which is a compliment to both of these great leaders (D&C 28:2; cf. Moses 1:40–41). Likewise, Moses is said to be like unto Christ (Deut. 18:18–19; Acts 3:22–23; JS—H 1:40), and in these same passages Christ himself is likened unto Moses. Such was the life of the man who "by faith…forsook Egypt" (Heb. 11:27).

NOTES

1. Bruce R. McConkie, *Mormon Doctrine* (Salt Lake City: Bookcraft, 1966), 515.

2. See also the LDS Edition of the Bible, p. 799 of the appendix.

3. Josephus, *Jewish Antiquities*, II,IX,6.

4. Ibid., II, X, 1,2.

5. Joseph Smith, *Teachings of the Prophet Joseph Smith*, comp. Joseph Fielding Smith (Salt Lake City: Deseret Book, 1976), 308.

6. Ibid., 168.

7. Ibid., 264.

Chapter Eight

Ruth—Woman of Faith

Linda Aukschun

The Lord considers a person's life to be the illustration of what that person believes. In the first Lecture on Faith, Joseph Smith asks: "Why is faith the first principle in this revealed science? Because it is the foundation of all righteousness." He stated in the same text, "If men were duly to consider themselves, and turn their thoughts and reflections to the operations of their own minds, they would readily discover that it is faith, and faith only, which is the moving cause of all action in them." He put it in the most basic of terms: "Would you have ever planted, if you had not believed that you would gather?... Would you have ever sought unless you thought you would have found?"[1]

Though the word *faith* never appears in the Old Testament book of Ruth, her faith is evident. Matthew 7:20 says, "By their fruits ye shall know them," and in nearly every verse, Ruth's words and actions provide ample evidence of her faith. Although I intend to tell Ruth's story against this backdrop of faith, I have broadened this chapter to include two other people, Naomi and Boaz, both of whom also show faith by their willingness to live lives motivated by love and consecrated to God.

To any who might wonder if simple habit, lack of alternatives, or fear might explain Ruth's life and its directions, they must consider how short-lived are such shallow motivations. As Glenn Tinder wrote in the *Atlantic Monthly,*

> We all know many people who do not believe in God and yet are decent and admirable. Western societies, as highly secularized as they are, retain many humane features. Not even tacitly has our sole governing maxim become the one Dostoevsky thought was bound to follow the denial of the God-man: "Everything is permitted."
>
> This may be, however, because customs and habits formed during Christian ages keep people from professing and acting on such a maxim even though it would be logical for them to do so. If that is the case, our position is precarious, for good customs and habits need spiritual grounds, and if those are lacking, they will gradually, or perhaps suddenly in some crisis, crumble.[2]

The book of Ruth begins with Elimelech and his wife, Naomi, leaving their native Bethlehem because of famine to live in the nearby country of Moab. While there, Elimelech became ill and died, leaving Naomi a widow with two sons. Within the space of ten years, the two sons married Moabite women and then followed their father in death. The widowed Naomi decided that it was time for her to return to Bethlehem. Her plan had been to go alone, but Ruth, one of her widowed daughters-in-law, announced her intentions to go to Bethlehem with Naomi in this beautiful passage of scripture: "Intreat me not to leave...thee: for whither thou goest, I will go; and where thou lodgest, I will lodge: thy people shall be my people, and thy God my God" (Ruth 1:16).

This simple comment declares that Ruth was a convert. She did not say, "I want to come with you," as she urgently begged Naomi to let her travel to Bethlehem with her. She clearly stated why she did not want to return to Moab with her sister-in-law Orpah: she had chosen Jehovah and wanted to live among his chosen people.

Love for Naomi would not adequately explain such self-sacrifice because Ruth could have maintained their relationship while keeping her own way of life. Moab, after all, was only thirty to forty miles away, which was considered at the time to be a relatively short distance.[3] Other possibilities, such as a desire for adventure or a hope for a better life, likely would not have prompted her action, because Moab, at the time, was "theocratically hostile"[4] to Israel. Ruth's faith stands alone as her motivation. Ruth's courage is a fruit of her faith.

Any who have ventured into the unknown for any righteous cause realize that fearlessness does not come easily; such courage comes from faith in God. Ezra Taft Benson said:

> The righteous are bold as a lion (Prov. 28:1). People who live righteously have nothing to fear. In spite of the turmoil, anxiety, and insecurity which may seem to be everywhere, we will be able to stand erect and go forward with courage and faith.[5]

Throughout her story, Ruth behaved as one who knew this kind of courage, persevering through the frightening social and political circumstances of her time. The Old Testament is filled with references to the hatred existing between Moab and Israel. For example, "An Ammonite or Moabite shall not enter into the congregation of the Lord; even to their tenth generation shall they not enter into the congregation of the Lord for ever" (Deut. 23:3; Neh. 13:1). Or "Woe to thee, Moab! thou art undone, O people of Chemosh" (Num. 21:29). And during the time of the Judges, it was written:

> And he [Ehud] said unto them, Follow after me: for the LORD hath delivered your enemies the Moabites into your hand. And they went down after him, and took the fords of Jordan toward Moab, and suffered not a man to pass over.
>
> And they slew of Moab at that time about ten thousand men, all lusty, and all men of valour; and there escaped not a man.
>
> So Moab was subdued that day under the hand of Israel. (Judg. 3:28–30)

Besides the danger of being a Moabite in Israel, Ruth's being a woman also complicated matters: "The treatment of both women and foreigners was generally demeaning through most of Israelite history, but during the times of Naomi and Ruth, it was especially horrific."[6] There was also the problem of the Israelite attitude towards the marrying of Moabite women. King Solomon was denounced for having married Moabite women (1 Kgs. 11:1), and the prophet Ezra condemned the men of Israel for having taken wives from among the Moabites (Ezra 9:1–2).

But Ruth's courage is summed up by Phyllis Trible:

> She has disavowed the solidarity of family; she has abandoned national identity; and she has renounced religious affiliation. In the entire epic of Israel, only Abraham matches this radicality, but then he had a call from God.... No deity has promised her blessing.... Not only has Ruth broken with family, country, and faith, but she has also reversed sexual allegiance.... One female has chosen another female in a world where life depends upon men. There is no more radical decision in all the memories of Israel.[7]

Such courage would be almost incomprehensible without the element of faith factored in.

Ruth's unselfishness is likewise a sign of her faith. Though extraordinary unselfishness such as that exhibited by Ruth, Naomi, and Boaz is not reserved exclusively for the faithful, it is a strong indication of true believers. Neal A. Maxwell supports this view:

> How much sustained attention to civic duty will there be without the foundation of a prior regard for the duties that flow from the first and second great commandments? Otherwise, the growing narcissism, adulation, and worship of self, fostered by relativism, will mock the attempts to deal with mankind's increasing interdependency.
>
> How much sense of personal responsibility will there finally be for many individuals who do not believe in their ultimate accountability to God? And how long can we keep the culture of service alive in the acid of secular selfishness? How much environmental deference will there be for those of tomorrow without belief in the everlasting tomorrow of immortality?
>
> Can man's sense of stewardship for this planet be sustained if it is not, ultimately, a stewardship for and in behalf

> of a loving God? We can scarcely persuade some today to assume responsibility for their aging parents, let alone feel responsible for generations unborn, unknown, and unseen![8]

Many verses in the book of Ruth illustrate that the author wanted selflessness to be a virtue strongly present in his text. This virtue first appears in Naomi's blessing of her daughters-in-law (Ruth 1:8–9) and continues in her pointing out to both why life with her would be the wrong choice (Ruth 1:11–13). When Ruth asked Naomi to not send her back to Moab, she had, at least in her own mind, given up her own life for her friend. As such, this act exemplified love as Christ taught. "Greater love hath no man than this, that a man lay down his life for his friends" (John 15:13).

Elder Maxwell notes that doubt, faith's opposite, creates selfishness.

> One can see in individuals like Hyrum Smith, or Joseph in Egypt, this spirit of generosity, this selflessness, which did not require them to compute beforehand the benefits to them of their actions. Perhaps the individual who is filled with doubt about life's purpose himself uses too much of his psychic energy in processing his doubts, energy that might well be channeled into acts of service. Surely the person who is too caught up in sensual things dispenses too much of his energy, mental and physical, in the realization of self-satisfaction to have much time or thought left for others.[9]

Miracles, too, follow the faithful Ruth. As the scriptures say, "Signs follow those that believe" (D&C: 63:9), and Ruth's life is filled with them, subtle though they may be. Elder Bruce R. McConkie said:

> Gifts of the Spirit which the Lord bestows upon those who believe and obey the gospel of Christ are called *signs*. That is, their receipt stands as an evidence or sign of the presence of that faith which results from believing the truth. Signs are wonders and miracles; they always and invariably are manifest to and among the faithful saints.[10]

Elsewhere, Elder McConkie noted that

> miracles, signs, the gifts of the Spirit, the knowledge of God and godliness, and every conceivable good thing—all these are the *effects of faith;* all of these come because faith has become the ruling force in the lives of the saints. Conversely, where these things are not, faith is not.[11]

Though the scriptures do not call it such, Ruth's fortune at being found in Boaz's field seems to be more of a miracle than just a lucky happenstance (Ruth 2:2–3). She was poor, he was rich. She was an immigrant of little consequence. He was well established in his environment. In Ruth 2:5 Boaz asks "whose" (not "who") is this woman, indicating that he thought she "belonged" to someone. And Ruth reveals how she views her own position as it relates to Boaz when she asks why he would show her special interest, because she is a "stranger." In the Hebrew, she calls herself *siphah,* maidservant—a term "more menial than *amah,*" though it also means "maidservant."[12]

We are advised by our leaders not to see such results as coincidences. As Thorpe B. Isaacson said:

> Miracles are performed today. The power of healing is in the priesthood and in the Church. Some wonder whether or not miracles are performed today. If they could hear the testimonies of these missionaries in the stakes and these mission presidents, they would have no reason ever to wonder about miracles. But sometimes our faith is not strong enough. Sometimes we are too weak to accept the blessings of the Lord as miracles. Sometimes we are inclined to call them just a coincidence. Sometimes we say, "Oh it's just one of those things." That's because our faith is not strong enough to recognize the hand of the Lord in these miracles and the healing power of the priesthood that is in the world today.[13]

Bruce Hafen also reminds us of this as he recounts from the film *The Windows of Heaven:*

> And then we see President Lorenzo Snow receive the telegram in his office, telling of the rain; and then we see him

> instinctively proceed to his bedside and say something like "Oh, what can I do to show my gratitude that thou hast heard the prayers of thy people and thy humble servant? I would give anything, even my life...."
>
> Neither that prophet nor those farmers stood by watching the rain, wondering if perhaps it was just a coincidence. Their attitudes, their experiences, and their instincts told them otherwise. They knew in whom they trusted.[14]

Ruth, not as a one of the house of Israel but as a Moabite, found and embraced the true religion of Jehovah. Herself a widow, she followed her widowed mother-in-law to a land where she was a stranger and where Naomi described their situation as follows: "I went out full, and the Lord hath brought me home again empty" (Ruth 1:21). Yet in Bethlehem both Ruth and Naomi were provided for through the kindness of a kinsman. Ruth was remarried, and she became a mother in the lineage that would bring forth the Messiah.

If we do not see miracles in the life of Ruth, it could be that, in view of the marvels that surround us and the great events that sign-seekers look for, we miss the real miracles.

Additionally, Ruth's story would never have made it into scripture if its purpose had simply been to present the simple story of a good woman who was willing to accept inevitable circumstances. By definition, scripture requires more than that. According to 2 Timothy 3:16–17, "All scripture is given by inspiration of God, and is profitable for doctrine, for reproof, for correction, for instruction in righteousness: That the man of God may be perfect, thoroughly furnished unto all good works." Elsewhere the scriptures teach, "They [meaning scriptures] are they which testify of me" (John 5:39).

A comparison can easily be made between the willingness of Ruth to leave Moab behind her and head out into the unknown and the pioneer spirit that brought the Latter-day Saints west nearly one-hundred and fifty years ago. Such courage deserves respect, and the faith that would impel a person or people to make such a sacrifice deserves our acknowledgment. As Spencer W. Kimball said:

> Brigham Young and the pioneers demonstrated courage of faith. What great, stirring program could cause people to leave all that they had previously held dear—material possessions, family ties, friendships, and luxuries? Was there a pot of gold at the end of this newly-found rainbow? A life of comfort, worldly acclaim, popularity, with wealth and affluence? Quite the contrary: There was to be hunger, heartaches, despair, and privations. Only a great faith and an abiding testimony and assurance of divinity could lead men through such hardships.[155]

It is legitimate, however, to ask: If their faith was so great, and God so willing to respond to the wishes of his children, why would Ruth and so many others not pray themselves out of their difficulties in the first place?

In his remarkable book, *Den of Lions*, journalist Terry Anderson recounts his experiences as a hostage for seven years in Lebanon. In it he catalogs the progress of his own faith during his imprisonment, eventually reaching the point where he no longer saw God's job as preventing trials or releasing him from them, but rather as one of helping him with comfort, joy, realization, understanding, and growth toward perfection.

> The night is filled with the sound of guns and with the same thoughts all of us who believe in God must confront sooner or later. If God is omnipotent, and loving, where does evil fit in? Where does justice come in?...
>
> Somehow I know I'm asking the wrong questions, trying to understand God in my terms. None of this was God's doing.... These men are not in any way I can understand God's instruments. This is not my punishment for adultery, or indifference, or all petty dishonesties I've been guilty of in my life.
>
> Nor do I believe it is a deliberate test, that I'm a kind of modern Job, being subjected to some sort of spiritual test. God knows my soul, to its innermost depths, if he cares to. He doesn't need to check, to give me a midterm examination.

> This is man's work, the product of a combination of political and economic forces, mixed with the needs and greeds of petty, evil men and the indifference of others. God is there to help me, to give me guidance and solace, and to keep me in the knowledge that no matter how much I may be humiliated, no matter how much I may come to dislike myself as my knowledge of myself grows, His love is unquestioning. He did not place me here, but He will help me get through it, even unto death, with grace and dignity, if I accept His help.[16]

Elsewhere Anderson writes:

> My faith has to do with a knowledge, a deep assurance that there is a God and a Christ and that He requires something of me. What I'm not sure of. I know I still have not become the kind of person I am capable of being, and should be.[17]

And:

> Sometimes I feel a joy in prayer, an understanding of what it means to be loved by God as I am, as I know myself to be—faulted, proud, self-indulgent. Those times ease the pain of this existence so much, give me hope that I can not only stick this out, but perhaps emerge whole and live a better life when it's over.[18]

The miracle generally takes place within—but it does take place. The circumstance of our lives is not nearly so significant as how we respond to that circumstance. And as all students of the gospel eventually come to realize, there is no sacrifice or suffering that ultimately goes unrewarded. God stands ready, offering each of us "all that He hath" (Luke 12:44). "The Lord is nigh unto them that are of a broken heart; and saveth such as be of a contrite spirit" (Ps. 34:18). Did Ruth know this? She must have or she would not have lived the life she did.

Without doubt, whoever wrote Ruth's story into scripture saved the best for last. Closing the story is the simple genealogy of Ruth's son, which includes King David, a forebear of Christ himself. Ruth, by faith, not only took Naomi's people as her own but she provided them their greatest king. She not only made

Naomi's God her God by living a life of faith and sacrifice but also by carrying within her the seed to the coming in the flesh of the Savior of the world.

NOTES

1. Joseph Smith, *Lectures on Faith* (Salt Lake City: Deseret Book, 1985), 1-2.

2. Glenn Tinder, "Can We Be Good without God?" *Atlantic Monthly,* Dec. 1989, 80.

3. *Old Testament Student Manual* (Salt Lake City: The Church of Jesus Christ of Latter-day Saints, 1980), 262.

4. G.C.D. Howley, F.F. Bruce, H.L. Ellison, eds., *The New Layman's Bible Commentary* (Grand Rapids, Michigan: Zindervan Publishing House, 1979), 371.

5. Ezra Taft Benson, *Teachings of Ezra Taft Benson* (Salt Lake City: Bookcraft, 1988), 69.

6. William E. Phipps, *Assertive Biblical Women* (Westport, Conn.: Greenwood Press, 1992), 48.

7. Ibid, 55.

8. Neal A. Maxwell, *We Will Prove Them Herewith* (Salt Lake City: Deseret Book, 1982), 90-91.

9. Neal A. Maxwell, "That My Family Should Partake," *Gospel Library,* Third Edition (Provo, Utah: Infobases International Incorporated, 1990).

10. Bruce R. McConkie, *Mormon Doctrine,* 2nd ed. (Salt Lake City: Bookcraft, 1966), 713.

11. Ibid, 264.

12. *The New Layman's Bible Commentary,* 375. James Strong, *The Exhaustive Concordance of the Bible: a Concise Dictionary of the Words in the Hebrew Bible with Their Renderings in the Authorized English Version* (Grand Rapids, Michigan: Baker Book House, n.d.), 495-96.

13. Thorpe B. Isaacson, in *Conference Report,* April 1950, 39.

14. "Is Yours A Believing Heart?" *Ensign,* Sept., 1974, 53.

15. Spencer W. Kimball, *The Teachings of Spencer W. Kimball,* ed. Edward L. Kimball (Salt Lake City: Bookcraft, 1982), 431.

16. Terry A. Anderson, *Den of Lions, Memoirs of Seven Years* (New York: Crown Publishers, Inc., 1993), 140-41.

17. Ibid, 178.

18. Ibid, 264.

CHAPTER NINE

PETER: FISHER OF MEN

RICHARD D. DRAPER

Introduction

PETER STIRRED THE faith of multitudes "insomuch that they brought forth the sick into the streets, and laid them on beds and couches, that at the least the shadow of Peter passing by might overshadow some of them" (Acts 5:15). The confidence this man inspired grew out of his own unshakable faith, which gave him dominion over three worlds: the physical in which he healed sick and broken bodies, the spiritual in which he cured depressed and sinful souls, and the demonic in which he rebuked and exorcised evil spirits.

How did he come to such eminence? Not all at once, certainly. He grew line upon line, precept upon precept, trial by trial, power by power, and grace to grace. The *Lectures on Faith* reveals the key ingredient in Peter's growth to spiritual greatness. It states very clearly that

> a religion that does not require the sacrifice of all things never has power sufficient to produce the faith necessary unto life and salvation; for, from the first existence of man, the faith necessary unto the enjoyment of life and salvation never could be obtained without the sacrifice of all earthly things. It was through this sacrifice, and this only, that God has ordained that men should enjoy eternal life.... Under these circumstances, then, he can obtain the faith necessary for him to lay hold on eternal life.[1]

This essay explores Peter's growth through sacrifice to a fullness of faith and the rewards such faith brings. It ends by examining his counsel to others, counsel which Joseph Smith testified contained "the most sublime language of any of the apostles."[2]

Preparation for Faith: Peter's Background

Peter's beginnings were inauspicious enough. He was born of common Jewish stock living in the Galilean town of Bethsaida. His parents named him Simon, the name of one of the sons of Israel.[3] He had little formal education, though he was not illiterate. Some perceived him as both "unlearned and ignorant" (Acts 14:13), the first term meaning untrained through formal schooling and the latter (Greek *idiotes*)[4] meaning rude or, more precisely, unrefined. At some point, probably shortly after his marriage, he moved to the seaside town of Capernaum.[5] There he and his brother, Andrew, along with Zebedee and his two sons, James and John, ran a fishing business successful enough to require hired help.

If tradition is correct, Peter lived with his family near the center of town in one of the apartment complexes. Peter's home was quite large, given the standard of the day, consisting of three courtyards surrounded by living rooms, two of which were fairly large and served as the primary family dwelling areas.[6] Peter's household consisted of his mother-in-law, his wife, and, very likely, their children though the record is silent on this point (Matt. 8:14).[7]

The majority of the Jews of the Galilee appear to have been conservative and devout, resisting the influence of a significant Gentile population.[8] Most would have followed the persuasion of the Pharisees. Peter's own nature was marked by inherent piety, and it is likely that he attended the synagogue not thirty yards north of his own house. However, the family was not tied strictly to the sect of the Pharisees. Peter's brother was a follower of John the Baptist. John's promise that the kingdom was at hand had stirred his disciples, and Andrew may have spoken to Peter about John's witness and its portent.

If they did discuss John's teachings, Peter's faith was such that he listened, perhaps even pondered, but was not swept into John's circle. He was a fisherman pursuing a fisherman's life. He was neither a mystic nor an intellectual, just a practical man making a good living. Honest, straightforward, and hardworking, though impetuous and a bit rash, neither his character nor his faith shone above his brethren. He appeared an ordinary man. But appearances were wrong. The eye of the great Jehovah was upon him, and the hand of the divine soon began to school him, building an unshakable faith through the refining fire of the law of sacrifice.

The excitement of Andrew's announcement one day in Capernaum must have startled Peter. "We have found the Messias," Andrew testified. Peter dropped everything and followed his brother. The meeting was full of portent. Beholding Simon, the Savior said, "Thou art Simon, the son of Jona: thou shalt be called Cephas" (John 1:41–42). The word *Cephas* is Aramaic for "stone," equivalent to the Greek *petros*, translated "Peter" and designating a rock ranging in size from a large pebble to a small boulder, but specifically one suitable for building. Simon would have to wait nearly two and a half years to find out the full significance of that prophetic nickname.

Peter immediately entered into the ranks of the Lord's disciples and began an intensive tutorial course. Peter's faith began to focus on the Lord, confirmed by, but not dependent on, the Lord's miracles. One, specifically directed at Simon, foreshadowed his ministry. It occurred one morning after the fishermen had been unsuccessful with the catch. A large crowd had gathered along the seashore that morning to hear the Savior. The multitude pressed upon him, making it hard to teach. Seeing Peter washing his nets near the small wharf, the Lord asked for assistance, and Peter complied, rowing the Savior a few yards out to sea where the Lord could more comfortably teach the people lining the shore.

After the sermon was over, the Savior asked Peter to take him fishing. Peter explained that he had toiled from early morning with no success, and with the day on, fishing would not be good. "Nevertheless," Peter responded, revealing a real, if fledgling, faith, "at thy word I will let down the net" (Luke 5:5). The result he could not have anticipated. The net enclosed such a huge number of fish that it broke as they tried to haul it on board. Peter signaled John and James for assistance. They arrived with another boat and were able to unload the net. Both boats were nearly swamped with fish.

The lesson was not lost on Peter. He knew both purity and majesty were in the boat with him, and kneeling among the fishes he beseeched, "Depart from me; for I am a sinful man, O Lord" (Luke 5:8). The Savior calmed his concerns with the tender words, "Fear not; from henceforth thou shalt catch men" (Luke 5:10). Peter's faith in the Lord's instructions had brought a multitude of fishes into the boats, and further faith would bring a multitude of people into God's kingdom.

Growing Faith: Peter's Ministry with the Lord

It was only a few months later when the call to fish for men came. Jesus approached Andrew and Peter at their small seaside wharf. "Come ye after me," he beckoned, "and I will make you to become fishers of men" (Mark 1:17). The response of the two brothers was immediate: "And straightway they forsook their nets, and followed him" (Mark 1:18). The Lord's request was a test of faith. They were required to leave their successful business and engage in the ministry. Admittedly, this call was but to part-time service and consisted mostly in training, but any time at all was time away from their livelihood. By responding to the call, Peter made the first of many sacrifices for the Lord. The result would be increased faith.

Within the year, the call to more extensive service came. Sacrifice demanded that the select disciples leave family and fishing and devote themselves fully to the work. The Savior commissioned Peter, along with his brother, their partners (James and John), and eight others as Apostles (Matt. 10:1–4; Mark 3:14–19; Luke 6:13–16). The term *apostle,* chosen by the Lord, meant delegate, messenger, envoy, but carried the idea of a representative of the divine.[9] The nuance of the title would not have been lost on those who heard it.

The Lord sent the Twelve to preach the gospel to the Jews in all the regions round about Galilee. He required faith on their part, for they were to take neither money nor extra clothing. Furthermore, he told them that there would be opposition. Men "will deliver you up to the councils, and they will scourge you in their synagogues." The ministry of the Twelve would cause division, and as a result, they would be "hated of all men for my name's sake" (Matt. 10:17–22). However, they were not to fear. The Spirit would attend them and they would be powerful in speaking.

Accepting the call in faith, the brethren went forward. The mission proved most successful. They "went through the towns, preaching the gospel, and healing every where" (Luke 9:6). The sacrifice demanded by this first mission was not great, for it lasted only a few weeks. Nonetheless, Peter and his brethren were richly rewarded. They manifested God's power to heal both bodies and spirits. Sacrifice demanded faith, and faith had brought power. Peter had begun to fish for men.

Shortly after the missionaries' return they participated in another miracle, the Savior's feeding of the 5,000 with just five barley loaves and two fishes (see Matt. 14:16–21). The miracle precipitated two events which affected Peter. First, the Savior sent his Apostles away by sea, a trip that proved grueling. As the evening settled in, the wind blew against them and the sea became choppy. Rowing against the wind, the disciples made little headway. Suddenly, they spotted a figure walking among the waves. Frightened, they were sure a ghost approached. The specter called reassuringly: "Be of good cheer; it is I; be not afraid." Putting the apparition to the test, "Peter answered him and said, Lord, if it be thou, bid me come unto thee on the water" (Matt. 14:27–28). The Savior consented, and without hesitation Peter slipped over the side of the boat onto (not into) the sea.

Peter displayed tremendous faith, certainly much more than those in the boat who did not even consider challenging the waves.[10] Yes, Peter failed. As the wind gusted and the sea billowed, his faith faltered, "and beginning to sink, he cried, saying, Lord, save me. And immediately Jesus stretched forth his hand, and caught him" (Matt. 14:30–31). But Peter's faith failed on the sea—not in the boat. What kind of faith in his Lord did Peter express by taking even one step onto the sea? Perhaps, had the wind and the waves remained steady, he would have made it. The text suggests he was not far from the Lord when he began to sink. It may even be that he was walking back toward the boat when he failed. Such would put the Savior's rebuke, "O thou of little faith, wherefore didst thou doubt?" (Matt. 14:31), in perfect context. Whatever the case, Peter exercised real faith. It was, as yet, "little faith" and had to grow, but it was faith. Once back in the boat, with the others, but perhaps in a more qualitative way, he and they "worshipped [Jesus], saying, Of a truth thou art the Son of God" (Matt. 14:33).

One point needs to be emphasized. Peter actually put his life in jeopardy, sacrificed his fear, and walked, if but for a moment, on water. Overall he failed, but failure born out of faith and sacrifice generated greater faith. That faith expressed itself the next day in the second event that affected Peter.

A few of the more zealous among the multitudes found the Savior and expressed their desire to make him king. He reacted by giving them the bread of life sermon (see John 6:1–68). The Lord taught pure and powerful doctrine. It proved too much, and "from that time many of his disciples went back and walked no more with him. Then said Jesus unto the Twelve, Will ye also go away?" (John 6:66–67). The Savior had tested many, and many had failed. What of the Twelve? None of those who stayed in the boat spoke, but he whose faith had allowed him to walk for a moment on the water did, saying, "Lord, to whom shall we go? thou hast the words of eternal life. And we believe and are sure [Greek *ginosko*] that thou art that Christ, the Son of the living God" (John 6:66–69). The KJV translation here is too weak. The verb *ginosko*, as used by the Jews, meant "to know" through actual application—hands-on experience, as it were. Thus, Peter announced that he and his brethren knew through personal, if spiritual, experience that Jesus was the very Messiah. Faith expressed in sacrifice had become knowledge.

From this period on, the work began to escalate. Need demanded full-time service and full-time sacrifice. Once again the Lord called his disciples away from family and fishing. Never again would Peter return to his nets for more than a brief period. He had become a fisher of men.

Only a few months later, Peter once again had opportunity to express his testimony. At Caesaria Philippi, the Lord asked about the speculations concerning him. The disciples told him, and the Savior responded by asking, "But whom say ye that I am?" Again, the only recorded response was from he who walked on water:

"Thou art the Christ, the Son of the living God." The Savior who had rebuked Peter's lack of faith now commended his testimony: "Blessed art thou, Simon Bar-jona: for flesh and blood hath not revealed it unto thee, but my Father which is in heaven" (Matt. 16:13–17).

Peter's experience teaches an important lesson about testimony: it is God's gift, and as such it cannot be conveyed from one person to another through any course of instruction. Peter did not get his sure knowledge from the Lord even though the Lord was instructing his chief disciple at the very moment. No flesh and blood, not even the Lord's flesh and blood, had been the instrument of transmission nor could it be. Peter knew firsthand the truth of Jesus's declaration: "the Father himself, which hath sent me, hath born witness of me" (John 5:37). As Hugh Nibley noted, "the knowledge of salvation is not transmitted from one man to another horizontally, as it were; it is not passed from one generation to the next as a great earthbound tradition."[11] It comes by vertical descent from God upon those whom he chooses. Peter's testimony came from God himself.[12] But it came after faith and sacrifice, not before.

Next the Lord revealed the great work this apostle of faith would move forward. "I say unto thee, That thou art Peter." The tense is arresting. On their first meeting, the Savior promised Simon he would become Peter. Now he was Peter; revelation had made the difference. Indeed, Simon, the rock (Greek *ho petros*)—still rough but becoming more shaped, more polished, and more steady—could bear the weight of increasing faith and responsibility. The JST supplies insights into what the Savior had in mind, for it adds that Cephas "is, by interpretation, a seer, or stone" (JST John 1:42). Via revelation, Peter had become, and would continue to be, the seer stone.

Going on, the Savior said, "and upon this rock (Greek, *he petra*) I will build my church" (Matt. 16:18). The term *petra* designates a rock of such size that a tomb or dwelling could be cut into it. In this case it referred to the mountain of revelation, from which the one called *petros* derived his testimony.[13] Peter was not the rock—*petra*—but a piece of the rock—*petros*. Into his mind would flow the visions of heaven and the knowledge of the divine.

He would be the rock, the revelator and seer who would in just a few months direct the Lord's kingdom.

With the position came power. The Savior declared that "the gates of hell shall not prevail against it [the Church]" (Matt. 16:18). Many interpret this statement as an assurance that Satan would not overcome the Church. Such is not the case, for Satan did indeed overcome the early Church. It fell to apostate forces within seventy years after the Lord's death.[14] The phrase "gates of hell" (Greek *pule hadou*) does not refer to the entrance of Satan's domain, but to the portals of the spirit world.[15] Gates function to keep things in or out. When the gates do not prevail, they fail at their task.

But what would overpower the gates? The Savior made it clear: "I will give unto thee the keys of the kingdom of heaven: and whatsoever thou shalt bind on earth shall be bound in heaven: and whatsoever thou shalt loose on earth shall be loosed in heaven" (Matt. 16:19). The Lord promised Peter that at some future time he would hold keys which would not affect this world alone, but the next. Indeed, the gates of the spirit world would not be able to withstand these keys. The gospel light and sealing power would come to those who sat in darkness, and the work for the dead, initiated during Peter's presidency, would free them from their chains.

Only a few days passed before Peter received those keys in a way he could not have anticipated. Just one week later,[16] the Savior, secluded with his three chief apostles on a mountaintop, revealed his true majesty and power. Being transfigured before them, his "raiment became shining, exceeding white as snow; so white as no fuller on earth could whiten them" (JST Mark 9:3), and "his face did shine as the sun, and his raiment was white as light" (Matt. 17:2).

Peter and his brethren did not receive this vision without preparation or sacrifice. The Lord has clearly stated the cost of such an experience: hands, feet, and hearts must be cleansed and purified, and more, the apostles had to become clean from the blood of that wicked generation (see D&C 88:74–75). Not only must sin be sacrificed, but the things of the world as well. But out of sacrifice came the reward the Savior still promises to those whose eyes are single to his glory: "your whole bodies shall be filled with light, and there shall be no darkness in you; and that body which is filled with light comprehendeth all things" (D&C 88:67).

Others stood with Jesus in divine majesty: Moses, Elijah, and John the Baptist. Two of these bestowed upon the apostles keys and powers: Moses gave the keys of Israel's gathering, and Elijah gave those of sealing.[17] It appears that the apostles also received their temple endowments at the time, which prepared them for the climax of the vision[18] when "a bright cloud overshadowed them:[19] and behold a voice out of the cloud, which said, This is my beloved Son, in whom I am well pleased; hear ye him" (Matt. 17:5). Out of this grew Peter's most profound and sure witness. He testified:

> For we have not followed cunningly devised fables, when we made known unto you the power and coming of our Lord Jesus Christ, but were eyewitnesses of his majesty.
>
> For he received from God the Father honour and glory, when there came such a voice to him from the excellent glory, This is my beloved Son, in whom I am well pleased.
>
> And this voice which came from heaven we heard, when we were with him in the holy mount.
>
> We have also a more sure word of prophecy; whereunto ye do well that ye take heed, as unto a light that shineth in a dark place, until the day dawn, and the day star arise in your hearts. (2 Pet. 1:16–19)

It appears that the Savior blessed these apostles with the same sealing powers with which they would bless others, for they received the more sure word of prophecy and were, therefore, sealed unto eternal life.[20]

So sacred was the event that the Lord placed them under strict command to "tell no man what things they had seen, till the Son of man were risen from the dead" (Mark 9:9). True to the covenant, "these things they kept close, and they told no man in those days any of those things which they had seen" (JST Luke 9:36).

Faith through sacrifice had not only earned them a place on the mount but also a place in heaven. But the trial of faith was not over. Indeed, the greatest sacrifices for Peter were yet to come. The first was letting his beloved master go to Jerusalem to die. He had been taught that it would happen. Before the trip up the sacred mountain, the Savior had told the Twelve of his impending death and resurrection. Totally missing the promise of the Resurrection, Peter reacted by rebuking the Savior: "Be it far from thee, Lord: this shall not be done unto thee" (JST Matt. 16:22). The response earned him a rebuke in return: "Get thee behind me, Satan," the Savior told him, "thou art an offence unto me: for thou savourest not the things that be of God, but those that be of men" (Matt. 16:23). The Lord chose the epithet "Satan" well. The word means adversary, or one who opposes the will of God. Peter had appealed to the human element in the Lord's nature, as had the devil when he tempted the Lord in the wilderness. But the Lord would not be turned from his divine purpose.

The rebuke did not land on deaf ears, but there was no conversion either. Peter would go to Jerusalem believing that the Savior would die, but understanding neither the Atonement nor the Resurrection; he would go protesting and resisting the inevitable.

The Trial of Faith: Peter during the Final Weeks of the Savior's Life

The Savior stopped in Perea on his way to Judea and taught the people there. A rich young man asked him how to obtain eternal life. When the Savior responded that he had to give up not only his wealth but also his time in service to the Savior, the youth departed in sorrow. Watching him, the Savior observed: "How hardly shall they that have riches enter into the kingdom of my Father" (JST Mark 10:23). The disciples responded with the question, "Who then can be saved?" (Mark 10:26). Looking at his disciples he explained, "With men that trust in riches it is impossible; but not impossible with men who trust in God and leave all for my sake, for with such all these things are possible" (JST Mark 10:27). This statement piqued Peter's interest. He recognized as his own the sacrifice which the Lord described as making all things possible. Peter responded by asking, "we have forsaken all, and followed thee; what shall we have therefore?" (Matt. 19:27). Peter already had the assurance of eternal life; that had been given to him on the mount. Now he wanted to know of what eternal life would consist. The Lord promised:

> that ye which have followed me, in the regeneration when the Son of man shall sit in the throne of his glory, ye also shall sit upon twelve thrones, judging the twelve tribes of Israel.
>
> And every one that hath forsaken houses, or brethren, or sisters, or father, or mother, or wife, or children, or lands, for my name's sake, shall receive an hundredfold, and shall inherit everlasting life. (Matt. 19:28–29)

The Savior's promise brings out two points: just what Peter and the others had sacrificed for him (home, family, position, and affluence) and the reward for doing so (governing the glorified house of Israel).[21]

After leaving Perea, the Lord and his disciples entered Judea, there to celebrate the Passover. The Savior put Peter and John in charge of making preparations for the meal. They found a large upper room and there gathered all that was necessary for the feast. When evening came the Lord and his disciples gathered and celebrated the meal with great solemnity.

After the meal was over, the Savior washed the disciples' feet. He probably began with Peter, he being the chief among them. Impetuous as usual, the disciple refused seeing his Lord in an act performed by the lowest of servants. But the Savior responded: "What I do thou knowest not now; but thou shalt know hereafter" (John 13:7). Peter mistook the act of the Lord, who was not performing a servant's task but initiating the first of a series of sacred ordinances which only later would be fully instituted. Nonetheless, this was the preparatory one which gave to the Lord's beloved disciples the gift of being clean from the blood and sins of that wicked generation. These men had sacrificed much, and now it had brought them the first of the ordinances which would prepare them to receive the fullness of the mysteries of godliness just two months later.[22]

Peter, still not realizing what the Lord was doing, overreacted, saying, "Thou shalt never wash my feet." Jesus answered him, "If I wash thee not, thou hast no part with me. Simon Peter saith unto him, Lord, not my feet only, but also my hands and my head. Jesus saith to him, He that is washed needeth not save to wash his feet, but is clean every whit" (John 13:8–10). Enough was enough, clean was clean, no more had to be done. Peter submitted, as did the rest of the Twelve, save one, who by choice did not become clean. Even the loving act of this God who had power to forgive sin could not cleanse the faithless soul of Judas, and this son of perdition went out into the night.

The meal, the implementation of ordinances, and all instruction being over, the Lord and his disciples departed for the Mount of Olives. On the way, the Savior declared: "All ye shall be offended because of me this night: for it is written, I will smite the shepherd, and the sheep of the flock shall be scattered abroad." Peter protested, assuring his Lord that "though all men shall be offended because of thee, yet will I never be offended" (Matt. 26:30–31). The Savior responded: "Simon, Simon, behold Satan hath desired you, that he may sift the children of the kingdom as wheat. But I have prayed for you, that your faith fail not; and when you are converted strengthen your brethren" (JST Luke 22:31–32).

The Lord clearly revealed the terrible burden carried by his chief apostle. Satan wanted him badly as a means of destroying the Church. The trial would be over faith, but the Lord had requested that Peter's faith remain sufficient for the task at hand. Because the record focuses on the Lord, it does not reveal all the trials, struggles, and temptations of this apostle nor the faith that had to be continually exercised in order to resist, but Satan was never far, and his enticements were ever ready.

The most interesting part of the Savior's statement reveals that Peter was not yet converted. Here was a disciple who had been baptized, walked with the Lord, observed his miracles, performed miracles himself, had revelation from the Father assuring him that Jesus was the Messiah, saw the transfigured Christ, received the more sure word of prophecy, and remained as yet unconverted. How could it be so? One must never confuse revelation, sealing, and membership in the Church as synonymous with conversion. As Elder Marion G. Romney has pointed out:

> Being converted, as we are here using the term, and having a testimony are not necessarily the same thing either. A testimony comes when the Holy Ghost gives the earnest seeker a

> witness of the truth. A moving testimony vitalizes faith; that is, it induces repentance and obedience to the commandments. Conversion, on the other hand, is the fruit of, or the reward for, repentance and obedience. (Of course one's testimony continues to increase as he is converted.)[23]

Peter's conversion lay a few weeks away, but when it came, it came because of his repentance and obedience, both expressions of his devout faith.

But as Peter's conversion was not yet full, neither was his faith. It would be put to the test before conversion came. Peter did not realize this and so, being aggrieved, declared: "Lord, I am ready to go with you, both into prison, and unto death," but the Lord assured him, "Peter, the cock shall not crow this day, before that thou shalt thrice deny that thou knowest me" (Luke 22:34).

Were those words of prophecy or command? Unfortunately, the Greek phrase is ambiguous.[24] On the one hand, the Savior may have issued a commandment which would have a twofold effect. It would save the life of his devoted and impetuous apostle, but also put him under a most severe test of faith—to deny, in obedience to a most difficult commandment, the Master he was ready to die for. The accounts show that Peter was indeed ready to give up his life. As the guardsmen came to arrest Jesus, Peter drew his sword to defend him. When Malchus got too close, Peter struck, cutting off the guard's ear. Such an act could have earned him a spear point through the heart, but Peter did not flinch. The Lord asked Abraham to offer up his son as a token of his faith, but Peter placed his own life on the altar.

On the other hand, the Lord's statement may have been prophecy. Peter was willing to fight, but when the Lord refused to allow him to do things his way, he may have felt helpless and vulnerable. Peter did not understand that the Atonement had to be carried to fruition and that the Savior had to stand alone: Christ alone could carry out the task the Father had placed upon him. In this light, the profound sleep which prevented Peter, James, and John from watching and praying as the Lord went through the agony of Gethsemane may have been providential. Even the determined Peter was not to give him aid.

Three of the gospel writers suggest that the Lord's statement was prophetic. Each implies that Peter had forgotten the Lord's words until the cock crowed. The sound served to bring them vividly to mind (compare Matt. 26:75; Mark 14:72; and Luke 22:61–62). According to the accounts, he and probably John were able to get entrance as far as the courtyard of Caiaphas, the High Priest, who questioned the Lord. It was here that Peter was accused three times of being the Lord's disciple. His denials were firm and pointed: he knew not the man. Upon the third denial, the cock crowed, "and he went out, and wept bitterly" (Matt. 26:75). John, who most likely was the only one actually present during these trying events, tells the story up to the cock's crowing and leaves it there. He does not mention Peter's having to recall the Lord's words. If Peter did show weakness at that time, and was not responding to a commandment which tested his faith to the extreme, it would be the last time.

Peter, however, had to pass one more test. Three days after his Lord was buried, and still early in the morning, Mary of Magdala brought news: someone had robbed the Lord's grave. Peter and John ran to the site, and Peter actually went into the tomb itself. His Messiah was gone. Peter was dumbfounded. Who would steal his Lord's body? Who would be so cruel? Leaving, he joined with the remaining ten apostles to tell them of these untoward events. Then strange stories began. A group of women came saying they had seen the Lord, and Mary confirmed their story with testimony of her own. These were to Peter and most of his brethren but wishful thinking, the tales of naive children. When two disciples came also proclaiming that they had seen and talked with the risen Lord, Peter still refused to believe. Then, at some point, the Lord appeared to his chief apostle (1 Cor. 15:5). No details of the meeting have been preserved, but Peter came away with a sure testimony and understanding of both the Resurrection and the Atonement.

Mature Faith: Peter as Head of the Church

Peter's preaching from that point on had two themes: the Resurrection and the eventual return of his Messiah. Peter knew that Christ lived and testified in his first recorded speech: "God hath raised [him] up, having loosed the pains of death: because it was not possible that he should be holden of it" (Acts 2:24). Indeed, "this Jesus hath God raised up, whereof we all are witnesses" (Acts 2:32). Peter testified and taught in his favorite place, the porticoes of the temple. His testimony, along with those of his brethren, brought opposition. As they preached, "the priests, and the captain of the temple, and the Sadducees, came upon them, Being grieved that they taught the people, and preached through Jesus the resurrection from the dead. And they laid hands on them, and put them in hold" (Acts 4:1–3).

The next day Peter stood before the very rulers in fear of whom he had denied his Lord. There was no denial now. Boldly Peter testified of "Jesus Christ of Nazareth, whom ye crucified, whom God raised from the dead," who manifested and would continue to manifest his power through his chosen leaders. "This is the stone which was set at naught of you builders, which is become the head of the corner," Peter scolded (Acts 4:10–11). When threatened with beatings, Peter declared, "Whether it be right in the sight of God to hearken unto you more than unto God judge ye. For we cannot but speak the things which we have seen and heard" (Acts 4:19–20). When Peter and his brethren not only refused to quit preaching but also converted around 10,000 people to the Lord in just a few weeks, the Jewish rulers decided on harsher measures. Peter was again arrested with some of his brethren and beaten. The result? "And they departed from the presence of the council, rejoicing that they were counted worthy to suffer shame for his name. And daily in the temple, and in every house, they ceased not to teach and preach Jesus Christ" (Acts 5:41–42).

What made the difference in Peter? In a word, conversion. Through faith and perseverance, the Spirit had touched and transformed him during the celebration of Pentecost. The disciples knew the gift was coming. The Lord had promised it to them before his death and even described what it would do for them (see John 14:15–20; 16:7–15). Now, not more than a week after the Lord had ascended into heaven, the gift came as a rushing wind and a cloven tongue of fire. It enabled the disciples to bear pure testimony, which touched the hearts of thousands and converted the humble followers of the Lord. Peter, now having been born again, quickened in the inner man, stepped forward as the greatest man of faith in the Church, touching, lifting, healing, and loving the Lord's people, and being loved in turn.

Through sacrifice, Peter's faith had yielded love, the pure love of Christ. That love would be the hallmark of his ministry. It came naturally as a result of his conversion and expressed itself in obedience to the Lord's commandments. After Peter and some other disciples had returned to their families in Galilee, the Lord appeared to them. On this occasion the Lord asked Peter:

> Simon, son of Jonas, lovest thou me more than these? He saith unto him, Yea, Lord; thou knowest that I love thee. He saith unto him, Feed my lambs.
>
> He saith to him again the second time, Simon, son of Jonas, lovest thou me? He saith unto him, Yea, Lord; thou knowest that I love thee. He saith unto him, Feed my sheep.
>
> He saith unto him the third time, Simon, son of Jonas, lovest thou me? Peter was grieved because he said unto him the third time, Lovest thou me? And he said unto him, Lord, thou knowest all things; thou knowest that I love thee. Jesus saith unto him, Feed my sheep. (John 21:15–17)

Three times Peter had denied his Lord; now three times he confessed his love. In each instance he was commanded to take care of the Lord's children. But a prophecy went with the commandment. The Lord warned,

> Verily, verily, I say unto thee, When thou wast young, thou girdedst thyself, and walkedst whither thou wouldest: but when thou shalt be old, thou shalt stretch forth thy hands, and another shall gird thee, and carry thee whither thou wouldest not.
>
> This spake he, signifying by what death he should glorify God. And when he had spoken this, he saith unto him, Follow me. (John 21:18–19)

The Lord prophesied of Peter's final act of faith: martyrdom. He was to follow his Lord even into death. His Lord demanded full sacrifice, but Peter received therefrom perfect faith unto everlasting life.

Conclusion
Peter's Message: Add to Your Faith

In his last preserved writings, Peter wrote a promise to those who "have obtained like precious faith with us through the righteousness of God and our Savior Jesus Christ." Note, the source of faith, like testimony, is not man but God. It is his gift. Out of it grows "life and godliness, through the knowledge of him that hath called us to glory and virtue" (2 Pet. 1:1, 3). The word translated as *knowledge* in this passage is not the common *gnosis*, but the intense form, *epignosis*, meaning sure or certain knowledge—not that which can be gained from textbooks but only through actual association and experience.

The point is that faith is not an end in itself. It is a power, like steam or electricity, which makes other things possible, such as association with God. This opens additional channels. As Peter testifies, "Whereby [through the "knowledge" of God] are given unto us exceeding great and precious promises: that by these ye might be the partakers of the divine nature" (2 Pet. 1:4). Faith brings the promises, or covenants, of God in reach of the disciple. Out of this grows knowledge, and out of knowledge grows the powers of godliness, the divine nature, and eternal life.

Faith is not the end but the beginning of the process of salvation. Therefore, Peter counsels that one must give all diligence and "add to your faith" those powers which it opens: virtue (*areta*, moral excellence, but also the power of God); knowledge (*gnosis*, that which is learned by study and also by faith); temperance (*egkrateia*, self-control or self-mastery); patience (*hupomone*, steadfastness, endurance); godliness (*eusbeia*, reverence, piety, proper service to God); brotherly kindness (*philadelpheia*, brotherly love); and charity (*agape*, the pure love of Christ) (2 Pet. 1:5–7).

All these come only as one opens the door by faith. But out of them come the promise: "if these things be in you and abound, they make you that ye shall neither be barren nor unfruitful in the knowledge [*epignosis*] of our Lord Jesus Christ" (2 Pet. 1:8). Only through the powers of love, the greatest fruit of faith, does one come to know—that is, experience or associate with on a spiritual but very real level—God and Christ. Therefore, Peter admonishes:

"give diligence to make your calling and election sure; for if ye do these things, ye shall never fall" (2 Pet. 1:10).

Peter knew well whereof he spoke. He sacrificed his life in service, adding virtue after virtue until he came to love through faith. Through unremitting faith he acquired the powers of godliness—even being able to raise the dead, heal broken bodies and broken souls, and exorcise the very powers of hell. Multitudes gathered to him, and he gathered them to his Lord. Truly, through faith he became the great fisher of men.

NOTES

1. Joseph Smith, *Lectures on Faith* (Salt Lake City: Deseret Book, 1985), 69.

2. Joseph Smith, *Teachings of the Prophet Joseph Smith*, comp. Joseph Fielding Smith (Salt Lake City: Deseret Book, 1976), 301.

3. *Simon* is the Greek equivalent of the Hebrew *Simeon*. The name translates as "hearing" in English. Leah so named her secondborn child because God had heard her pleas and blessed her with a son.

4. The source of all Greek translations in this paper is Walter Bauer, *A Greek-English Lexicon of the New Testament and Other Early Christian Literature*, 2d ed. (Chicago: The University of Chicago Press, 1979).

5. Capernaum sat on the northern shore of the Sea of Galilee. It was small, running just over 500 yards along the coast from east to west and about 200 yards south to north. It was composed primarily of one-story insulae, or apartment complexes, though there were some individual homes, a synagogue, a customs house, and a few shops. The population was around 1,500. The people of the town made their living primarily from the sea. They did little farming, the area being covered with basalt rock with only a shallow layer of soil. See Stanislao Loffreda, *Recovering Caphernaum* (Jerusalem: Edizioni Custodia Terra Santa, n.d.), 18–27; Jerome Murphy-O'Connor, *The Holy Land* (New York: Oxford University Press, 1986), 188–93; David Noel Freedman, et. al., eds., *The Anchor Bible Dictionary* (New York: Doubleday, 1992), s.v. Capernaum.

6. For arguments, descriptions, maps of the city, and isometric reconstructions of the house believed to belong to Peter, see Loffreda, *Caphernaum*, 50–63, 70–74.

7. In 1 Peter 5:13, the apostle mentions "Marcus my son." This is generally though to refer to John Mark, the writer of the Gospel of Mark. He was closely affiliated with Peter in Rome and used Peter's teachings as the basis for

his gospel (see Eusebius, *Ecclesiastical History*, 2.15.1). If this is the case, then the phrase "my son" refers to a spiritual bond, not a filial one, for Mark's mother was named Mary, and, from the way Acts 14:14 is written, she was a widow.

8. E. Meyers, "Galilean Regionalism: A Reappraisal," *Studies in Judaism in Its Greco-Roman Context* (Atlanta: Brown Judaic Series 32, 1985), 115–31.

9. The term originally denoted an expedition at sea and referred specifically to its captain, the one in charge holding all power. The philosophers called Cynics, about the third century B.C., applied the term to their preachers as messengers of the gods who were commissioned to act in their name. See Epictetus, 3.22.23.

10. J. Lewis Taylor, "Peter and His Writings," *Sidney B. Sperry Symposium* (Provo, Utah: Brigham Young University Press, 1978), 125.

11. Hugh Nibley, *The World and the Prophets* (Salt Lake City and Provo, Utah: Deseret Book and Foundation for Ancient Research and Mormon Studies, 1987), 27.

12. Normally it is the privilege and duty of the Holy Ghost to bear witness of the Father and the Son (Moses 6:66). From the ministry of Moses to the day of Pentecost about fifty days after the Lord's crucifixion the powerful and sure revelation coming through the Gift of the Holy Ghost was generally not available. During the Lord's ministry, revelation seems to have come from the Father, probably through the instrumentality of the Holy Ghost, but not the gift of the same. After Pentecost, when the Gift of the Holy Ghost was again operating, Paul could testify that "No man can say [Greek *eipein*, here "testify"] that Jesus is the Lord, but by the Holy Ghost" (1 Cor. 12:3).

13. *Ho petros*, a stone, stands in contrast to *he petra*, a rock face into which tombs were cut. The stone is a fragment from the rock.

14. The Apostle John, living near the turn of the century, noted that "it is the last time: and as ye have heard that antichrist shall come, even now are there many antichrists; whereby we know it is the last time" (1 John 2:18). The word translated "time" (Greek *hora*) denotes a fixed or set moment. Thus, John states that the set time, or final hour, for the Church has come. In 3 John 1:9–10, he notes a prominent regional leader, Diotrephes, would not receive the true leaders, spoke openly against them, and excommunicated any who defended or associated with them. John's witness in Revelation 12:13–17 shows that Satan soon forced the Church out of the reach of even the pure in heart.

15. Early Christian and Jew alike thought of the place of spirits as a large detention center, but not necessarily a place of torment. See 1 Peter 3:19; Tertullian, *De Anima* (*On the Soul*) 7.35, 55; The Wisdom of Solomon 17:15; Book of Enoch (1 Enoch) 10:13; 69:28; Jerome, *Commentarius in Osee* (*Commentary on Hosea*) 1.13. "In the Jewish tradition the righteous dead are described as sitting impatiently in their place of detention awaiting their final release and reunion with their resurrected bodies and asking, 'How

much longer must we stay here?'" Hugh Nibley, *Mormonism and Early Christianity* (Salt Lake City: Deseret Book, 1987), 105–6. See also, 4 Esdras 4:35–36; 7:75–99; cf. Josephus, *Jewish Antiquities* 18.1.3.

16. Matthew 17:1 and Mark 9:2 say six days later, while Luke 9:28 states it was eight days later.

17. Bruce R. McConkie, *The Mortal Messiah* (Salt Lake City: Deseret Book, 1980), 3:57–58.

18. Joseph Fielding Smith, *Doctrines of Salvation* (Salt Lake City: Bookcraft, 1955), 2:165.

19. The Greek phrase *nephele photeine epeskiasen outous*, "a brilliant cloud overshadowed [i.e., screened or shielded] them," is arresting. The purpose of the cloud, as bright as it was, acted as a shield to protect them from something yet brighter, something that even in their elevated spiritual state they could not endure. That something was not the Son who, though brilliant beyond description, they could clearly see, but the Father come to earth on this most important occasion to be with and bear witness of his Son. From this experience Peter would have known that the Father and the Son were two separate and glorious personages.

20. D&C 131:5–6; Bruce R. McConkie, *Doctrinal New Testament Commentary* (Salt Lake City: Bookcraft, 1970), 1:400.

21. The idea that the Twelve shall be rulers over, rather than judges who assign glory to, the divine family of Israel comes from two sources. The first states that "the keeper of the gate is the Holy One of Israel; and he employeth no servant there" (2 Ne. 9:41), suggesting that the Lord performs all judgment and assigns all glory. The second notes that "mine apostles, the Twelve which were with me in my ministry at Jerusalem, shall stand at my right hand...to judge the whole house of Israel, even as many as have loved me and kept my commandments, and none else" (D&C 29:12). They preside over those who love the Lord and have kept his commandments and so are celestial heirs. The judgment has already taken place before they begin their period of rule. The Greek *krino* used in the New Testament does not mean simply to sit in judgment of, but also to plead for and to assist. The Septuagint uses the word to translate the Hebrew *diyn* which means to act as judge, but in the sense of to rule, preside over, make and enforce laws for. Therefore, this kind of judge combines both the judicial and executive powers.

22. Bruce R. McConkie, *Mortal Messiah*, 4:37–38. There is a problem here which has not been resolved by Church authority. If Peter received his endowment six months earlier on the Mount of Transfiguration, why did he not recognize what the Lord was doing during the Last Supper?

23. Marion G. Romney, in *Conference Report*, October 1963, 24.

24. In this irregular verb, *aparneomai*, both the second person singular future indicative and the present imperative form are the same, *aparnese*.

Chapter Ten

Paul: Growing Seeds of Faith

Doug Reeder

Introduction

The earth has never been the same since the Apostle Paul walked it. There are few individuals who forever alter the course of history, but Paul is such a person. In his lifetime he made the gospel of Jesus Christ as much at home in Rome as it had been in Palestine. Paul's influence increased over time, and his writings fired Martin Luther and other reformers with zeal, courage, and knowledge to pioneer new directions for Christianity, which would open the door for the Prophet Joseph Smith and the Restoration.

Paul brings to mind character traits of the most noble kind: faith, hope, charity, commitment, obedience, and the entire spectrum of positive attributes needed to carry on the work in the kingdom of God. Where did Paul get his relentless and untiring energy? What made him so great? It would be hard to select a single word that would answer these questions, but if pressed to do so, *faith* would come as near as any to explaining Paul's whole-souled devotion.

Paul and *faith* are nearly synonymous. Nearly 70 percent of the references to faith in the New Testament are attributed to Paul. He was a man of faith; his teachings are saturated with the principle of faith; and his faith nourished the faith of others. For Paul, there were three pillars on which a person's life could be supported: faith, hope, and charity. He claimed the greatest was charity, or the pure love of Christ, but his life and teachings did not leave faith far behind.

Foreordination

Paul says of Christ's visitation to him and his apostleship that he was born "out of due time" (1 Cor. 15:18), or, as the Greek phrase signifies, he was born an abnormality or a miscarriage. He did not consider himself a "normal" apostle of the Lord because he, unlike the original twelve Jesus had chosen, had persecuted and "wasted" the Church (1 Cor 15:9; Gal. 1:13). Furthermore, Paul was not an eyewitness of Christ's mortal ministry, which caused some Christians to doubt that Paul was a bona fide apostle. In spite of these hindrances, Christ used him in a mighty way to labor "more abundantly" than any of the other apostles (1 Cor. 15:10) in taking the gospel to kings, the gentiles, and the children of Israel (Acts 9:15).

Paul says he was "separated from [his] mother's womb," or, as the Revised Standard Version translates the phrase, "I was ordained before I was born" (Gal. 1:15). Paul was no doubt one of those noble and great ones Abraham saw and spoke of in such laudatory terms (see Abr. 3:18–19). This foreordination was effected by God to bring about his divine will (Eph. 1:11); and although the great apostle had gone contrary to his foreordained call and the will of God, God did not give up on him, but rather shook him up through faith and love to show in Paul "a pattern to them which should hereafter believe on [Christ] to life everlasting" (1 Tim. 1:13–16).

Early Life and Education

Paul was instructed by Gamaliel, one of the foremost rabbis of learning Judaism has produced. Paul's being educated at Jerusalem by a scholar among scholars speaks well of the aspirations and hopes of loving, concerned parents. However, anything said about his immediate family is mere speculation. What we do know is that Paul had the basis of faith rooted in God and scripture, but it would take time and effort to get rid of pesky theological weeds Judaism had allowed and nourished in the garden of God's truth.

We first meet Paul as young man, using his Jewish name Saul, at the stoning of Stephen, one of the seven disciples selected to distribute commodities among Church members (Acts 7:58). Paul's purpose at the stoning of Stephen has been widely discussed. Some assert that Paul was in charge of the murderous, illegal riot; others claim he was merely a bystander; still others speculate that he was there in some sort of official capacity as a member of the Sanhedrin.[1] Whatever his position, he gladly approved of the action of his fellow synagogue worshippers. I use the word *gladly* because it is clearly implied in the Greek word that has been translated that he was consenting.[2] Luke, the writer of Acts, chose to use a word that conveys the meaning of taking pleasure in or thinking well of the action being taken.

This zeal for cutting out the cancerous Christian sect culminated in murderous threats against the disciples of Jesus and persecuting them unto death (Acts 9:1, 22:4). Just how directly Paul was involved with the death of any Christian is not clearly stated in the Holy Scriptures, but knowing the murderer is denied salvation in the celestial kingdom,[3] it is highly unlikely that Paul did anything more than to bind Christians, punish them, and drag them to prison (Acts 22:4–5; 8:3). He did vote in favor of the death penalty for professing Christians (Acts 26:10), but he surely felt justified in this action because the law of Moses approved death for blasphemers (Lev. 24:10–16). And a Messiah who had been crucified—hanged on a stake? That would have been evidence enough for the Jewish Saul to brand Jesus a false pretender because the Old Testament clearly says anyone who is hanged on a stake is accursed by God (Deut. 21:33).

In his zealous commitment and misguided faith, Paul was determined to get rid of this malignancy even if doing so required drastic surgery. Once this zeal was coupled with a knowledge of the truth, Paul would prove so well prepared for his foreordained calling that nothing would deter him from his divine mission, not weariness, punishment, prison, want, or even threat of death.

Paul's Conversion—Sprouting Seeds of Faith

Each individual's faith starts as a seed. Whatever his position in life the seed of faith needs to be planted, nourished, weeded, and cared for—sometimes with a tender hand, sometimes with a hoe. With some the sprouting and growth of the seed may involve a lot of time; with others it may come about by a single event that so totally focuses the person on the things of God and the direction he or she is going that he or she is a different person than before the event. Such was the case with Paul.

In a sense, the road to Damascus is every convert's road. Each person must come to a knowledge for himself that Jesus is the promised Messiah, the Redeemer, not only of the world but, more importantly, of the individual himself. Paul's journey from Jerusalem to Damascus was less than 200 miles, but in his heart, mind, and soul it was a journey of light-years. He started out as a Pharisee, ended as a Christian. He started out a persecutor, ended being persecuted. He started out as a wrecker of the faith, but ended as a master builder. He started out as an attacker, but ended as a defender of the faith.

Paul's journey to Damascus would take him the better part of a week. Was it a time to re-evaluate his course of action, to ponder Stephen's violent yet calm death? Could it have been a time of weighing and considering and examining? Would Paul have ended up an apostle of the Lord had not the dramatic event on the road to Damascus taken place? Every blessing is predicated upon obedience to law, obedience which extends from premortality as well as mortality, and Paul undoubtedly received the blessings that were rightfully his.

When Christ appeared to Saul, Saul asked two questions. First, "who art thou Lord?" When this was answered, the second question was, "Lord, what wilt thou have me to do?" (Acts 9:5–6). Paul was now submissive. He has been in the yoke, but breaking up the wrong field. Now he had been goaded to new fields of plowing, and plow he would. He would break up the fields of Palestine, Syria, Asia, and Europe, even to the great capital of the empire, Rome. That is putting on the yoke and going to work and not looking back! The work will be long and hard and tiresome, but the yoke is a good fit and the Master "meek and lowly in heart" (Matt 11: 29–30).

Paul's newfound faith will be his life and breath; he will labor as a master builder to build his converts (1 Cor. 3:10; 2 Cor. 12:15). He will labor as a farmer in preparing people's hearts to receive the seed (1 Cor. 3:6). He will have the care and concern of a nursing mother to see that his converts will receive the nourishment they need to mature (1 Cor. 3:1–2).

Paul always had faith in God, scripture, covenants, and prophets (Rom. 3:2; 9:4; 2 Tim. 3:15). Once he found his Savior, he was complete (Col. 2:10). The faith he has had in God's word would take on new depths and meaning. His faith and works would generate power that would give light throughout much of the Roman Empire.

Early Missions—a Flame Fired By Faith

Straightway Paul preached Christ in the synagogues, proclaiming that he is the Son of God (Acts 9:20). For Paul there was no time to waste—in comparison to his newfound faith, all else was as dung (Phil. 3:8). The message was one of urgency. The gospel immediately became part of his lifestyle, and Paul would do all in his power to further the cause of Christ. Time is such a precious commodity it should be invested, not merely spent, and Paul became the patron saint of the present moment. He had too long trafficked in error, and now that he was a repository of truth which must be shared, there was no time to lose or squander.

Paul was now preaching the very thing he went to Damascus to destroy. His first mission to Damascus was limited to two activities: the first, preaching and proving that Jesus is the anointed one of God; second, his escape from Damascus and the scathing abuse of the Jews by being lowered over the wall in a basket (Acts 9:25). To a large extent the first mission at Damascus would be a precursor of his life.

When a life is fired by faith, perspective changes. Life and events are evaluated from an eternal frame of reference. It is with this eternal frame of reference that Paul would carry out his work. After fleeing Damascus to protect his life he went to Jerusalem and there examined and discussed with the Grecians, that is Greek-speaking Jews. (Though the King James translators translated the Greek as *disputed,* the Greek does not convey a meaning of a debate of disputation, but rather an examination in order to discuss and arrive at truth.) Once again his life was endangered and they went about to slay him (Acts 9:29). Here is the Damascus experience relived—preaching and fleeing.

In order to protect Paul's life, the brethren sent him from Jerusalem to his hometown of Tarsus. The number of years he spent in Tarsus is debated; suffice it to say he spent a considerable amount of time there. The scriptures are silent concerning his activities in Tarsus.

The scriptures reveal just enough about Paul's early mission to Damascus and Jerusalem to let us see a pattern of Paul's faith in and total dedication to the Savior, the Lord Jesus Christ. The Savior was Paul's peace, his joy, his strength (see Eph. 2:14; Rom. 5:11; Phil. 4:13). The riches of faith are clearly revealed in the accounts of Paul's formal missions and the letters he wrote to branches of the Church while serving in the mission field. It appears from Paul's writings that faith is not a principle captured once and for all time, but rather a continuing process. When we attain to faith we have not arrived; that is, we do not have all that is available, it is not an all-or-nothing proposition. Paul teaches instead that faith is a continuing achievement in our lives. For example, in writing to the Church at Philippi he tells the Saints that he wants to continue to abide with them, furthering their faith (Phil. 1:25). He also tells the Saints at Thessalonica he wants to visit with them and perfect that part of faith which is lacking (2 Thes. 3:10).

It is encouraging to know that we can have faith that is powerful and effective in our lives and still have the feeling of lacking faith. Deficiency in faith does not mean lack of faith. Paul seems ever willing to start at the level of faith a person has attained and build thereon.

To the Roman church Paul taught that God gives to every person the measure of faith required to act in the office to which he or she has been called (Rom. 12:3–8). Our callings and assignments come to us as individuals, and God will help us in attaining the measure of faith they require. So often we compare ourselves with others and the gifts and abilities and faith they have. We would be wise to heed the counsel of Paul when he says, "[They] comparing themselves among themselves are not wise" (2 Cor. 10:12).

Paul's Missions and Letters—the Power of Faith

Realizing that faith is given in different proportions and in different ways to different people, let's briefly look at Paul's formal missions and letters with regard to the rewards, or riches, of faith.

Paul's energizing faith, that which motivated and directed him, was centered in Christ and his gospel. His very life was lived by faith in the Son of God: "Christ shall be magnified in my body.... For me to live is Christ" (Phil. 1:20–21). These statements are not idle posturings; they are a philosophy of life. Paul who had been freeborn a Roman citizen was willing to be a slave for Jesus Christ; he was willing to devote his time, talents, and means for furthering the cause of Christ. Sometimes in this hectic, demanding life it is easy to get caught up in the thick of thin things and even relegate Jesus, the Son of God, to the background, but for Paul, Christ and him crucified was the central hub around which all else revolved. Consequently, Paul's life—whether it was the physical (Phil.1:20–21), mental (2 Cor. 10:5), social (Acts 15:36), or spiritual (Rom. 8:6)—was well balanced, orderly, and full measured. Because of Paul's faith in Christ he was willing to spend and be spent for his Savior's children even when his efforts were unappreciated (2 Cor. 12:15). Serving Christ was Paul's life—not popularity, nor worldly goods, nor pride, nor any other thing.

As one examines such a life to glean the riches of faith, the selection process becomes a difficult dilemma, and each student of Paul would probably make different selections. Out of a lengthy list that could be catalogued, I will mention just a few.

One of the riches of faith is summed up in 2 Corinthians 1:24, which proclaims, "By faith ye stand." Paul nowhere suggests that the righteous will live a problem-free life; in fact he teaches the opposite. During his first mission Paul was exposed to a number of cruelties, but told Church members, "We must through much tribulation enter into the kingdom of God" (Acts 14:22). He told the Saints living at Thessalonica, "We are appointed [to affliction]" (1 Thes. 3:3) and that "we should suffer tribulation" (1 Thes. 3:4). One of the promises Jesus made to us as his disciples is that we will have tribulation in the world (John 16:33). Paul does not promise immunity to the Saints, but he does indicate that tribulation will teach us patience (Rom. 5:3), that through sufferings we become joint heirs with Christ (Rom. 8:17), and that through trouble we will attain rest (2 Thes. 1:7). Persecution, suffering, problems, perplexities, and difficulties may come our way and even camp in our lives, but the blow will be softened, the pain will be tolerable, the anguish will be endurable through faith.

Being sanctified is another of the riches of faith. When Paul was defending his conversion to Christianity before Agrippa, the apostle recounted his conversion experience on the road to Damascus. While rehearsing the details he related what Jesus had said to him during the vision and then quoted what Christ had told him concerning his mission:

> Delivering thee from the people, and from the Gentiles, unto whom now I send thee.
>
> To open their eyes, and to turn them from darkness to light, and from the power of Satan unto God, that they may receive forgiveness of sins, and inheritance *among them which are sanctified by faith that is in me.* (Acts 26:17–18; emphasis added)

Sanctification is the process of becoming clean and holy; it is through sanctification that we become candidates for the celestial kingdom. This vital process begins by having faith. Without the first step of faith none of the other essential principles or ordinances would follow. Even as we attain to personal righteousness in denying ungodliness and loving God with all our might, mind, and strength (Moro. 10:32), it is faith in Jesus Christ that keeps us going on toward perfection (Heb. 6:1). Faith is to sanctification as steam is to an engine; it creates power in our lives to live righteously, and by doing so we become sanctified and worthy to enter into the presence of our Heavenly Father in the celestial kingdom.

Another of the riches of faith mentioned by Paul is faith to be healed. During Paul's first formal missionary journey he traveled to a city called Lystra, and while there he met a man who had been a cripple from birth. Paul perceived that the man had faith to be healed and "said with a loud voice, Stand upright on thy feet. And he leaped and walked" (Acts 14: 8–10).

The gift of healing is one of the nine gifts of the Spirit Paul mentions to the Church at Corinth (1 Cor. 12:9). It is also listed as one of the necessary elements of the Church (1 Cor. 12:28). However, Paul is quick to add that not everyone has the gift of healing; like other gifts of faith, it is a gift we should covet, or earnestly seek after (1 Cor 12:31). The gift of healing is a vital part of faith and also of the Church, but this is not to be understood that lack of healing is indicative of a lack of faith. For instance, Paul left one of his fellow workers, Trophimus, at Miletum sick (2 Tim 4:20). It would be hasty to conclude that either Paul or Trophimus or both lacked the necessary faith to be healed. The scripture is silent as to why he was not healed, and each student can speculate as to why, but to conclude it was because of lack of faith would fly in the face of what little evidence we do have. Epaphroditus, another of Paul's companions, was so sick he nearly died, but through God's mercy he was spared (Phil. 2:25–27).

One of the great and vital riches of faith, truly a gold mine, and akin to standing by faith, is walking "by faith not by sight" (2 Cor. 5:7). When one examines the lives of great men and women of God, whether in the Old Testament, the New Testament, the Book of Mormon, or our own dispensation, it is impressive how totally they have put their lives in God's control. Paul's life is an example of continuously walking by faith. From the mighty issues to the simple, Paul felt faith was a key ingredient—even something as routine and mundane as diet could be an act of faith. On the surface this might seem foolish, but notice the last verse of Romans chapter 14: "And he that doubteth is damned if he eat, because he eateth not of faith: for whatsoever is not of faith is sin" (Rom. 14:23).

This is the culmination of the principle being taught in that chapter. The members of the Church in Rome were a mixed group: some had been Jews with all the Mosaic Law woven into their theological fabric (Rom. 7:1–2). Others were Gentiles who weren't sure of their status under the law of Moses and how that law related to their salvation (Rom. 11:13–32). There seems to have been some dissension on certain points of the law, including the dietary law. Was Leviticus 11 still in force? Were there meat dishes that should not be eaten by the gentile converts, and if they did eat, did this jeopardize their salvation? Paul answers that it is not our place to judge, but we should leave that to Christ, as we will all stand before his judgment seat and give an account of ourselves (Rom. 14:10,12). He ends the argument by saying we should not be a stumbling block to our brother or offend or weaken him by our actions. Paul then sums up the matter by saying that even eating or not eating is based on understanding of the law and faith.

As Latter-day Saints we have been blessed with a Word of Wisdom that prohibits the use of certain foods and encourages the use of others. Living the Lord's health code is not merely a matter of health, it is also a matter of faith—faith in the Lord and faith in the prophet. Our faith may be strengthened or weakened by the mere act of eating and drinking.

Walking by faith is personified in Nephi when he was heading toward Laban's house to get the brass plates and made the statement, "I was led by the Spirit, not knowing beforehand the things which I should do" (1 Ne. 4:6). As with Nephi, Paul's life was a walk of faith. When he went on his first mission he experienced persecution, even to the point of nearly being killed (Acts 14: 18–20). Yet when he reached the city of Derbe he and his missionary companion Barnabas "returned again to Lystra, and to Iconium, and Antioch" (Acts 14:21). He revisits the very cities in which he had suffered such violence, "confirming the souls of the disciples, and exhorting them to continue in the faith" (Acts 14:22).

At times wisdom dictates that we flee and get away from problems (Matt. 10:23), but if we are so inspired and if we are walking by faith, facing problems directly and not running from them can be very rewarding. Paul "ordained them elders in every church" in the very cities where he had previously been so ill treated (Acts 14:23). Walking by faith helps us to be courageous, take positive action, and fulfill the Lord's purposes even when common sense may dictate otherwise.

Walking by faith may not remove our infirmities, but it helps us cope with difficulties in our lives. Paul had an infirmity in his flesh that prevented him from accomplishing all he desired (1 Thes. 2:18), yet Paul learned to glory in his infirmities because it was revealed to him that God's strength was made perfect in weakness (2 Cor. 12:9). Concerning the notion of weakness being an ally to God, Elder McConkie wrote:

> Weaknesses cause men to rely upon the Lord and to seek his grace and goodness. If all men excelled in all things, would

> any develop the humility and submissiveness essential to salvation? As shown by Paul's life, even the greatest prophets—for their benefit and schooling—though strong in the spirit, are weak in other things. Some have physical infirmities, others are denied financial ability, or are lacking in some desirable personality trait, lest any think of themselves more highly than they ought.
>
> When Moroni complained to the Lord that the Gentiles would criticize the literary weaknesses of the Nephites, the Lord replied: "Fools mock, but they shall mourn; and my grace is sufficient for the meek, that they shall take no advantage of your weakness; And if men come unto me I will show unto them their weakness. I give unto men weakness that they may be humble; and my grace is sufficient for all men that humble themselves before me; for if they humble themselves before me, and have faith in me, then will I make weak things become strong unto them. Behold, I will show unto the Gentiles their weakness, and I will show unto them that faith, hope and charity bringeth unto me—the fountain of all righteousness (Ether 12:26–28).[4]

Walking by faith can thus ameliorate our weaknesses and infirmities, and even these things can work together with God for our good.

Among many other things that could be mentioned, walking by faith also helps us live a life of commitment and perseverance. Who better exemplifies these character traits than Paul? In writing to the Corinthians he said, "We are troubled on every side, yet not distressed; we are perplexed, but not in despair; Persecuted, but not forsaken; cast down, but not destroyed" (2 Cor. 4:8–9). Quitting seems foreign to Paul's vocabulary and life. Paul catalogs some of the trials that his commitment led him through: (1) labors more abundant, (2) stripes above measure, (3) prisons more frequent, (4) death oft, (5) being whipped with thirty-nine stripes on five different occasions, (6) being beaten with rods on three occasions, (7) being nearly killed by stoning, (8) being in three shipwrecks, one of which left him in the sea a night and a day. At this point the reader is nearly exhausted at what Paul has suffered because of his commitment, but he is not half finished with his vexatious vignettes for he goes on with (9) journeyings often, (10) perils of water, (11) perils of robbers, (12) perils by Jews, (13) perils by the heathen, (14) perils in the city, (15) perils in the wilderness, (16) perils in the sea, (17) perils among false brethren or apostates. At this point it is easy to think surely there is nothing more to be inventoried, but Paul is not merely making a list to exhaust all possible afflictions, but is describing the price he has willingly paid to be a legitimate ambassador for Jesus Christ (Eph. 6:20). He continues on: (18) weariness, (19) painfulness, (20) watchings often, (21) in hunger and thirst, (22) fasting often, (23) cold, (24) nakedness, and finally on top of all this, he had care of all the churches. For the Apostle Paul, faith is far more likely to be a verb than a noun.

In this limited space it would not be wise to sermonize on each of the ills, but a word on his being whipped on five occasions may be appropriate because it sheds additional light on Paul's commitment to the cause of Christ.

Because Paul was a Roman citizen he would not be subject to Jewish punishment; however, if Paul refused a beating that had been formally authorized by Jewish leaders, he would have been banned from the synagogue, which would have severely hindered his missionary activity. Submitting voluntarily to this kind of lashing gives greater appreciation to Paul's commitment, especially considering the manner of executing the whipping. The following is a description from the Mishna as quoted by Adam Clarke:

> The two hands of the criminal are bound to a post, and then the servant of the synagogue either pulls or tears off his clothes till he leaves his breast and shoulders bare. A stone or block is placed behind him on which the servant stands; he holds in his hands a scourge made of leather, divided into four tails. He who scourges lays one third on the criminal's breast, another third on his right shoulder, and another on his left. The man who receives the punishment is neither sitting nor standing, but all the while stooping: and the man smites with all his strength, with one hand.[5]

Paul's Death—Keeping the Faith

Of all the riches of faith that could be mentioned, one of the weightiest is that it energizes an individual who is striving toward attaining eternal life. Notice the words of Paul to Titus, the bishop of Crete: "In hope of eternal life, which God, that cannot lie, promised before the world began" (Titus 1:2). It is this hope that keeps us walking even when we cannot clearly see the way. Laying hold on eternal life (1 Tim. 6:12) is the purpose of mortality, and we attain glory, honor, immortality, and eternal life by "patient continuance in well doing" (Rom. 2:7). The things of God, particularly his purposes, are not generally understood by the world nor by the scientific method nor by enticing words of man's wisdom, but by the power of God. And this is what demands that we walk by faith, not by sight. Then as we walk by faith, faith is increased, which gives us greater hope for and desire to attain eternal life.

Faith fortifies life even in the face of death, and nowhere is this clearer than in the letters Paul wrote while he was in prison waiting to be executed. First let us examine the letter written to the Church at Philippi. That Paul is in prison while writing this letter is understood from the following passages: "Even if it is meet for me to think this of you all because I have you in my heart; inasmuch as both *in my bonds,* and in the defense and confirmation of the gospel ye all are partakers of my grace" (Phil. 1:7). Further on Paul writes, "So that *my bonds* in Christ are manifest in all the palace, and in all other places" (Phil. 1:13). And finally, "The one preach Christ of contention, not sincerely, supposing to add afflictions to *my bonds"* (Phil. 1:16). Though there is dispute as to which prison Paul was in at the time he was writing Philippians, there isn't any dispute that he was in prison. The traditional and most weighty view is that Paul was in prison at Rome, and the internal evidence of the letter indicates that it was written at Rome.

Even as Paul wrote Philippians his case was probably being considered by a Roman tribunal, and their verdict would either free him or execute him. Notice what Paul says about the possibility of the verdict:

> According to my earnest expectation and my hope, that in nothing I shall be ashamed, but that with all boldness, as

> always so now also Christ shall be magnified in my body, *whether it be by life, or by death.*
>
> For to me to live is Christ, and to die is gain.
>
> But if I live in the flesh, this is the fruit of my labour: yet what I shall choose I wot not.
>
> For I am in a strait betwixt two, having a desire to depart, and to be with Christ; which is far better. (Phil. 1:20–23; emphasis added)

The death sentence is definitely hanging over Paul's head.

Under these dire circumstances, it would have been so easy to get discouraged, disheartened, lose faith, and quit. But not Paul; his message is "stand fast in the Lord" (4:1), rejoice in Christ (3:3), "press toward the mark" (3:14), learn contentment regardless of circumstances (4:11). Living by faith doesn't eliminate injustice but it keeps a person focused on what life is all about.

Just before leaving Philippians it would be rewarding to look at verse 30 in chapter one. "Having the same conflict which ye saw in me, and now hear to be in me." Let's try to plumb this verse and mine the wealth.

The first thing that must be done is to examine the text in its context. Going back to verse 27, we find Paul is telling the Saints to strive for the faith as though they were one person with one goal; then he admonishes them not to be frightened in any way by their enemies because believing in Christ will bring suffering by those who oppose him. Then comes verse 30 wherein Paul says it is now their turn to be engaged in the battle that has caused Paul to be incarcerated and may yet cost him his life. But Paul is still engaged in the battle. It is amazing that Paul will not quit, quiet, or quake even in prison but continues to do the thing he has been called to do.

Finally, we meet Paul the aged. He is once again in prison and is now writing a letter to Bishop Timothy who has been his long-time friend and colleague, whom he affectionately calls "my dearly beloved son" (2 Tim. 1:2). He reminds Timothy of his priesthood calling (1:6–9) and encourages him to continue to teach correct doctrine (1:13), and then tells the bishop about the apostasy that has taken place in Asia where Paul had labored so long and diligently. After giving much sound advice and teachings he says:

> For I am now ready to be offered, and the time of my departure is at hand.
>
> I have fought a good fight, I have finished my course, I have kept the faith:
>
> Henceforth there is layed up for me a crown of righteousness, which the Lord, the righteous judge, shall give me at that day: and not to me only, but unto all them also that love his appearing. (2 Tim. 4:6–8)

"Keep the faith," what a powerful sermon, but Paul gave his counsel far more than lip service—it was a way of life for him, even at this point when it would be so easy to sink into depression and discouragement. Rather than fret and fume over the apostasy or impending death, he asked his friend Timothy to come visit him and bring a few necessities, a coat and some books, but especially the parchments, or scriptures.

In the mind's eye one can see an aged, worn apostle whose body has been torn and bruised but whose faith is intact and vibrant because he has discovered the riches of faith.

Notes

1. Sidney B. Sperry, *Paul's Life and Letters* (Salt Lake City: Bookcraft, 1955), 11–12.
2. Vine, *Expository Dictionary of New Testament Words* (n.p.: Flemming Revell, Co., 1966), 229.
3. Spencer W. Kimball, *The Miracle of Forgiveness* (Salt Lake City: Bookcraft, 1969), 27.
4. Bruce R. McConkie, *Doctrinal New Testament Commentary,* 3 vols. (Salt Lake City: Bookcraft, 1971), 2:448.
5. Adam Clarke, *A Commentary on the Holy Bible* (Grand Rapids, Michigan: Baker Book House, 1979), 1146.

Chapter Eleven

Lehi: A Spiritual Portrait

Daniel C. Peterson

> Oh, that I could have had my days in the days when my father Nephi first came out of the land of Jerusalem, that I could have joyed with him in the promised land; then were his people easy to be entreated, firm to keep the commandments of God, and slow to be led to do iniquity; and they were quick to hearken unto the words of the Lord—
>
> Yea, if my days could have been in those days, then would my soul have had joy in the righteousness of my brethren.
>
> But behold, I am consigned that these are my days, and that my soul shall be filled with sorrow because of this the wickedness of my brethren. (Hel. 7:7–9)

It is, I think, a universal human tendency to suppose that people of other times had it easier, or that our own happiness lies not now but in the future. I may be facing challenges now, but later—when I'm in college, when I'm on my mission, when I get home from my mission, when I graduate from college, when I get married, when I get a real job, when we have a house, when the children are grown—then things will be easier. How I wish I could have lived in the days of the Prophet Joseph Smith, or in the days of the ancient prophets, or in the days of the Savior, when choices were clearer!

The quotation opening this essay is, perhaps, yet another illustration of this human tendency.[1] Were Nephi's brethren really righteous? Did Lehi or Nephi find things easy in their day? Were their people "easy to be entreated, firm to keep the commandments of God, and slow to be led to do iniquity"? Well, perhaps some of them were. We can certainly understand the desire of this later Nephi who dreamt of a better time than the one in which he lived, for it was one in which, the Book of Mormon tells us, the corruption and immorality and murderousness of his people filled him with "sorrow" and "agony" (Hel. 7:6). But we must always keep in mind that every time has its challenges. Every human soul faces tests.

If we romanticize great figures of the past, prophetic or otherwise, we lessen their relevance to us. How can we profit from the example of people who really didn't face our challenges, who had it easy? This is the thought that undergirds the Lord's answer to Joseph Smith when the Prophet lay near despair in the jail at Liberty, Missouri. After a recitation of all the horrible things that could (and, in fact, did) happen to the Prophet, the Lord reminded him that "the Son of Man hath descended below them all. Art thou greater than he? Therefore, hold on thy way" (D&C 122:8–9). If the Savior had not experienced every pain and sorrow and struggle that we will ever face, he would, in an important sense, lack the authority to tell us to "hold on our ways."[2] He would have little to say to us.

Likewise, when considering the experience and ministry of Lehi, we must never imagine that spirituality was easy for him. He faced all of the material challenges and family problems that any of us will ever encounter—and considerably more than most of us—but triumphed nonetheless. That is one of the major reasons why his life and example are still relevant to us. The scriptures are the field notes of Saints who have preceded us. They tell us of both their successes and their failures, and we can learn a great deal by paying close attention.

What do we know of Lehi? He was a descendant, through Manasseh, of Joseph who was sold into Egypt (Alma 10:3). His being from Manasseh tells us that his family, after the division between Israel and Judah, probably lived in the northern kingdom, since the territory assigned to the tribe of Manasseh was north of Ephraim and lay in the rich pasture land of Bashan and Gilead on the eastern side of the Jordan River. Yet Lehi was born and raised "at Jerusalem" (1 Ne. 1:4. Unless expressly indicated, all chapter and verse references in the text are to the book of 1 Nephi).[3] This probably means that his ancestors had fled southward prior to the northern kingdom's collapse before Assyrian invaders in 721 B.C. (The wickedness of the kingdom of Israel had drawn prophetic warnings and denunciations for some time, and, among the righteous who paid attention to the prophets, its fall to the westward-expanding Assyrian empire would hardly have been unexpected.)

Lehi was a wealthy man. We are told that he had "gold...silver ...and precious things" (3:22,24) and that his "property" was "exceedingly great" (3:25). This allowed him to acquire an excellent education, which included a sophisticated awareness of things Egyptian (1:2; Mosiah 1:4). Furthermore, he was a "goodly parent," and he passed on his learning to his children (1 Ne. 1:1). (It is also interesting to note that his sons, in their attempt to obtain the plates of brass, were able to gain access to the aristocratic Laban, something that would probably have been impossible for peasants or for members of the artisan class. They were most likely the children of one of Laban's economic equals.)

Yet Lehi did not behave in precisely the ways his aristocratic wealth might lead us to expect. Perhaps he and his family, members of a "foreign" tribe and probably relative newcomers to Jerusalem, had never fully fit into Jerusalem society. As Hugh Nibley observes, "Nephi always speaks of 'the Jews who were at Jerusalem' (2:13) with a curious detachment, and no one in 1 Nephi ever refers to them as 'the people' or 'our people' but always quite impersonally as 'the Jews.'"[4] It may be significant that he evidently lived outside the walls of the city (3:22–23). Property within the walls would have been hard for late arrivals to come by. Far more importantly, however, he did not share the attitudes of the Judean aristocracy.

Lehi's story, as we know it from the Book of Mormon, began during the commencement of the first year of the reign of Zedekiah. The new king was an inexperienced twenty-one-year-old. The situation was highly volatile. The Babylonian monarch Nebuchadnezzar had his eyes on the weakened states of Syria and Palestine, which had been paying tribute to Babylonia for a number of years but were seeking a chance to escape his control. It was a time of great trouble, a time that required diplomatic skills of the highest order. The kingdom of Judah's young king badly needed on-the-job training. It is not surprising that, at this pivotal moment of change, many prophets appeared (1:4). The names of most of these men are probably lost to history, but Lehi's contemporaries included such well-known prophetic figures as Nahum, Zephaniah, Habakkuk, and Jeremiah, all of whom sought to advise the rulers and people of Judah that salvation lay in repentance, national and individual, and in obedience to the will of God. Otherwise, the prophets warned, "the great city Jerusalem must be destroyed" (1:4).

It should also not be surprising that amidst the excitement of a new reign just following Zedekiah's coronation prophetic pessimism would not be well received. Already, a few years earlier, the prophet Urijah, guilty of nothing more than preaching the words of Jeremiah, had been dragged out of his self-imposed Egyptian exile and killed by royal order (Jeremiah 26:20–23). And things did not improve under Zedekiah, for

> he did *that which was* evil in the sight of the Lord his God, *and* humbled not himself before Jeremiah the prophet *speaking* from the mouth of the Lord.
>
> And he also rebelled against king Nebuchadnezzar, who had made him swear by God: but he stiffened his neck, and hardened his heart from turning unto the Lord God of Israel.
>
> Moreover all the chief of the priests, and the people, transgressed very much after all the abominations of the heathen; and polluted the house of the Lord which he had hallowed in Jerusalem.
>
> And the Lord God of their fathers sent to them by his messengers, rising up betimes, and sending; because he had compassion on his people, and on his dwelling place:
>
> But they mocked the messengers of God, and despised his words, and misused his prophets, until the wrath of the Lord arose against his people, till *there was* no remedy. (2 Chron. 36:12–16)

Lehi was one of those who heard the warnings of these prophets, and, concerned about the fate of "his people," he was deeply moved by them (1:4–5). His reaction to their preaching was, as we shall see, characteristic: His first recorded impulse or action was to pray on behalf of "his people" (1:5).[5] We are not told precisely what was the object of his prayer. Perhaps he merely wanted comfort, or perhaps he sought to know what, under the current circumstances, he himself ought to do. In any event, one should always be prepared, when one prays, for the Lord's answer—which (as Joseph Smith learned in the grove and many times thereafter) may or may not be the kind of answer one expected. In reply to his prayer, Lehi received a vision of "a pillar of fire" in the midst of which "he saw and heard much" (1:6). It was an exhausting experience, perhaps a rather harrowing one, and Lehi returned home to cast himself on his bed. But the Lord was not finished with him.[6] He was given a spectacular view of the council in heaven—comparable to that given to Isaiah, Micah, Abraham, and others—and of the celestial Book that contains the decrees and judgments of God (1:8–15).[7] In response to these awesome experiences, he himself began to prophesy (1:18).

We know from later incidents that Lehi could be a powerful preacher (2:14). But, like his fellow prophets at this time, he had little if any impact on the people of his native city. Indeed, the Jews at Jerusalem mocked him and even threatened him with death (1:19–20; 2:1). Lehi's son Jacob later testified to the sexual immorality of the Jerusalemites during his father's time (Jacob 2:22–35). One can well imagine that the residents of Jerusalem, and perhaps especially those of the leisured and wealthy class, did not take kindly to Lehi's rebuke of their pleasures. ("The guilty taketh the truth to be hard," Nephi said in a different context, "for it cutteth them to the very center" [1 Ne. 16:2].) Their disrespectful and insulting behavior did not, however, dissuade Lehi from his prophetic mission, and he reacted much the way he would later respond in his famous dream of the Tree of Life, when he was scorned by people in a "great and spacious building," "but…heeded them not" (8:33). Finally, though, he received a dream commanding him to leave Jerusalem (2:1–2; 17:44).[8] Like his ancestors, Lehi would be a refugee from the land in which he had been born and raised.[9]

Lehi was obedient to this commandment to leave Jerusalem (2:3). We must not pass lightly over this fact. A departure like

Lehi's, in response to a divine command, sounds somehow easier at such a great distance from us in space and time than a contemporary edict might. The figures of scripture often seem larger than life, people who found self-sacrifice a snap and spirituality a matter of course. But they were real, flesh-and-blood human beings, and we should not imagine that it was any easier for Lehi than it would be for us when he "left his house, and the land of his inheritance, and his gold, and his silver, and his precious things, and took nothing with him, save it were his family, and provisions, and tents" (2:4). He left behind him "gold and silver, and all manner of riches...because of the commandments of the Lord" (3:16) and entered, by choice, into the far more primitive and far less comfortable life of the desert. Repeatedly, we are told that, after his exile from Jerusalem, Lehi dwelt in a tent. These descriptions, I suspect, are intended to remind us of his return to the nomadic lifestyle of his patriarchal ancestors as well as to portray his humble circumstances in the wilderness after, loyal to the command of God, he had given up his urban wealth and comfort (see 2:15; 10:16; 15:1).

Small wonder that Lehi was commended for his faithfulness (2:1). He was a very different personality from the other aristocrats of Jerusalem, of whom Laban is perhaps more typical. That rich but unethical man had plenty of wealth of his own, nonetheless, "he did lust after" Lehi's "property," which was "exceedingly great" (3:25). So, too, the "great and abominable church" that Nephi beheld in his great vision, that loved "gold and silver, and...harlots" (13:7–8) and, indeed, preferred them to the true service of God, was the polar opposite of Lehi, who left his precious things behind in order to escape the immorality of Jerusalem and to obey God.

Lehi's contemporary, the prophet Habakkuk, had rebuked the wealthy of Judah for their greed and for the injustice by which, all too often, they had obtained their riches. They sought security in their possessions rather than in righteousness and in the might of God:

> Woe to him that coveteth an evil covetousness to his house, that he may set his nest on high, that he may be delivered from the power of evil!

> Woe to him that buildeth a town with blood, and stablisheth a city by iniquity! (Hab. 2:9, 12)

Zephaniah, another of Lehi's contemporaries, spoke of the greedy Jerusalem upper class of that day, denouncing their complacency and their smug confidence that the Lord would never call them to account:

> Howl, ye inhabitants of Maktesh[10] for all the merchant people are cut down; all they that bear silver are cut off.
>
> And it shall come to pass at *that* time, that I will search Jerusalem with candles, and punish the men that are settled on their lees: that say in their heart, The Lord will not do good, neither will he do evil.
>
> Therefore their goods shall become a booty, and their houses a desolation: they shall also build houses, but not inhabit *them*; and they shall plant vineyards, but not drink the wine thereof....
>
> Neither their silver nor their gold shall be able to deliver them in the day of the Lord's wrath. (Zeph. 1:11–13, 18)

Lehi, clearly, was not a typical member of his economic class in Jerusalem. Rich though he was, he did not let his wealth own him, nor did he let it dictate his attitudes or interfere in his relationship with God. Indeed, one of the most striking things about Lehi was his obedience to revelation. He was a spiritual person, one sensitive to impressions and manifestations from God. And he received many of these.[11] Why? Not, I would suggest again, because he was a fundamentally different kind of human being than most of the rest of us (although he had been called by God to carry out a most unusual mission), but because he was willing to act upon the instruction of the Lord. The Lord confirmed early in the Book of Mormon story that both Nephi and Lehi had faithfully kept his commandments (5:20). And Nephi commented of Lehi, after he and the other sons had all taken wives: "And thus my father had fulfilled all the commandments of the Lord which had been given unto him" (16:8). (In this sense, at least, Lehi had attained a kind of perfection.) And not only did he obey, he was quick to obey. Thus, when he was commanded at night, by "the voice of the Lord," to leave the valley of Lemuel in which he and his group had dwelt for some time,[12] he did so—the very next morning (16:9, 11–12).

The secret of Lehi's obedience was his absolute and utter trust in the Lord. He knew with certainty, for example, that Jerusalem would be destroyed—because the Lord had told him so (3:17; 5:4). He did not have to see it to know that it would surely happen. He was confident, despite the obvious and serious risks of the undertaking, that his sons would return safely from their expedition to procure the brass plates from the treacherous Laban (5:5). Their return to Jerusalem had been divinely commanded (3:4), and Lehi knew "that the Lord giveth no commandments unto the children of men, save he shall prepare a way for them that they may accomplish the thing which he commandeth them" (3:7; compare 3:8).

Once again, however, we should not assume that this kind of faith and trust came easily to Lehi, or that it was somehow more natural for him than it would be for us under similar circumstances. His trust in the Lord did not exempt him from normal human emotion. When his four sons were delayed in their return from Laban and Jerusalem, both Lehi and his wife were anxious and concerned. And he rejoiced with Sariah when their sons returned unharmed (5:1, 7, 9). But, whereas Sariah—perhaps for the first time—was certain of her husband's prophetic calling only after the return of her sons (5:8), Lehi seems never really to have had any doubts on that score. When, in the darkest moment of her anxiety, Sariah criticized him as "a visionary man" (5:2), he did not deny it. Indeed, in a striking illustration of the truth of the accusation, he faithfully credited his being "a visionary man" with saving him from the destruction of Jerusalem—which had not yet occurred. "If I had not seen the things of God in a vision," he reflected, "I should not have known the goodness of God" (5:4). And this gratitude was voiced at the very time when, having given up his wealth, he sat in a tent in the Arabian desert very worried about his long-absent boys. "I have obtained a land of promise" (5:5), he exclaimed, solely on the strength of the divine word, while still many thousands of desert and ocean miles away from that promised land.

There is something to be noted here. Faith is not primarily intellectual conviction about a list of propositions, although it does include such conviction. Faith is trust in a person—or, we might say when speaking of spiritual things, in a Person. Lehi trusted in the Lord. He had had the kind of experiences with the Lord that had built up such trust, and he had strengthened his trust in the same way that we must do with any merely human person: We take that person at his or her word, act upon it, and find that our faith or trust is justified. We delegate a task to an employee or an assistant and see how the task is handled. We entrust the car keys to a teenager and learn whether or not that teenager can be trusted. We turn the care of the pets over to a child and hope for the best. We accept the promises of God and find that his promises are fulfilled. Repeated experiences of this kind, when the results are positive, build up a confidence that is virtually unshakable. (Clearly, by the way, when faith is understood in this manner it makes very little sense to talk about "faith without works." If I say that I trust my teenager completely but the thought of loaning him or her the car keys terrifies me, my claim is not true. Trust without trusting behavior, faith without works, truly is "dead.") Lehi knew that God's promises to him were reliable because he had found God to be reliable in the past.

Another noteworthy aspect of Lehi's personality was his gratitude for divine blessings, even for divine promises that had not yet been fulfilled. When in the wilderness, Lehi "built an altar of stones, and made an offering unto the Lord, and gave thanks unto the Lord our God" (2:7). For what? a skeptical observer might have asked. (Laman and Lemuel certainly did ask, at least silently, or under their breaths.) For leaving his property? For the mockery and indignities and death threats to which he had been subjected? For an as-yet-unseen land of promise? Again, when his sons had in fact returned safely with the plates of brass, he offered "sacrifice and burnt offerings unto the Lord" and "gave thanks unto the God of Israel" (5:9). Yet again, when his sons had returned once more from another risky trip to Jerusalem (this time accompanied by the family of Ishmael), "they did give thanks unto the Lord their God; and they did offer sacrifice and burnt offerings unto him" (7:22).

Such gratitude does more than merely show us the character of Lehi in a favorable light. Commentators on the biblical book of Job commonly point out, in their attempts to date that story, that Job is marked as a figure of the patriarchal age by the fact that he was both father and priest, offering sacrifices on behalf of his family.[13] There was, as yet, no distinct priestly family like the Levites. So, too, Lehi acted like one of the ancient patriarchs when he returned to the desert nomadic life of his ancestors, even to the extent of offering sacrifices on stone altars in the wilderness just as they had done.[14]

This is, I am convinced, not mere chance. The Lord had, after all, covenanted with Lehi to give him a land of promise for his posterity (13:30).[15] In this regard, as in certain others, Lehi was very much like Abraham, who also departed from his native land—the great city of Ur of the Chaldees—for religious reasons, suffered from family quarrels, and wandered for many years in the desert without a permanent home.

> By faith Abraham, when he was called to go out into a place which he should after receive for an inheritance, obeyed; and he went out, not knowing whither he went.[16]
>
> By faith he sojourned in the land of promise, as in a strange country, dwelling in tabernacles with Isaac and Jacob, the heirs with him of the same promise:
>
> For he looked for a city which hath foundations, whose builder and maker is God. (Heb. 11:8–10)

I think the similarity of his story to Abraham's was not lost on Lehi. He seems to have been very much aware of his return to the lifestyle of the patriarchs. This may, in fact, show up in the names of his younger children. Lehi's two eldest sons, Laman and Lemuel, bear names with clear Arabic links.[17] This is unsurprising, of course, since, "of all the tribes of Israel, Manasseh was the one which lived farthest out in the desert, came into the most frequent contact with the Arabs, intermarried with them most frequently, and at the same time had the closest traditional bonds with Egypt."[18] It may well be, if Hugh Nibley is correct in his contention that Lehi was a caravan trader,[19] that the prophet's two eldest sons were born and named in his earlier days, when he was engaged in the Arabian trade that would multiply his wealth.[20] On the other hand, Sam and Nephi, the two middle sons, appear to have Egyptian names.[21] They may well have been born in the days of Lehi's increased prosperity and were given names that reflected his international contacts. But Lehi also fathered two sons in the wilderness, after the loss of his wealth and his departure from Jerusalem. For them he chose neither names from Arab nomadism nor names out of Egypt. Instead, he opted for the names of two great Israelite patriarchs, Jacob and Joseph (18:7), names that reflected the rather austere simplicity of his new circumstances. He termed Jacob "my first-born in the days of my tribulation in the wilderness" (2 Ne. 2:1) and promised this second youngest son that God "shall consecrate thine afflictions for thy gain" (2 Ne. 2:2).[22] And Joseph, in his turn, was born in Lehi's worst time, "in the days of my greatest sorrow" (2 Ne. 3:1; compare 3:3).

The great sorrow or tragedy of Lehi's life, of course, was the fact that his own family was bitterly divided with respect to his prophetic calling and message. Like Abraham, Lehi's faith was very much bound up with his family. He was deeply conscious of the fact that he was "a descendant of Joseph who was carried captive into Egypt." And he was profoundly aware of the great destiny that awaited his posterity if only they would live worthily, of how "great were the covenants of the Lord which he made unto Joseph" (2 Ne. 3:4–25). Yet the two eldest sons, Laman and Lemuel, began to murmur and to complain very early in the story. Plainly, they were bothered by the loss of their wealth (1 Ne. 2:11, 12). We should perhaps be a little more understanding of them than we usually are, however, since we can well imagine how we might react if a member of our own family threw away our home and all our possessions on some baseless whim—which is precisely what Lehi's visions seemed to be to them. They had grown up as members of one of Jerusalem's wealthy families. In their home city, they had lived in luxury, in apparent security, with position and social status. But it was not merely greed that motivated the murmurers. Following Lehi entailed genuine discomfort, pain, and death, as well as financial sacrifice. The loss of Ishmael, for instance, provoked mourning then murmuring against Lehi.

Members not only of Ishmael's family but of Lehi's own complained of their suffering and their hopelessness (16:35–36). They wanted to go back to the comforts of their city home in Jerusalem, to the wealth they still hoped they had not left permanently behind.

> He hath led us out of the land of Jerusalem[23] and we have wandered in the wilderness for these many years; and our women have toiled, being big with child; and they have borne children in the wilderness and suffered all things, save it were death; and it would have been better that they had died before they came out of Jerusalem than to have suffered these afflictions.
>
> Behold, these many years we have suffered in the wilderness, which time we might have enjoyed our possessions and the land of our inheritance; yea, and we might have been happy. (17:20–21)

Laman and Lemuel's hostility toward their father soon extended to their younger brother Nephi as well. For Nephi and his father could easily be considered co-testators, two witnesses for the Lord against the corruption that surrounded them (22:31). Nephi agreed, for instance, with his father's perception that the Jerusalemites were evil (17:44). Indeed, he compared Laman and Lemuel to them for their murderous intentions toward their father (17:44). In return, and quite accurately, Laman and Lemuel said, "thou art like unto our father" (17:20; cf. 17:22[24]) though they did not intend it to be a compliment. Therefore, he too became an object of their complaining and their murder plots (16:36–37). Nephi had already been divinely designated as Lehi's heir (2:21–22; 3:29). But Laman and Lemuel regarded him as a usurper, as one who had no right to such an inheritance. And they had some justification for their hostility, since even Nephi himself recognized the priority of elder brothers as the ideal rule for inheritance (7:8). They had simply forfeited their rights.

Even at their best, on those few occasions when they were actually interested at all, Laman and Lemuel disputed Lehi's words. Given their lack of spiritual preparation, they naturally could not comprehend them (15:2–3). They could not understand

Lehi's vision of the tree of life and the rod of iron and the river of water, for example (15:21, 23, 26). They did not understand, and they would not inquire of the Lord (15:7–11). One can only imagine how baffling Lehi must have found this attitude. When he was troubled, or perplexed, his favored course was to ask the Lord (as, for example, 1:5). This trait is apparent even in his vision of the Tree of Life:

> I beheld myself that I was in a dark and dreary waste.
>
> And after I had traveled for the space of many hours in darkness, I began to pray unto the Lord that he would have mercy on me, according to the multitude of his tender mercies. (8:7–8)

Here, as so many times, Lehi's trust in God was rewarded, and his prayer was answered. The obscurity lifted, and he could see:

> And it came to pass after I had prayed unto the Lord I beheld a large and spacious field. (8:9)

This, however, was not Laman and Lemuel's style. They denounced Lehi as judgmental and resented his denunciation of the inhabitants of Jerusalem, who, they said, were actually righteous and undeserving of any supposed divine punishment (17:22). Laman and Lemuel, of course, identified with the very people that the prophets denounced. And, indeed, it soon became clear that they felt more of a kinship with the corrupt urban aristocracy they had left behind than they did with their own father. They disbelieved his prophecies (2:13). They complained that he had been "led away by the foolish imaginations of his heart" into stupidly and pointlessly giving up his wealth and position—and, more horrible still, their own(17:20; compare 2:11). Worst of all, Laman and Lemuel conspired to kill Lehi (16:37).[25] Nephi, the younger brother, was quick to see precisely what this meant. "They were," he says, "like unto the Jews who were at Jerusalem, who sought to take away the life of my father" (2:13; compare 17:44). Something of the corruption of Jerusalem had accompanied Lehi even in his flight from the city. It had entered his very family.

One cannot escape the impression that it was perhaps partially from his own family that Lehi, under divine inspiration, derived his concept of opposition in all things (as described in 2 Ne. 2:11–16, 22). His worries about Laman and Lemuel began very early (2:8–11) and very likely well before the opening of the Book of Mormon. Not long before his death, while summing up a lifetime rich with experience and inspiration, he spoke of the need for challenges, for choices between good and evil. He had faced his own challenges, and he had made his own choices. And so had each of his sons, each in his own way. Speaking of Adam and Eve in the garden, Lehi commented that, had they remained in Eden

> they would have had no children; wherefore they would have remained in a state of innocence, having no joy, for they knew no misery; doing no good, for they knew no sin. (2 Ne. 2:23)

Lehi's concern for other people continued to bring him both joy and sorrow throughout his prophetic ministry. This, of course, was natural. We might think of love or care as a kind of invisible bubble that surrounds objects of affection or concern. Some people, in order to avoid pain, shrink their sphere of concern to the smallest dimensions possible. Perhaps they draw it in tightly about themselves, caring about nobody else. There is a certain logic to this. Fortunately, however, there are many others who extend their sphere of concern and take in others—family, friends, even strangers. This is the right choice, the divinely-ordained way. It is an important path toward a fullness of joy, but it also has risks. With every extension of the bubble, with every expansion of the sphere of our concern, we greatly increase its surface area. This, in turn, increases its exposure—our exposure—to possible injury or pain. Potential sorrows are greatest where concern is greatest.[26] This is illustrated well in the life and mission of the Savior, who loved us all so much that he took upon himself the sins of the whole world and endured sufferings we cannot even imagine. God himself, exalted, perfected, living in glory beyond description, nonetheless weeps at the self-imposed sufferings of his children (Moses 7).

Lehi chose the sometimes painful but ultimately rich and joyful path of God. On at least one occasion after his departure from the land of Jerusalem, when he was living in relative poverty in desert exile and when one might have expected that he would not much care about the fate of those who had mocked him and sought his life, Lehi spoke prophetically and hopefully of the future of all Israel (15:18). But his primary attention was given to his own family. We are told time and again of his concern for his children (see, for example, 5:21). "I desire that ye should remember to observe the statutes and the judgments of the Lord; behold, this hath been the anxiety of my soul from the beginning" (2 Ne. 1:16). "I have none other object save it be the everlasting welfare of your souls," he assured them (2 Ne. 2:30). Under the inspiration of God, he prophesied many times concerning his posterity (as at 1 Ne. 5:18–19; 7:1). He "preached" to his children and prophesied to them, especially to Laman and Lemuel (8:38; 10:2, 15). He exhorted them to "awake," to remember and to hearken (2 Ne. 1:12–14, 23). "He did exhort them [Laman and Lemuel]...with all the feeling of a tender parent, ...yea, my father did preach unto them." He pleaded with them "that they would hearken to his words, that perhaps the Lord would be merciful to them, and not cast them off" (8:37). When, in his vision, he partook of the fruit of the Tree of Life and recognized it as something desirable that would make people happy, his first thought was to share it with his family (8:12). He beckoned to them, trying to guide them, calling to them to come to where he stood (8:15). Specifically, he invited Laman and Lemuel to partake of the fruit of the tree (8:17; compare 8:38). At times he was joyful, as when he contemplated the righteousness of some of his posterity (2 Ne. 1:21); at other times he could only be sorrowful and resigned when he beheld the sins and the inevitable fate of others among his descendants (2 Ne. 1:17–19).

At the end of his life, Lehi spent his dying days pronouncing blessings and offering advice to those who would remain behind.[27] He blessed and counseled Sam (2 Ne. 4:11), Joseph (2 Ne. 3), and the children of Laman and Lemuel (2 Ne. 4:3–9). Characteristically, though, his interests and concerns extended beyond his own family. Thus, he also "spake" to the children of Ishmael (2 Ne. 4:10), counseled Zoram (2 Ne. 1:30–32), and offered blessing and counsel to the sons of Ishmael (2 Ne. 1:28–29).[28]

Lehi's concern for those around him places him in stark contrast to the figure of Lucifer, as Lehi himself learned through revelation. Where Lehi consistently sought the welfare of others, Lucifer wants all people to be miserable, like himself (2 Ne. 2:27). But this is not the divine plan. "Adam fell that men might be," Lehi taught, reflecting at the end of his life, "and men are, that they might have joy" (2 Ne. 2:25). Lehi's effort and purpose was to assist them along the path to that joy.

Despite his rejection at Jerusalem, and notwithstanding the apostasy of Laman and Lemuel, Lehi was far from a failure in his efforts. For a thousand years his followers kept the gospel alive in the New World. And, since 1830, the record kept largely by his posterity has served as the foundation for a religious movement that is spreading throughout the world. Very few human beings, even very few prophets, can claim such success.

How did he do it? He did it as every successful spiritual leader, or parent, must do it. He himself made righteous choices and those choices had an impact on individuals. As it is depicted in the Book of Mormon account, the effect of Lehi's spirituality upon Nephi is striking. Nephi rebuked Laman and Lemuel for their murmuring against the prophet (7:49), and he commanded his older brothers to honor their father and mother (7:55). "I believe all the words of my father," said Nephi (11:5), who wanted to see the same things Lehi had seen (11:1–3). Nephi consistently recognized that it was the Lord who was speaking through his father (3:15; 4:17, 34). In fact, for Nephi the "words of the Lord" clearly seemed to be equivalent to Lehi's words (7:4). Nephi did not lose sight of the human element; he was not unaware that his father was a man and not God.[29] But he believed his father to be the mouthpiece of God. Thus, according to 1 Nephi, it was the Spirit of the Lord who was the author of Lehi's comparison of Israel to an olive tree (15:12). But Lehi himself is also described as its author (15:13, 17,18), for Lehi had made himself so transparent to the will and mind of God that when he spoke under inspiration, his words were indistinguishable from those of the Lord. This is the goal from all those who hold the priesthood, and, indeed, for all those who speak or pray or testify "in the name of Jesus Christ":

> And this is the ensample unto them, that they shall speak as they are moved upon by the Holy Ghost.
>
> And whatsoever they shall speak when moved upon by the Holy Ghost shall be scripture, shall be the will of the Lord, shall be the mind of the Lord, shall be the word of the Lord, shall be the voice of the Lord, and the power of God unto salvation. (D&C 68:3–4)

Lehi's pivotal importance in the life and subsequent career of his son Nephi is apparent even in small details. For instance, Lehi's departure from Jerusalem was the chronological benchmark for Nephi (19:8) and for many generations of his posterity. Nephi's deference to Lehi is shown furthermore in the manner of his dating and placing his own experiences: "Now, all these things were said and done as my father dwelt in a tent in the valley which he called Lemuel" (16:6).

But Nephi's trust in Lehi is by no means to be dismissed as the somewhat uncritical veneration of a boy for his father. For Nephi's estimate of his father's status as the Lord's mouthpiece was actually confirmed by a divine source: An angel identified the items in Nephi's vision as the things that Nephi's father had in fact seen (12:16, 18), so that Nephi could bear strong and assured testimony: "I bear record that I saw the things which my father saw" (14:29). Additionally, Lehi's words were confirmed in others by the work of the Spirit (2:16). Nephi always sought divine confirmation of his father's prophecies, and many of his own greatest revelations came in response to this seeking.

We must not pass over this achievement of Lehi's—his winning the absolute loyalty of an intelligent son like Nephi—as if it were something light or easy. Thrown by arduous circumstances into close daily contact with his father, Nephi was in an excellent position to detect hypocrisy or self-serving compromise. He manifestly saw nothing of the sort. Lehi's spiritual strength clearly came from the fact that he really did let the Lord speak through him, by the power of the Holy Ghost—"which power he received by faith on the Son of God" (10:17; compare 2 Ne. 1:6). Lehi knew that it was the Lord, not he, who issued commands (3:5). Furthermore, he was quick to discern the blessing and inspiration of the

Lord in others (3:7–8). Even when Lehi erred, being after all human, Nephi showed him the respect that a disciple owes to a prophet of the Lord. Thus, for instance, Nephi's account of his own vision gently mentions that Lehi had failed to notice a detail of his dream of the Tree of Life (15:27). And when Nephi's bow broke and even Lehi began to complain against the Lord, Nephi (who had kept his head) went to his father for directions, which motivated Lehi to humble himself and get back in tune with the Spirit in order to give the inspired answer that his family's welfare required (16:18–20, 23–27). It is interesting to note that Nephi did not directly rebuke his father as he did his "brethren" (16:22).

One of the characteristics of Lehi's spirituality—as, in fact, it is a characteristic of the spirituality of the entire Book of Mormon—was its association with records and record keeping. From the very beginning, Lehi made a record of his spiritual experiences, his prophecies, his genealogy, and his teachings (1:16; 6:1). His practice in this respect is highly relevant to us, for his record was something like a journal. Lehi was simply trying to record and pass on his experiences with the Lord and with the Spirit, just as we ought to do. He did not merely keep a journal himself, though, for he passed the practice on to his children: Nephi followed his example (1:17; compare 19:1–3), as did a long line of prophet-scribes down to Moroni. And when Lehi had obtained an edition of the scriptures, the brass plates—which, in an age long before printing, was very much a rarity—he commenced to search them (5:10; compare 5:21, where Nephi once again follows suit).[30]

This reading of the scriptures filled him with the Spirit and inspired him to prophesy (5:17). Of course, the scriptures have often had this effect; one thinks of Joseph Smith, moved to pray by a passage in the epistle of James, or of Joseph F. Smith, whose meditation on the writings of Peter opened the way for his great "Vision of the Redemption of the Dead." But they only have that effect for those who treasure them, who love them, who spend time and effort on them, and who deeply desire to understand them. Laman and Lemuel, like so many others, did not, and they consequently never even began to sense the riches of the scriptures. The "great and abominable church," Nephi told us, though it treasures material luxuries, removes things from the scriptures (13:26–28). This is precisely the opposite of Lehi, who valued the scriptures so highly that he sent his sons back on a dangerous journey to Jerusalem to get them, and, sitting in his place of desert exile, rejoiced over receiving them, although it had been at the cost of his wealth. Many years later, in fact, King Benjamin taught his own sons the importance of the scriptures by pointing out that without them, even so spiritual and righteous a person as Lehi could not have remembered all he needed to teach his family (Mosiah 1:4).

After spending years in the desert, Lehi started to lose his health and energy and Nephi, his spiritual heir, began to assume the leading role in the family. It was, for instance, Nephi who was told to go and build a ship (17:7–10).[31] And, once at sea, it was Nephi who guided the ship (18:22). It was Nephi who took the active role in rebuking his brothers on board and who bore the brunt of their resentment. ("We will not that our younger brother shall be a ruler over us," they complained [18:9–11].) Lehi, by contrast, was reduced to futile exhortations, pleading with his elder sons to behave. He was a grandfather, "stricken in years," grey-haired, and near to death (18:17–18). Even Laman and Lemuel, in their more lucid moments, recognized that the spiritual center of gravity in the family had, in a sense, shifted to Nephi. At one point, thus, they came to their younger brother Nephi for spiritual guidance, and he gave it to them (22).

But Lehi, though certainly weary from years of opposition in the wilderness, had not yet finished his work. Some of the greatest teachings in the Book of Mormon come from Lehi at the end of his prophetic career, after a long life full of experiences and difficulties, of revelation and demanding obedience to the revealed will of God. He had learned much. He had encountered resistance at every phase of his ministry, and he knew about Satan (2 Ne. 2:17).[32] But he also knew Christ as the harbinger of the resurrection (2 Ne. 2:8) and the bearer of God's grace. Despite his own achievements, he knew that nobody is justified by the law (2 Ne. 2:5; cf. 2:8) but, rather, that redemption comes through the righteousness of the Redeemer (2 Ne. 2:3), that it lies only in the power of the Holy Messiah, who is full of grace and truth (2 Ne. 2:6; cf. 2:8). In direct contrast to Laman and Lemuel, who thought that they had to be comfortably located in Jerusalem in order to be "happy," Lehi experienced great joy even as a refugee in the Arabian wasteland and understood that the Messiah frees us from the bondage of outward circumstance, from the captivity of spiritually bad environments:

> The Messiah cometh in the fulness of time, that he may redeem the children of men from the fall. And because that they are redeemed from the fall they have become free forever, knowing good from evil; to act for themselves and not to be acted upon, save it be by the punishment of the law at the great and last day, according to the commandments which God hath given.
>
> Wherefore, men are free according to the flesh; and all things are given them which are expedient unto man. And they are free to choose liberty and eternal life, through the great Mediator of all men, or to choose captivity and death, according to the captivity and power of the devil; for he seeketh that all men might be miserable like unto himself. (2 Ne. 2:26–27)

External factors do not ultimately decide the happiness of those who have been freed by Christ. As Lehi's contemporary, the prophet Habakkuk, expressed it:

> Although the fig tree shall not blossom, neither shall fruit be in the vines; the labour of the olive shall fail, and the fields shall yield no meat; the flock shall be cut off from the fold, and there shall be no herd in the stalls:
>
> Yet I will rejoice in the Lord, I will joy in the God of my salvation. (Hab. 3:17–18)

Through the grace of God, Lehi had escaped from the captivity of the devil as well as from the captivity of the Babylonian armies that were soon to conquer Jerusalem and carry its wealthy aristocrats off to the land of Mesopotamia. Lehi knew well that "salvation is free" (2 Ne. 2:4), but he also knew what was required of one in order to obtain it. He understood the conditions on which Christ would satisfy the demands of the law, which would otherwise have taken us captive (2 Ne. 2:7; cf. 2:9).

He had stepped back into the past of his own scriptural heritage, taking up the ancient role of prophet-patriarch, and he had learned something thereby about the age and constancy of the gospel. "The Spirit is the same, yesterday, today, and forever," he said (2 Ne. 2:4). Lehi knew that access to the grace of God, and thereby to salvation, occurred on the same basis that it has ever done and will ever do, for "the way is prepared from the fall of man" (2 Ne. 2:4). This is also one of the major messages with which the Book of Mormon closes, and, for those who have experienced the Spirit of God in today's Church, it is one of the major messages of their own experience. The gospel has been restored. The same gifts and blessings are available to today's Saints that were available to the Saints of Lehi's day, as they had been available to those who were already ancient history by the time of Lehi's birth.

At the very end of his life, Lehi saw in a vision that Jerusalem had been destroyed just as he had predicted it would be (2 Ne. 1:4). He and his family, however, had escaped captivity and death. Now, not as a revelation of the future but as a present and glorious reality, Lehi had obtained the land of promise for which he had abandoned all his earthly goods. It was faith that had led him to take his family and leave Jerusalem. It was faith, too, that had activated the Liahona, which in turn had guided them toward their new home (16:16, 28–29). Lehi could plainly take his place in the ranks of those heroes of faith of whom the author of Hebrews speaks so eloquently:

> These all died in faith, not having received the promises, but having seen them afar off, and were persuaded of them, and embraced them, and confessed that they were strangers and pilgrims on the earth.
>
> For they that say such things declare plainly that they seek a country.
>
> And truly, if they had been mindful of that country from whence they came out, they might have had opportunity to have returned.
>
> But now they desire a better country, that is, an heavenly: wherefore God is not ashamed to be called their God: for he hath prepared for them a city. (Heb. 11:13–16)

Lehi did, of course, receive and see the land of promise, just as Noah did actually see the flood and his promised salvation from it and just as Abraham did actually settle the promised land of Canaan. But surely the point here is that Canaan and the ark and the land of promise across the great waters were merely types and shadows of what is to come. Our real salvation, and our real inheritance, waits for us in the celestial kingdom of God. Nonetheless, Lehi was filled with gratitude for the blessings that God's grace had showered upon him and his family here upon the earth, even when they were unworthy.

> Our father, Lehi...rehearsed unto them, how great things the Lord had done for them in bringing them out of the land of Jerusalem.
>
> And he spake unto them concerning their rebellions upon the waters, and the mercies of God in sparing their lives, that they were not swallowed up in the sea.
>
> And he also spake unto them concerning the land of promise, which they had obtained—how merciful the Lord had been in warning us that we should flee out of the land of Jerusalem. (2 Ne. 1:1–3)

Lehi was conscious of his age and of his nearness to death (2 Ne. 1:14, 21); he knew he was "in the last days of [his] probation" (2 Ne. 2:30). But he was also at rest, having full confidence in his salvation. "I have chosen the good part," he said (2 Ne. 2:30). "Behold, the Lord hath redeemed my soul from hell; I have beheld his glory, and I am encircled about eternally in the arms of his love" (2 Ne. 1:15). He realized that he had done all that he could do, and that the fate of his sons was really, in the last analysis, up to them. "Men," he reflected, "are instructed sufficiently that they know good from evil" (2 Ne. 2:5). Certainly his sons were.

Finally, old and tired, he died. And, in the absence of the prophet-patriarch who had barely managed to hold the family together, "not many days after his death" there was trouble (2 Ne. 4:12–13). Lehi, however, had obtained the true land of promise, one into which the wicked and the rebellious cannot bring their conflicts, one compared to which all the riches of any earthly promised land are only an inadequate foretaste. Those who are likewise faithful and obedient will someday join him there.

NOTES

1. It is also a strong indication that in the Book of Mormon we are reading about real people. They are often righteous and highly spiritual people, but they are still human like the rest of us.

2. See Alma 7:12.

3. Notice that the text does not say that he lived *in* Jerusalem.

4. Hugh Nibley, *An Approach to the Book of Mormon*, 3d ed. (Salt Lake City: Deseret Book and F.A.R.M.S., 1988), 72.

5. Lehi's use of the phrase "his people" is not necessarily a contradiction to the point made by Hugh Nibley above. "His people" may well refer to his family as it can in Arabic even today. Compare the reactions of Jared and his brother to the impending crisis at Babel (as recounted in Ether 1:33–37).

6. Again one is reminded of Joseph Smith who, having collapsed from exhaustion on the morning after a series of visions that had occupied the whole night, awakened near his father's field to receive yet another. See Joseph Smith—History 1:47–49.

7. Alma had a similar experience, as recounted in Alma 36:22. Compare Isaiah 6, 1 Kings 22:19–22, and Abraham 3:22–28. Blake Thomas Ostler, "The Throne-Theophany and Prophetic Commission in 1 Nephi: A Form—Critical Analysis," *BYU Studies* 26/4 (Fall 1986): 67–95, offers a fine discussion of these visions but still does not exhaust what could be said about them.

8. Later, the Jerusalemites' threat to Lehi's life was also given as a reason for his departure from Jerusalem (7:14). One of the later Nephites says that he was "driven" from the city (Hel. 8:22). Alma the Younger says that he "was brought out of Jerusalem by the hand of God" (Alma 9:9). All of these explanations are true, depending on the perspective from which the account is viewed.

9. And this would not be the last time that members of his family would be obliged, by their obedience to the will of God and their conflict with those who were not obedient, to go into exile. Such withdrawals from sinful society are a recurring motif in the Book of Mormon.

10. Maktesh was a district of Jerusalem.

11. Besides the others discussed in this essay, these "visions and dreams" (1:16) include the vision referred to in 1 Nephi 10:17; some sort of commandment against sexual immorality and polygamy (Jacob 2:34); and his prophetic knowledge of the future, including the destruction of Jerusalem, the captivity, the return, the coming of Christ, John the Baptist, the death

and resurrection of Christ, the scattering of Israel, and the gathering (as discussed in 1 Ne. 10:3–14). Otherwise unrecorded revelations seem to be referred to in 17:12–14 and 2 Nephi 1:20.

12. The exact period of time is indeterminable, but Lehi and his party were in the valley of Lemuel from 1 Ne. 2:6 to 16:12.

13. As in Job 1:5. Compare Noah (Gen. 8:20), Abraham (Gen. 12:7, 8; 22:9), Isaac (Gen. 26:25), and Jacob/Israel (Gen. 31:54; 33:20; 35:1, 3, 7; 46:1).

14. Presumably, he was able to act in this manner because he held the Melchizedek priesthood. See Paul Y. Hoskisson's response to the question "By what authority did Lehi, a non-Levite priest, offer sacrifices?" in the *Ensign* (March 1994): 54. It might be added, too, that the Bible itself records at least one instance of a non-Levite legitimately offering sacrifice even after the giving of the law of Moses: Samuel, an Ephraimite, frequently functioned as a priest (as, for example, in 1 Sam. 7:9–10). Presumably he, too, held the Melchizedek Priesthood.

15. The commandment to send his sons back to Jerusalem in order to fetch brides seems to have come to Lehi at a time when the prophet might justly have been wondering how, exactly, he was to have posterity at all if his sons remained unmarried. See 7:1–3.

16. Compare 1 Nephi 4:6, a remarkable expression of faith. Again, Nephi's is trust in a person. It is rather like being led blindfolded: If we trust our guide, things go much better.

17. Nibley, *An Approach to the Book of Mormon*, 75–76, 291.

18. Nibley, *An Approach to the Book of Mormon*, 71. It will be recalled that, when Lehi's sons needed to find wives, they sought out the family of Ishmael, who bore the same name as the son of Abraham who is regarded as the ancestor of the Arabs by both the Bible and the Arabs themselves.

19. Nibley, *An Approach to the Book of Mormon*, 46–49, 59–83, 91–92; idem, *Lehi in the Desert/The World of the Jaredites/There Were Jaredites* (Salt Lake City: Deseret Book and F.A.R.M.S., 1988), 11–12, 34–42; idem, *The Prophetic Book of Mormon* (Salt Lake City: Deseret Book and F.A.R.M.S., 1989), 102.

20. His family must already have had some money. His Egyptian education points to this, as does his apparent entry into caravan trading, which would require considerable capital to begin with.

21. Nibley, *Lehi in the Desert/The World of the Jaredites/There Were Jaredites*, 27–28, 44; John Gee, "A Note on the Name *Nephi*," *Journal of Book of Mormon Studies* 1/1 (Fall 1992): 189–91.

22. Jacob's afflictions are described in 2 Nephi 2:1.

23. Incidentally, critics of the Book of Mormon have frequently pointed to the nonbiblical phrase "land of Jerusalem" (especially as it occurs in Alma 7:10) as a liability of the book. Recently, however, the same phrase has been discovered in the Dead Sea Scrolls, in a text known as "Pseudo-Jeremiah"

(4Q385), which claims to come from precisely the time of Lehi. See Robert Eisenman and Michael Wise, *The Dead Sea Scrolls Uncovered* (Shaftesbury, Dorset: Element Books, 1992), 57–8, who comment that the occurrence of the phrase in Pseudo-Jeremiah "greatly enhances the sense of historicity of the whole." I thank Gordon Thomasson for bringing this to our attention. See also Daniel C. Peterson, review of John Ankerberg and John Weldon, *Everything You Ever Wanted to Know about Mormonism*, in *Review of Books on the Book of Mormon* 5 (1993): 62–78, which, although written before the Pseudo-Jeremiah text had been published, offers a fairly complete discussion of the issue.

24. This was confirmed, in a sense, by Lehi, when late in his life he paid tribute to Nephi (2 Ne. 1:24–32).

25. The law of Moses stipulated the death penalty for any child who merely cursed his father or his mother (see Lev. 20:9). The act of patricide was virtually unthinkable in the Hebrew society, where the honoring of parents was one of the Ten Commandments (Ex. 20:12). One can only speculate why Lehi even brought Laman and Lemuel along. Very likely, he still had hope for them. Perhaps, of course, their "opposition" during the journey and in the New World was even part of the foreordained divine plan.

26. Buddhist doctrine recognizes this and therefore teaches that we should cease to care. The doctrines of the Restoration advise precisely the opposite course, despite the likelihood of eventual pain.

27. Much like the patriarch Jacob/Israel in the final chapters of Genesis.

28. It is appropriate, in the light of Lehi's compassionate concern for all people, that some repentant and righteous gentiles are to be numbered among the seed of Lehi in the latter days (14:1–2).

29. The relationship of the human and the divine in inspired utterances is nicely characterized in Nephi's description of the blessings given by Lehi, just before his death, to his family and others. The patriarch spoke, says Nephi, "according to the feelings of his heart and the Spirit of the Lord which was in him" (2 Ne. 4:12). Although God speaks through the prophets, their human individuality is not lost; Moses and Alma and Joseph Smith, for example, all maintain their distinctive personalities.

30. Perhaps it was his newly acquired opportunity to study the Bible that inspired him to name his two wilderness-born sons Jacob and Joseph.

31. The text notes that "many years" had passed (17:4). We should probably not read too much into this episode, however, as it was Lehi whom the Lord commanded to lead his people into the ship when it was completed (18:5).

32. It was perhaps with an eye on his elder sons, so very concerned about their rights and their prerogatives to rule, that Lehi pointed out that it is Lucifer who is ambitious to reign (2 Ne. 2:29).

Chapter Twelve

The Mighty Power of Deliverance: How Nephi Grew Faith

Kenneth W. Godfrey

Richard L. Bushman, a recognized authority on early Mormonism writes that a major Book of Mormon theme is deliverance.[1] Nephites, he says, do not rebel against evil oppressors; instead, the righteous are delivered after exercising faith. Nephi, less than a thousand words into his narrative, explicates this theme by declaring that faith makes us mighty "unto the power of deliverance" (1 Ne. 1:20).

Engraving his record after successfully reaching the promised land, Nephi, now a mature prophet with a family of his own, knew well the power of deliverance. Paraphrasing Nephi we learn that faith, he believed, brought about the deliverance of which he wrote. By their faith Lehi and his family were delivered from Jerusalem and its destruction. By faith the brass plates were delivered into their hands. By faith the Lehites were delivered safely to a promised land. Thus we see, to borrow a phrase from the Book of Mormon, that faith delivers us from evil, from our enemies, from sadness, from the bondage of sins, and from other obstacles on the straight yet narrow path leading to eternal life.

Lacking faith, Laman and Lemuel, like Lot's wife, were forever looking back to Jerusalem and a culture working darkness whose doings were described by Nephi as "abominations" (2 Ne. 25:2). In the vacuum of their unbelief, the desire, the will, the faith to be delivered from evil and its attendant unhappiness is conspicuous by its absence. How is it that two brothers nurtured by "goodly parents," exhorted more than once "with all the feelings of a tender parent" (1 Ne. 8:37), could be so different, so opposite in personality to Nephi and Sam, and so apathetic and lacking in commitment? In contrast, how did Nephi, who dreamed dreams on a pillow watered with his own tears of remorse because of his brothers (2 Ne. 33:3), develop the mighty faith that led to deliverance?

While it can be argued that far more personal benefits accrue from learning just how faith functions, it might not be inappropriate to attempt for a moment to describe precisely what faith is. More than a few scriptures declare that faith, a spiritual gift, is bestowed by God.[2] Faith is given to those who show by their sincerity that they are worthy of it.[3] The Apostle Paul tells us that faith is the substance of things hoped for, the evidence of things not seen (Heb. 11:1). As the very foundation of a religious life, faith has antecedents of hope, sincerity, and humility of soul.[4] Definitions of faith include full confidence and trust in "the being, purposes and words of God."[5] Such confidence in Deity removes all doubt and catalyzes actions that are good.

In attempting to procure the plates of brass, Nephi exemplifies his deep confidence in the Lord. He and his brothers tried wisdom, charm, and persuasion, even offering to trade valuable family treasures for the plates. After exhausting all their conventional wisdom, Nephi turned to pure faith. Using the words of Elder John K. Carmack:

> He convinced himself that the Lord had assigned him to get the plates. Next he conceived the mental energy and trust to try again.... Without knowing what he would do, Nephi began moving forward while his brothers skulked outside the city walls.... Now he was moving by faith—confidence in the unknown, hope in things unseen....
>
> Notice that faith and trust in the Lord came first. Then came action. He had no plan except confidence in the Lord. It was really a "ready, fire, aim" approach.[6]

Though those with faith are not altogether delivered from pain, suffering, tragedy, and sorrow, they are delivered in time from doubt, alienation, and meaninglessness. Furthermore, faith helps provide the ability to successfully cope with the pain, sorrow and tragedy that accompany our sojourn here on earth. Realizing that life has purpose and meaning at its core, those possessing faith are able to endure, knowing that all things give experience, are for our good (D&C 122:7), and shall "be but a small moment" (D&C 121:7). Years ago in a medieval history class, I was told a remarkable story about a devout Jew. Having been forced by authorities to watch his wife and daughters raped and ravished by Spanish soldiers, he shook his fist toward heaven and shouted, "God of heaven, it will take more than this to keep me from following you, much more." His cry exemplifies just the sort of confidence and trust in Deity that can rightfully be called true faith.

Nephi's faith, like that of the Jewish man referred to above, delivered and sustained him in times of trouble and despair. Following the death of his father he saw his family torn apart and his elder brothers' anger accelerating towards violence. In his hour of deepest despair, Nephi believed himself a wretched man (2 Ne. 4:17). Yet his faith would not allow his soul to "droop in sin" (2 Ne. 4:28). Instead he declares that in spite of life's difficulties, pain, and sorrow he will trust God forever (2 Ne. 4:34). While serving as a mission president, I had a missionary with Nephi-like faith. Let me tell you his story.

As a severe snowstorm swept from Canada and Lake Erie to cover Western Pennsylvania, seventeen sisters and elders arrived at the Pittsburgh airport. Their plane, hours late, skidded to a stop, and soon they were traveling south in mission cars. The treacherous roads made their journey to Upper St. Claire and the mission home take much longer than usual. Following dinner, I found myself interviewing missionaries far into the night. About two o'clock in the morning one of the elders, as I paused, asked if I wanted to see his leg. Smiling through my exhaustion, I replied, "I cannot think of anything right now I would rather see." Lifting his pant leg, he showed me one valley of scar tissue extending from his thigh to his knee and another on the back of his leg reaching from the knee to the ankle. "I have had thirty-one operations," he exclaimed. "You are never going to have a missionary work harder than I will because I never thought I would be allowed to come on a mission. Finally approval was given and I've never been so happy," he concluded.

Only a few months passed and he and his companion were leading the mission in hours worked. Then one night he telephoned me. His voice filled with concern, he informed me that there was a red sore in the scar tissue. "That usually means the tumor is back," he explained. "What shall I do?" My wife and I began to fast, as did he and his companion. The next evening I, with his companion, laid hands on his head. Never had I wanted to heal anyone as badly as I wanted to heal this young, devoted missionary. However, the Spirit constrained me.

Results of tests at the University of Pittsburgh Medical Center were discussed by the missionary department, the stake president, and the young man's parents. All agreed that he should be sent home where the doctor who had already performed the thirty-one operations on his leg could perform the thirty-second. After he spent the weekend in his area and baptized a family into the Church, I took the elder to the airport for his flight home. As we drove north, I noticed a river of tears running down his cheeks and heard him say, "President, why can't I be healed? Is it because I lack faith? I don't want to go home. You have never had an elder who wanted to stay on a mission as badly as I do. Why can't I be healed?"

"Elder," I said, "as I understand it, true faith is when you say 'Heavenly Father, I will love and follow you and keep your commandments regardless of what happens to me.' So why don't you just try to be the best person and the best missionary you can be even if you are not healed?" Then we both shed more than a few tears.

Only a few weeks passed, and one day I received a letter. It read something like this: "Dear President, I am now recovering from my thirty-second operation. I have three nurses ready to be baptized and the bishop brings the priests quorum to the hospital on Sunday mornings so I can teach them. Three priests have been reactivated and now are going on missions. Do you think Heavenly Father is pleased with me? Am I displaying faith?" I responded in a letter and assured him that he was. Faith is pressing forward and doing good when things do not go our way, when the food on our plate of life is more bitter than sweet.

Nephi's own faith enabled him to withstand peer pressure, fear, suffering, and disappointment, knowing that God not only consecrated his prayers (2 Ne. 33:4), but had "redeemed [his] soul from hell" (2 Ne. 33:6). It is instructive to search the scriptures to discover precisely how Nephi attained his powerful faith. A thorough perusal of the record he left behind provides remarkable insights into the process by which one acquires a confidence and a trust in God that far exceeds belief. It is to this matter that we now turn.

Look unto the Lord

The core of faith, even the first principle of the gospel, is confidence in Jesus Christ. Dostoyevsky, the great Russian novelist, in an 1858 letter to Mme. Natalya Fonviztna, wrote that his personal credo was

> to believe that nothing is more beautiful, profound, sympathetic, reasonable, manly and more perfect than Christ; and I tell myself with a jealous love not only that there is nothing but that there cannot be anything. Even more, if someone proved to me that Christ is outside the truth, and that in reality the truth were outside of Christ, then I should prefer to remain with Christ rather than with the truth.[7]

Dostoyevsky need not have worried, for Christ *is* the truth, the way, the life. And remaining with Christ, preferring him above all else, exudes just the sort of faith that Nephi possessed. It was in this respect that Laman and Lemuel fell short; they too should have looked unto the Lord (1 Ne. 15:3).

Nephi was convinced that developing faith is an individual responsibility involving both the mind and the heart. Having heard the teachings of his prophet father, Nephi, desiring a testimony of his own, personally inquired of the Lord and was rewarded with clarifying dreams and visions (1 Ne. 11:1). Laman and Lemuel, in contrast, disputed among themselves and failed "to look unto the Lord as they ought" (1 Ne. 15:3). Hard hearts fathered hard heads which in turn begat doubt. The older brothers refused to "inquire of the Lord," being convinced that "the Lord maketh no such thing known unto us" (1 Ne. 15:9). Had they kept the commandments, asked in faith, believed, and looked unto the Lord, Nephi was certain that "surely these things [would] be made known unto [them]" (1 Ne. 15:11).

There is a great lesson here. We each have to turn our own eyes unto the Lord. The Holy Ghost, we learn in 2 Nephi 33:1, carries the truth *unto* the hearts of the children of men. It then behooves each of us to open our soul and invite *in* the Holy Spirit. Parents, friends, church leaders, and significant others can help, but like Dostoyevsky, we must individually choose to remain with Christ. The roots of Nephi's faith were grounded in the soil of knowledge that we must *look unto the Lord* (1 Ne. 15:3).

Swift to Remember God

Louis C. Midgley reminds us that remembering is an essential Book of Mormon metaphor.[8] Nephi recalled not only with his mind, but with his heart as well.[9] Those who forget, perish, while those who remember "awaken, soften the heart, see, hear, believe and trust."[10] However, remembrance does not refer simply to inner reflections; it includes action. Properly remembering demands participation in the work of the Lord. These actions, Midgley continues, turn a person to God.[11] Elie Wiesel, the noted Jewish writer, informs us that to forget "is to abandon, and to repudiate."[12] Memory, and only memory, "leads man back to the source of his longing"—God. Wiesel writes, somewhat reflecting the faith of Nephi, "Even if you forget me, O Lord, I refuse to forget you."[13]

When Nephi's heart sorrowed because of his sins and his soul grieved because of his iniquities, he made an effort to rejoice, yet could not because of his iniquities (2 Ne. 4:19). (I believe Nephi greatly overexaggerates his unrighteousness; his despair probably did not allow him to see things clearly.) In this moment when depression seems about to overwhelm him, he suddenly remembers. He recalls his God who has been his support through the wilderness afflictions. Nephi's memories include God's love for him and his confounding of Nephi's enemies. God, Nephi remembers, too, heard his prayers by day and rewarded him with nighttime visions. The wings of His spirit carried Nephi to high mountains where he beheld the condescension of God. The moments he remembers cause his heart to rejoice (2 Ne. 4:17–30). Thus Nephi's memories are molded by his faith.

To further illustrate the importance of memory and its relationship to action, let me tell you about my mother. For almost two decades she fought a valiant yet a losing battle with Alzheimer's disease. At first Mother forgot the time of day and appointments she had made. As her memory loss continued she could not always remember who she was or where she was. Reverting once more to childhood, she threw things, refused to bathe and slept only erratically. Dad changed the diapers she now wore and looked after her every need. No longer able to remember tunes, she sang no more, nor could she speak. She even forgot how to feed herself. She now recognized no one, not her husband, not her children, not her friends. Lying all day in her rest home bed, those last two years she did nothing, her capacity for action having vanished with her memory. After more than a dozen memoryless years, she finally died.

Nephi grew in faith because he did not forget. In contrast, Laman and Lemuel forgot that they had seen an angel; they forgot the great things the Lord had done in delivering (there is that word again) them from the hands of Laban; they forgot that God is able to do all things according to his will (1 Ne. 7:12). They also seemed to forget that they had fled in to the wilderness because Jerusalem was going to be destroyed, and "they did [even] forget by what power" they had been safely delivered to the promised land (1 Ne. 18:9). Whereas Nephi, possessing faith, was swift to remember God and slow to do iniquity (1 Ne. 17:45).

Like a good brother, Nephi tried to help Laman and Lemuel remember. He attempted, as Wiesel says, to magnify their past and enrich their memory.[14] For example, early in their journey to the promised land, Laman and Lemuel, with their new wives, rebel against Lehi, desiring to return to Jerusalem (1 Ne. 7:6). Nephi, in a valiant effort to redeem his doubting brothers, asks, "Have ye forgotten that ye have seen an angel of the Lord?" (1 Ne. 7:10) "Have ye forgotten what great things the Lord hath done for us in delivering [there is that word once more] us out of the hands of Laban? Have ye forgotten that the Lord is able to do all things?" (1 Ne. 7:12)

At times because of Nephi's importunings, Laman and Lemuel seemed to remember. For one bright moment in the darkness of their forgetfulness, at Nephi's urging they prayed to the God they only rarely remembered for forgiveness (1 Ne. 7:21). Yet soon their forgetfulness again returned.

Remembering became an essential pillar of Nephi's growing faith. Because he remembered, he believed in Christ, he talked of Christ, he rejoiced in Christ, he preached of Christ, he prophesied of Christ and he wrote of Christ (2 Ne. 25:26). Both swiftly and often he remembered and looked to the Lord (1 Ne. 17:45).

Delighting in the Things of the Lord

The things of God pleased Nephi and he continually pondered them (2 Ne. 4:15–16). An Italian bibliophile, according to author Paul Tabori, spent twenty-five years creating a library of the world's most boring books.[15] It would be instructive to peruse his library and ascertain just which books this bibliophile found boring. Some people, especially unrepentant sinners, find the things of God boring. Moreover, many people seem to believe, though I have found no scripture substantiation for such a notion, that if something is boring we are justified in ignoring it. Thus, some people stop attending church, divorce a spouse, cease keeping a commandment, all the while excusing themselves by labeling the action or the thing boring.

In contrast, Brigham Young, when he heard the restored gospel, "wanted to thunder and roar out the Gospel to the nations. It burned in my bones like fire pent up...nothing would satisfy me but to cry abroad in the world, what the Lord was doing in the latter-days...I had to go out and preach, lest my bones should consume within me."[16] Nephi, like Brigham Young, delighted in the things of God, whereby he grew faith. He possessed a great desire to know the mysteries of God (1 Ne. 2:16). Listening to his father recount his visions instilled in Nephi, as stated before, a desire to know for himself the things his father saw (1 Ne. 11:1).

Delighting, too, in pondering scripture (2 Ne. 4:15–16), his thoughts were continually upon those things he read, saw and heard concerning the things of God. Scripture reading never seems to have bored Nephi. That ancient prophet even found pondering Isaiah, one of the more intellectually challenging prophets of Israel, thrilling (2 Ne. 11:2). Why did Nephi delight in the things of God and delight in pondering the scriptures, while Laman and Lemuel found such activities lacking in appeal, even boring?

Perhaps a clue can be found in the Dean Hughes novel *Jenny Haller.* Eldon Haller, a Mormon major league baseball pitcher, falls in love with a Kansas City bishop's daughter named Jenny. As the story unfolds, their relationship has its ups and downs because Jenny is seeking her own identity, her own goals. She attends law school while Eldon patiently waits for her to love him with the same fervor he feels for her. At one point the two are talking in Hooper's apartment when Jenny notices Eldon's bookshelf. There she finds almost every book she read in college.

Eldon explains that after asking what Jenny was reading in college, he always bought the books and read them. "Why did you do it?" Jenny wants to know. "Well.... I guess I wanted to know what you were thinking about," Eldon answers.[17]

Nephi, like the hero of the Hughes novel, so loved God that he always wanted to know what He was thinking. We learn what God thinks when we read and ponder the scriptures. Furthermore, just as Eldon's love for Jenny propelled him through her collegiate textbooks, so a true love for God caused Nephi to delight in the things of God, including the scriptures.

Nephi's faith and his love catalyzed his delight. He delights in the words of Isaiah (2 Ne. 11:2). He delights in proving to his people the truth of the coming of Christ (2 Ne. 11:4). He delights in the covenants of the Lord (2 Ne 11:5). And he also delights in "proving unto my people that save Christ should come all men must perish" (2 Ne. 11:6). Propelled by love and faith, Nephi found life, the scriptures and participation in proclaiming the divinity of Christ, thrilling, meaningful, delightful!

Diligence in Keeping the Commandments

Nephite prophets who lived long after Nephi tell us that the small seed of faith first grows in the heart. As it sprouts, we experience a mighty change of heart and lose our disposition to sin. It is informative to note that Joseph Smith, describing himself, writes that he had no disposition to commit serious sins (JS—H 1:28). His faith made malignant sins abhorrent.

While serving as mission president, one Sunday I visited a small, struggling branch in southwestern Pennsylvania. As I sat on the stand with the branch president, we watched as two missionaries walked into the chapel on either side of their best, in fact their only, serious investigator, a boy eighteen years old. He was dirty, and we could tell by looking into his eyes that he was on drugs. "Is that the best contact your missionaries have?" the branch president asked emphasizing the *your.* "I think so," I replied. "We don't need another member like him," the president continued. "What we need are some members who drive Mercedes, who are looked up to in the community, members who matter." "Listen," I whispered, "our elders will teach anyone you find for them. Find some 'respectable' community stalwarts and we will be glad to teach them." Then the meeting began.

More than a year passed. One night, sitting in the mission home, I looked out the window and saw a car stop in the driveway. A door opened and out stepped a young man clad in a navy blue suit, white shirt, maroon tie and black shiny shoes. I heard his mother say, "Son, I would rather have you back like you were a year ago than to have you doing what you are going to do!" His eleven-year-old sister, tears steadily dripping off her chin, told him how much she loved him and how much she would miss him. "The time will pass quickly," he assured her, "and I'll always love you."

He rang the doorbell and I invited the trio into the living room. With his nonmember mother and sister watching, I laid hands on his head and set him apart as a full-time missionary. Two years later he returned home, having baptized two hundred people into the Church. Though I was now home, I imagined whispering to the branch president, "Are you sure he isn't just the sort of member your branch needs?" As he was taught the gospel, this young man who had walked into the chapel with the missionaries that day had experienced a significant, radical change of heart which had the residual effect of causing him to lose the disposition to sin. Like Nephi, he, too, now delighted in keeping the commandments.

For faith to flourish we need not be perfect yet! Reasonable righteousness, Elder Neal A. Maxwell tells us, will do.[18] Like Nephi, at times we may exclaim, "O wretched man that I am!" (2 Ne. 4:17). The more faith we possess and the closer we come to the Master, the more keenly we feel remorse for silly, even dumb things we do. Still, when this happens, like Nephi we can exclaim, "Nevertheless, I know in whom I have trusted" (2 Ne. 4:19).

While serving on a high council, I once had the duty of judging a man with a wife and family who had confessed committing adultery. Years before this man had been a member of a deacon's quorum I advised. Now with fifteen other good men, I sat around a long table, saddened upon learning of the things to which he freely admitted. Listening with more than average intensity, I heard him vividly describe how, while living in his sins, he found that Church was boring, distasteful, and going to meetings a miserable experience. His whole life, he declared, was shrouded in depression, shame, and sorrow.

Then his story suddenly changed. Upon going to the bishop, making a full confession, expressing a willingness to do whatever was required to bring about full repentance, he suddenly found sacrament meeting a joy. He sometimes remained in the chapel long after others had returned home. He felt peace transcend his soul as sin became abhorrent. The meetings had not changed—members of the high council still spoke, the bishop still continued to conduct ward business. No, the Church was pretty much the same; it was the man who had changed. Now he delighted in keeping the commandments. He had experienced a mighty change of heart. He was a different person. Faith and repentance have a way of doing that.

Not only does faith cause a radical heart change, it also softens the heart and makes it possible for us to believe (1 Ne. 2:16). Because of his faith, Nephi cried unto the Lord "with lowliness of heart," and received blessings pregnant with promise (1 Ne. 2:19–22). Armed with faith, Nephi, like the man referred to above desired to know "the things" that his father had seen, and experience the spiritual joy that engulfed Lehi (1 Ne. 11:1). Pondering his parent's words, Nephi's wish is granted. As we experience a change of heart and lose the disposition to sin our desire to keep the commandments dramatically accelerates. Living the gospel becomes easier, yes even a joy, as faith delivers us from our sins, our doubts, our depressions, and our shame.

The Fruits of Faith

Abundant is the word which perhaps best describes Nephi's harvest of faith. While many live out their lives seeing through a glass darkly, to borrow a metaphor from Plato and St. Paul, Nephi, because of his faith, walked in the blazing light of almost sure knowledge. He saw Christ, conversed face to face with the Holy Ghost (1 Ne. 11:11), and while caught away to a high mountain beheld the same visions as his father (1 Ne. 11:1). Furthermore, he was blessed by being allowed to look into the future where in a vision he witnessed the Savior's birth, ministry, agony and death (1 Ne. 11:18–34). John the Baptist, Mary, Columbus, John the Revelator, and sundry angels were all seen by Nephi in vision. Witnessing the entire history of his people, he saw, too, the gospel's restoration, the fall of the great and abominable church and his own record establishing the truth of the Bible (1 Ne. 13:40). Convinced by his own visions, Nephi entreated his brothers, admonishing them, "Look to the Lord," and you will see (1 Ne. 15:3). Through exercising faith, Nephi was able to obtain the brass plates, build a ship, and ascertain the meaning of the allegory of the olive tree (1 Ne. 15:11–12). Nothing seemed beyond the power of Nephi's confidence in Deity.

As we carefully study Nephi's writings, we learn that of his family, apparently he alone possessed a faith that did not waver. Perhaps he was shown so much so early in his life by heavenly messengers so that he would be strong enough to stand alone. Even on the one occasion when not only Laman and Lemuel (who were both members of the doubters hall of fame) lost faith, but his parents, Sariah and Lehi, did also, Nephi still discerned the hand of the Lord guiding their destiny (1 Ne. 16:20–30).

A young lady one morning confessed to her Sunday School class that she alone, the night before, had refused to watch an "R"-rated video with her friends. "I felt crummy walking out," she said, "not at all good like I thought I would feel." Her teacher asked the eight or nine class members to join with him and give the valiant young lady three cheers. Nephi, too, must have thought at times that standing alone was difficult. Surely it was difficult to return to the house of Laban a third time, alone, in an effort to retrieve the brass plates. Often our faith compels us to stand up for unpopular causes. Just as we come to the age in life when we want to blend in, not be too conspicuous, we see "everybody" doing things that do not please God. When we have the faith to thrust away temptation and stand as a witness, we achieve a peace that allows us to hear the still small voice confirm the rightness of our actions.

Bound tightly, in the face of "a great and terrible tempest" (1 Ne. 18:13), Nephi, with wrists and ankles swollen and sore (1 Ne. 18:15), nevertheless looked unto God, prayed and praised him throughout four long days, and avoided murmuring against the Lord. Only when Laman and Lemuel faced drowning in the swollen sea did they repent and free him (1 Ne. 18: 11–20). Upon being loosed, Nephi applied the power of his faith to calm the sea.

Because of his great faith, Nephi saw in vision the destruction of Jerusalem (2 Ne. 1:4). Thus, he did not look back to an easier life that could never again be. Nor did his heart long for home, old friends, and the comforts of a prior life. Instead Nephi's faith allowed him to look to the future, to the challenges awaiting and the coming of the Christ, and with his confidence placed in the Master, he met these challenges as they came.

Following the death of his parents, even Nephi's faith could not keep the family from splitting apart. After he was forced to leave with his followers and found a new community, Nephi watered his pillow with his tears. His faith no doubt deepened his sorrow, just as it had deepened his love for Laman and Lemuel. Trusting in God and his love, Nephi autobiographically informs us that he "waxed bold in mighty prayer," beheld nocturnal visions, and was ministered to by angels (2 Ne. 4:23–24). Another harvest of his faith was that he shook at the appearance of sin (2 Ne. 4:31).

Remembering God and faithfully keeping his commandments not only grows faith, but has the residual effect of causing happiness (Alma 50:22–23). Men and women are, in a sense, created to experience joy. Nephi included in his record Lehi's teaching that "Adam fell that men might be, and men are that they might have joy" (2 Ne. 2:25). Dennis Rasmussen informs us that one Jewish rabbi, Yochanan Muffs, contends that "joy is the essence of religion. There is nothing more fundamental to religious living than joy. That is its heart."[19] It is difficult to describe the joy parents feel when a son or daughter is baptized, does a good deed, or offers a particularly sincere prayer. It is almost impossible, too, to explicate the joy of finding solace or the answer to a personal problem in the scriptures, or to feel the indomitable faith of one who has immersed themselves in the four standard works.[20]

A few years ago a Salt Lake family including father, mother, brothers, sisters, uncles, aunts, and cousins gathered at the airport to welcome a returning missionary. After the boy's arrival, after the balloons had popped and tears were just beginning to dry, the elder's mother was approached by two older women from a European country. The conversation proceeded somewhat as follows: "Madam, we have spent three months touring the United States. We have seen Disneyworld, the World Trade Towers, Niagara Falls, Mt. Rushmore, Washington, D.C., the Grand Canyon, and Disneyland. What just happened here? This is the best thing we have seen in America."

Is it so strange that even those who do not know us can tell when we are "living after the manner of happiness?" Nephi knew the joy of looking to the Savior, accepting his mercy and then, by faith, keeping his commandments. His people, those who would call themselves Nephites, "were those who believed in the warnings and the revelations of God" and who kept "the judgments, and the statutes, and the commandments of the Lord in all things (2 Ne. 5:6, 10). Because of their faith and obedience, Nephi records, they "lived after the manner of happiness" (2 Ne. 5:27).

One of the foremost reasons for Nephi writing and his initial reference to the word *faith* was to show "that the tender mercies of the Lord are over all those whom he hath chosen, because of their faith" (1 Ne. 1:20). We could all use additional "tender mercies" from the Lord, and if faith is the causal factor, then it is well worth acquiring. When we begin to grow our faith, God helps provide an inner strength that significantly increases our ability to cope with life's challenges, concerns, sufferings, and sorrows.

Deliverance, the dictionary informs us, means to rescue, release, or preserve. Faith, true faith, rescues us from Satan, releases us from spiritual death, and preserves our confidence in the Lord and Savior Jesus Christ. Nephi knew that faith alone provided access to the mighty power of deliverance. In Scottish law, deliverance is the expressed decision of a judge. When we have faith, and look to Christ, he, being the great Judge, delivers us in to the arms of our Father who exclaims, "My son, my daughter, I have you again." We then may say, "Oh, my Father, I am home again!"

Notes

1. Richard L. Bushman, "The Book of Mormon and the American Revolution," *BYU Studies* (1976) 17:1:3.
2. Matt. 16:17; John 6:44; Eph. 2:8; 1 Cor. 12:9; Rom. 12:3; Moro. 10:11.
3. James E. Talmage, *A Study of the Articles of Faith*, (Salt Lake City: The Church of Jesus Christ of Latter-day Saints, 1942), 107.
4. Talmage, op. cit.
5. Talmage, op. cit., 96.
6. John K. Carmack, "Faith Yields Priesthood Power," *Ensign* (May 1993), 42.
7. *New York Times Book Review,* 1 January 1984, 33.
8. Louis C. Midgley, "The Ways of Remembering," *Rediscovering the Book of Mormon*, John L. Sorenson and Melvin J. Thorne, eds. (Salt Lake City: Deseret Book, 1991).
9. Ibid. 169.
10. Ibid. 170.
11. Ibid.
12. Elie Wiesel, *The Forgotten* (New York: Summit Books, 1992).
13. Ibid. 12.
14. Ibid. 236–37.
15. Paul Tabori, *The Natural History of Stupidity* (New York: Barnes and Noble, 1993), x.
16. Ronald K. Esplin, *The Emergence of Brigham Young and the Twelve to Mormon Leadership, 1830–1841*, Ph.D. Dissertation, Brigham Young University, 1981, 70.
17. Dean Hughes, *Jenny Haller* (Salt Lake City: Deseret Book, 1983), 128–29.
18. Neal A. Maxwell, *Ensign* (May 1976), 126.
19. Dennis Rasmussen, "An Elder Among the Rabbis," *BYU Studies*, (Summer 1981) 21:3:345.
20. Ibid. 347.

CHAPTER THIRTEEN

MORONI: A PROPHET WHO ENDURED THROUGH FAITH

GERALD HANSEN JR.

Introduction

IN CHOOSING EXAMPLES from the scriptures of prophets who exhibited great faith in their lives, one might wonder why Moroni should be included. Compared to Abraham, Nephi, Paul, Moses, Alma, Peter, and others, very little is recorded about Moroni's life. In comparison with the greater volume of information written about other prophets, it might seem that a treatise on Moroni would contribute little to a discussion on faith. However, for principally two reasons, nothing could be further from the truth. First, Moroni's example of enduring to the end may be the greatest and most poignant in scripture. For over thirty-six years he wandered alone without family or friends, protecting and finishing the plates, not knowing when the Lamanites might find him and kill him. One can only imagine his loneliness or guess at the depth of his temptation to give up. But Moroni endured. His faith in God, his knowledge that this experience could work to his salvation, strengthened him to pass his test.

Second, and what will become the focus of this discussion, few other prophets have used their writings to teach as much or as well the principle of faith as has Moroni.

Moroni explores faith especially well in the book of Ether, his abridgment of the Jaredite records. He uses this history to teach that faith unto salvation must be centered on Christ. He accentuates his teachings by recording most of the history of the Jaredites in only scant detail, while expounding at length on the events and issues he wants us to focus on.

Moroni's teachings on faith in the book of Ether can be divided into three main parts. First, he uses the story of the brother of Jared to teach us that true faith should lead us to know God and become like him. Then, in his summary of Jaredite history, he warns us about the types of temptations that distract us from obtaining this level of faith. Finally, having taught us and warned us, he exhorts us to seek Jesus and to obtain the faith necessary to endure to the end. The total effect of Moroni's discourse is to move us to more diligently center our faith in Christ.

Moroni Teaches Faith unto Salvation

Moroni's teachings on Christ-centered faith directly contradict a commonly held, spiritually damning misconception that faith is a power independent of God, accessible to us if we can just believe hard enough. This misconception could originate from the fact that all causes, whether connected to salvation or not, require belief for success. Some people have faith in and work for communism. Others believe in false preachers. Some work to save endangered species or to elect various candidates to public office. Still others work for or against government regulation or isolationism or protective tariffs. Their belief in these causes helps them accomplish many of their goals and their success may foster the notion that strong belief accesses a power that enables us to bring to pass our own desires. In some cases this may be true. But if our desires do not agree with God's will, then the power we receive is not God's and the faith we have does not lead to salvation.

Gospel faith is not a power through which we can, by sheer force of will, bring our own selfish desires to pass. Elder Marion G. Romney illuminates this principle:

> There is, however, a principle associated with this matter of faith that we should all understand. I used to feel that if I could develop enough faith, I could receive in every instance exactly what I prayed for. This belief was based upon such scriptures as Matthew 17:20, in which Jesus said

> to his disciples, "If ye have faith as a grain of mustard seed ye shall say unto this mountain, Remove hence to yonder place; and it shall remove; and nothing shall be impossible unto you." But at that time I had not learned that this promise was made upon the implied condition that one's request be made in harmony with the *will of God.*[1]

True faith, faith unto salvation, comes from knowing God's will by revelation. It is to trust God enough to do what we know he wants us to do. It is Moses splitting the Red Sea because God told him to do so (D&C 8:2–3; Moses 1:25). It is Enoch moving mountains and rivers because God told him he had that power to fulfill God's purposes (Moses 6:34, 7:13). True faith is to hope for things which are not seen, which are true (Alma 32:21). We know these things to be true by revelation and use God's power and our strength to bring to pass God's revealed instructions. In other words, to quote from *Lectures on Faith,* true faith is not possible without "an actual knowledge that the course of life which one is pursuing is according to [God's] will."[2] We can't have faith in nothing. In a religious sense, when we say we have faith we mean that we know God's will for us and will act according to that knowledge because we trust him.

The Brother of Jared

Moroni's account of the story of the brother of Jared succinctly illustrates the principle that Christ-centered faith must be based on revelation from God. The miracles that the brother of Jared performed and the blessings he received were all given according to the will of and because of his faith in God. The brother of Jared had enough faith, or he trusted God enough, to call on him at the request of his brother (Ether 1:34, 36, 38). When the Lord answered, the brother of Jared had faith enough to gather flocks and family at God's command, leave home, and travel to the valley of Nimrod (Ether 1:41–2:1). He trusted God enough to follow the command to wander in the wilderness, "into that quarter where there never had man been," toward a promised land he had never seen (Ether 2:5, 7). He trusted God sufficiently to build barges to cross the "raging deep" and ask for directions in providing them with light (Ether 2:16–25, 3:2–5). Even his coming into God's presence, Moroni tells us, occurred because he had knowledge—knowledge of God's will and desires (Ether 3:12–13, 19–20). The brother of Jared could have faith because he knew what God expected of him. His experience bore out the wisdom of following God's will.

A most instructive episode relating to this principle occurred in the place called Moriancumer. Here, the brother of Jared had forgotten for a period to ask for revelation; he "remembered not to call upon the Lord." After some time, God chastised him for this (Ether 2:14–15). His faith, like ours, could not mature without calling upon God. His knowledge of God and God's will was not growing, and the group's progress toward the promised land had stopped—short of carrying out the Lord's will and short of the ultimate blessing the Lord had in store. They had already come far, and the obstacle they now faced—the sea—was formidable. As is the common tendency with many of us, the brother of Jared apparently preferred to rest for a while on his current spiritual plateau. After the chastisement, the brother of Jared repented, and God moved him to again progress in faith.

We might hope that God would chastise each of us if we begin to slacken in this process of revelation, trust, and action that we call faith, because this process is the process of exaltation. Stagnation is damnation. Faith is how God teaches his children to become like him. In other words, faith is not just the means by which we act in God's name; rather, acting in his name is the foreordained method for becoming like God. In this process, God first teaches his children; then, if his children have faith, or trust God's word to be true, they act accordingly. Through this means, little by little, the attributes of godliness become ours. Faith unto salvation, therefore, first requires revelation of God's will through the Holy Ghost, which is followed by obedience to that revelation. As our level of faith grows, the level of the knowledge God gives us also increases. The culmination of true faith is, as shown by the brother of Jared, to be invited into God's presence so we can be taught more fully. Catherine Thomas describes the process in these terms:

> The knowledge given by the Holy Ghost, the first comforter, is not a perfect knowledge, though it prepares and draws the

> seeker to that perfect knowledge. Faith, produced by the revelations of the Holy Ghost, is an assurance or *pre*-knowledge that what the Lord says is true (see Alma 32:34). But faith is designed to proceed along and become perfect knowledge, which is seeing something for ourselves after we have believed in, and been obedient to, the assurances of the Holy Ghost. Faith is not an end in itself, it is a means to an end, and that end is to be like and to be with the Lord.
>
> When we say in our testimony meetings, I know that the Lord Jesus lives, without having actually seen him, we likely mean that the Holy Ghost has given that assurance to our souls. But we do not have a perfect knowledge until, after an extended period of probation, we see for ourselves as the brother of Jared did.[3]

As Thomas points out, in this life the ultimate blessing of faith is to stand in the presence of God and have him teach us greater truths. And as *Lectures on Faith* teaches, it is by this process "that men got the knowledge of all things which pertain to life and godliness, and this knowledge was the effect of faith. So all things which pertain to life and godliness are the effects of faith."[4] If we are going to be exalted we must pursue this sort of faith.

That this blessing of communing face-to-face with God is available to worthy, tested members of the Church seems quite clear from scripture. It is, after all, one of the spiritual blessings to which the Melchizedek Priesthood holds keys (D&C 107:18–19). Also, God himself makes the promise in scripture that he will come to the sanctified (D&C 88:68). Statements by numerous prophets likewise confirm this possibility, as does this one from the *Lectures on Faith:*

> Let us here observe that after any members of the human family are made acquainted with the important fact that there is a God who has created and does uphold all things, the extent of their knowledge respecting his character and glory will depend upon their diligence and faithfulness in seeking after him, until, like Enoch, the brother of Jared, and Moses, they shall obtain faith in God and power with him to behold him face to face.[5]

Elder Bruce R. McConkie echoes this statement in these words:

> He [God] is no respecter of persons. If the brother of Jared, because of his perfect knowledge, "could not be kept from beholding within the veil," so shall it be with any of like spiritual perfection. (Ether 3:19–26)[6]

Unfortunately, according to Elder McConkie, not everyone in the Church knows that the Lord offers these blessings to his people, and, therefore, not all are motivated to seek them:

> [S]o few know in the full and true sense of the word, that those who believe and obey the whole law shall see the face of their Lord while they yet dwell as mortals on earth....
>
> The fact is that the day of personal visitations from the Lord to faithful men on earth has no more ceased than has the day of miracles....
>
> There are even those who neither believe nor know that it is possible to see the Lord in this day, and they therefore are without the personal incentive that would urge them onward in the pursuit of this consummation so devoutly desired by those with spiritual insight.[7]

I believe that Moroni records the story of the brother of Jared for this reason, to let us know that the Lord does appear to his people and to inspire us to greater diligence and greater levels of faith.

At first, the knowledge that we can in this life have the Lord personally instruct us might seem overwhelming. However, we must remember that God does not expect us to come to this point in a day. He only expects us to be diligently progressing, to be determined "to serve him to the end" (see D&C 20:37). To this end, immediately after the vision of the brother of Jared, Moroni records the key for knowing where to begin developing the type of Christ-centered faith that leads to the Lord's presence and then to the revelation of all things (see Ether 3:25–26). In an illuminating quotation of the Lord's own words, Moroni shows that we must believe the words of God and his disciples. The words of God will persuade us to do good and lead us to be clean and sanctified, at which point, as Christ says, he will show unto us the greater things, the knowledge which is hid up because of unbelief (see Ether 3:6–13). The key is obedience to the word of God. As Elder Neal A. Maxwell says, "While we are saved no faster than we gain a certain type of knowledge, it is also the case that we will gain knowledge no faster than we are saved."[8] Joseph Smith verifies this truth in his well-known statement on what men and women must do to receive the Second Comforter:

> After a person has faith in Christ, repents of his sins, and is baptized for the remission of his sins and receives the Holy Ghost, (by the laying on of hands), which is the first Comforter, then let him continue to humble himself before God, hungering and thirsting after righteousness, and living by every word of God, and the Lord will soon say unto him, "Son, thou shalt be exalted." When the Lord has thoroughly proved him, and finds that the man is determined to serve Him at all hazards, then the man will find his calling and election made sure, then it will be his privilege to receive the other Comforter, which the Lord hath promised the Saints, as is recorded in the testimony of St. John, in the 14th chapter, from the 12th to the 27th verses.[9]

As these two statements point out, if we heed the word of God, taking the Holy Ghost as our guide, the time will come when we will see the face of the Lord. However, it will happen in the Lord's own time and in the Lord's own way when he sees that we are ready (see D&C 88:68). Therefore, the wisest counsel on this matter is to do all the little things—study the scriptures, pray, attend the temple, teach and nurture our families in the ways of God, serve in the Church, serve others, sustain those who hold the keys of the priesthood, consecrate ourselves to the kingdom—in short, honor our covenants, and the great things will take care of themselves. This is essentially the pattern that Moroni shows us in the Book of Ether. He shows that the brother of Jared exercised his faith and obeyed the revelations of God on all matters, whether it was gathering his flocks or building barges or repenting for not calling upon the Lord until, eventually, he prepared himself to be invited by God into his presence:

> And the Lord said unto him: Because of thyaith thou hast seen that I shall take upon me flesh and blood; and never has man come before me with such exceeding faith as thou hast; for were it not so ye could not have seen my finger. Sawest thou more than this?
>
> And he answered: Nay; Lord, show thyself unto me.
>
> And the Lord said unto him: Believest thou the words which I shall speak?
>
> And he answered: Yea, Lord, I know that thou speakest the truth, for thou art a God of truth, and canst not lie.
>
> And when he had said these words, behold, the Lord showed himself unto him, and said: Because thou knowest these things ye are redeemed from the fall; therefore ye are brought back into my presence; therefore I show myself unto you.
>
> Behold, I am he who was prepared from the foundation of the world to redeem my people. Behold, I am Jesus Christ. (Ether 3:9–14)

Secret Combinations Tempt Us from Faith

After the positive story of the brother of Jared, whereby Moroni teaches the effects of Christ-centered faith, the ancient prophet focuses most of the rest of his abridgment of Ether's record on the things that make faith unto salvation most difficult. He singles out secret combinations in particular as the greatest roadblock to faith and the surest means of destruction for any society plagued by them. Having had to deal with the cancer of secret combinations in his own time (see Hel. 2:13–14; 4 Ne. 1:42–46; Morm. 1:18–19), Moroni well understood the danger of such groups. He says that they caused the destruction of both the Jaredite and the Nephite societies (see Ether 8:21). The great temptations gratified by these secret combinations, those which draw us away from faith like unto the brother of Jared, are greed and pride, manifest in the desire for power and gain (see Ether 8:22–23; 11:15).

To understand why secret combinations are such a roadblock to faith and righteousness we have to examine their nature a little more closely. Too often we think of secret combinations only in terms of organized crime groups like the Mafia or gangs. Such a narrow definition might cause us to miss the real spiritual dangers posed by secret combinations, since joining organized crime is not much of a temptation for most members of the Church. Elder Bruce R. McConkie helps broaden our understanding:

> What are these secret combinations which have such powers that whole civilizations are destroyed by them? They wear many guises and appear in many forms. They were the Gadianton robbers among the Nephites, and the perpetrators of the Spanish inquisition in the dark ages. Among us they include some secret and oath-bound societies and such Mafia-like groups as engage in organized crime. They include some political parties, some revolutionists who rise up against their governments, and those evil and anarchist groups which steal and kidnap and murder in the name of this or that political objective. They are always groups that seek money and power and freedom from the penalties that should attend their crimes.[10]

Given this definition, the threat to our salvation posed by secret combinations becomes more real. Secret combinations could include businessmen who go to church on Sunday but make shady deals in back rooms on Monday, or the old established families of a particular town who hold onto the power they have in community affairs in a variety of devious ways, or popular groups of teenagers who stick together and make fun of others, doing anything necessary to retain their status. In short, secret combinations can be big or small. They can participate in different levels of secrecy and violence. Some generate more serious consequences for society than others, but all of them lead people away from real faith in God as they seek, in unrighteous ways, money and power, as well as freedom from the consequences that come with being immoral.

The scriptures indicate just how difficult it is to resist playing this game of wickedness by representing the forces of evil as a ferocious beast (see Rev. 13:1–2). The temptation to join with others and exclude, cheat, lie, or worse so that the game favors us, so we can guarantee our success at the expense of others, increases incrementally as more and more around us succumb to these sins. Faced with the mounting pressures of succeeding in this world, we may, like the Nephites and Jaredites of old, find ourselves willing to "believe in their [the secret combinations'] works and partake of their spoils" (Hel. 6:38; see also Ether 9:11).

We may then begin to accept false philosophies that justify unrighteous and uncharitable actions. The world is always ready to convince us that money is a sign of righteousness, that we serve God by making money, that poor people deserve what they get, and that success in this world equates with success in God's kingdom. Despite God's calling us back to him by the voice of prophets, as he did with the Jaredites (see Ether 7:23; 9:28; 11:1), we may, if we accept the world's philosophies, slide to various levels of wickedness without believing we have done so.

The temptation to accept false teachings and join forces with groups that seek money and power derives from the natural desire we all have for security and happiness. Of course God offers us exactly that—security and happiness—but he offers them according to his eternal perspective, which requires patience and faith, or trust in him. His expectation is that we will live by the principles of stewardship and consecration, whereby every man "esteem[s] his brother as himself" (see D&C 38:24), there are no idle, and every man may have as much as is sufficient for himself and his family (see D&C 42:32, 42). God has said that the earth has sufficient resources to provide a good life for all his children (D&C 104:17). He admonishes us that whosoever will lose his life in this world, for his sake, shall find it in the world to come (JST Matt. 16:28). His promise is that if we will "search diligently, pray always, and be believing," as well as "walk uprightly and remember the covenant wherewith [we] have covenanted one with another," that "all things shall work together for [our] good" (see D&C 90:24). With God, the promise of security is a promise of internal peace in this life, as well as an eternal reward for faith and goodness.

In contrast, those who promote secret combinations promise financial security and the gratification of ambition in this life through power, control, and freedom from penalty. They believe that this is a competitive world where for some to win, others must lose. Their motto is "me first" and their doctrine that of

Korihor, who taught that "every man fared in this life according to the management of the creature; therefore every man prospered according to his genius, and that every man conquered according to his strength; and whatsoever a man did was no crime" (see Alma 30:17). They are willing to lie, seduce, cheat, or kill for money and power, using intrigue and secrecy to protect themselves from discovery. In scriptural terms we might summarize the practices and beliefs of secret combinations as the "Mahan" principle. *Mahan* was what Cain, glorying in his wickedness, called himself after being the first person to enter a secret combination for the purpose of gaining wealth (see Moses 5:31).

The book of Ether shows the consequences that await any society that upholds and promotes the Mahan principle. In the nine short chapters that recount centuries of Jaredite history in the promised land, Moroni shows again and again that when the Jaredites sought wealth and power and were willing to do almost anything to get it, their degeneracy sank so low that brothers killed brothers, sons killed fathers, and fathers killed sons. The worst example of depravity is the story of Jared, who becomes king by having his daughter dance for Akish so that he will desire to marry her and be willing to kill Jared's father, Omer, the king, for that privilege. After Omer is warned in a dream and flees, Akish murders Jared and becomes king himself. Eventually Akish's own sons wage a war against him and the Jaredite nation is reduced to thirty survivors and those who had fled with Omer (see Ether 8–9).

This tale, while it is probably the worst example of evil in the book of Ether, is not the only one. Moroni records intrigue after intrigue—by Corihor, by Heth, by the brother of Shiblom, to name a few—to show that the Jaredites' destruction was well deserved. By recounting these intrigues, Moroni warns us that any nation that will allow and encourage secret combinations, built up to get power and gain, will be destroyed (see Ether 8:22).

At first glance, this warning appears to be unnecessary for the average Latter-day Saint, since sinking to the Jaredites' level of depravity is highly unlikely for most of us. However, we must remember that Moroni does not warn us so much of specific crimes as much as he does the specific temptation. He describes the extremes in that society so we will sit up and take notice. The minute we forget that the desire for riches and power is an enticement that we all face, we put ourselves in danger of being seduced into some level of the Mahan game. President Spencer W. Kimball warned us of the deceptive nature of this temptation in a great sermon given during the year of the United States' bicentennial:

> Few men have ever knowingly and deliberately chosen to reject God and his blessings. Rather, we learn from the scriptures that because the exercise of faith has always appeared to be more difficult than relying on things more immediately at hand, carnal man has tended to transfer his trust in God to material things.[11]

As President Kimball indicates, the test of trusting God rather than our possessions is not an easy one, and it is one that depends on faith. He also indicates in that same talk that as a whole, the members of the Church struggle to pass the test:

> I am afraid that many of us have been surfeited with flocks and herds and acres and barns and wealth and have begun to worship them as false gods, and they have power over us. Do we have more of these good things than our faith can stand?... Forgotten is the fact that our assignment is to use these many resources in our families and quorums to build up the kingdom of God.[12]

To further illuminate just how difficult it is to fight the natural man part of us that entices us to pursue the world, we need only to read this counsel from Elder Joseph B. Wirthlin:

> We may build a beautiful, spacious home that is far larger than we need. We may spend far too much to decorate, furnish, and landscape it. And even if we are blessed enough to afford such luxury, we may be misdirecting resources that could be better used to build the kingdom of God or to feed and clothe our needy brothers and sisters.[13]

These three quotes are enough to indicate that no one seeking to know God can afford to treat lightly the temptations of pride and money. The type of discipleship demonstrated by the brother of Jared demands more of us than simply not committing great and serious crimes like fraud and murder. It demands that we be exclusively seeking God's will for us and trusting him enough to do what he tells us. This may mean that life will not turn out for us exactly the way we had planned for ourselves. It also means that we cannot spend most of our time thinking about and making money, guaranteeing worldly success and greater and greater comforts. We must not take our eyes off the building of Zion in order to guarantee, as President Kimball says, "carnal security throughout, it is hoped, a long and happy life."[14] Making carnal security our goal and our pursuit tends to make us neglect the little things that increase our faith. Satan can then pacify us, lull us into carnal security, and lead our souls to hell (see 2 Ne. 28:21).

We cannot afford to miss this point, that we must seek to know God by doing his will as opposed to pursuing our own agenda in life, because the choice between the two approaches is the test of exaltation. Trusting God in a lone and dreary world has never been popular or simple. It can be lonely and discouraging. But it is the sacrifice required of all the righteous. As the *Lectures on Faith* teach, exaltation depends on whether or not we can gain this kind of faith:

> The faith necessary unto the enjoyment of life and salvation never could be obtained without the sacrifice of all earthly things. It is through this sacrifice, and this only, that God has ordained that men should enjoy eternal life. And it is through the medium of the sacrifice of all earthly things that men do actually know that they are doing the things that are well pleasing in the sight of God. When a man has offered in sacrifice all that he has for the truth's sake, not even withholding his life, and believing before God that he has been called to make this sacrifice because he seeks to do His will, he does know, most assuredly, that God does and will accept his sacrifice and offering and that he has not sought nor will not seek His face in vain. Under these circumstances, then, he can obtain the faith necessary for him to lay hold on eternal life....
>
> But those who have not made this sacrifice to God do not know that the course which they pursue is well pleasing in

> his sight.... and where unshaken confidence is not, there faith is weak. And where faith is weak, the persons will not be able to contend against all the opposition, tribulations, and afflictions which they will have to encounter in order to be heirs of God and joint-heirs with Christ Jesus. But they will grow weary in their minds, and the adversary will have power over them and destroy them.[15]

Conclusion: Moroni Exhorts Us to Seek Christ

The sacrifice of all earthly things does not necessarily mean that we all must die as martyrs or live in poverty. It means different things for each of us. For many it will mean not being distracted by the world from doing the little things mentioned earlier, like temple attendance, teaching and nurturing children in the ways of God, praying, and serving. For Joseph Smith it also included sealing his witness of the Book of Mormon and Doctrine and Covenants with his blood (see D&C 135:1). For Alma the Younger it meant spending his life in preaching the gospel. For Moroni it included wandering alone and preparing the plates. The common denominator is the consecration of oneself to the building of the kingdom, *according to God's revelations to us.* If we do this, the promise is that we will not seek the face of God in vain. We have to believe and have faith that he will fulfill this promise.

The more we trust God, trying to live by his word and do his will, the more power he gives us to make the required sacrifices and overcome the world. Faith breeds faith (see Alma 32:28–43, D&C 88:40) and generates hope. Having taught about faith and the temptations which hinder us from developing it, Moroni leaves us with an exhortation to obtain faith and find hope in Christ. He says, quoting the prophet Ether, that "hope cometh of faith [and] maketh an anchor to the souls of men, which would make them sure and steadfast, always abounding in good works" (Ether 12:4). He encourages us to develop faith in Christ by giving examples of Nephites and Jaredites who performed miracles, including the example of the Nephites at the temple in Bountiful and the brother of Jared, all of whom saw the Son of God (see Ether 12:6–22). Moroni's own difficult life witnesses that faith in Christ can lead us through our trials to endure to the end. Growing up in a completely decadent society, he saw his own people destroyed because of wickedness and then wandered alone for over half his life. Instead of giving up, Moroni sought and found peace through Christ. His life affirms that true faith makes living righteously amidst chaos and wickedness possible.

It is Moroni's testimony that faith in the Lord Jesus Christ gives us the hope to overcome the trials of life and eventually enter into God's presence. His writings testify that the brother of Jared saw Jesus Christ (see Ether 3:13). His writings testify that Emer, a Jaredite king who did execute judgment in righteousness all his days, saw Christ (see Ether 9:22). He testifies that he himself spoke to Jesus face-to-face (see Ether 12:39). With these testimonies in mind he admonishes all to do the same, to seek Jesus Christ in faith that the grace of the Father, Son, and Holy Ghost may abide in us forever (see Ether 12:41). Then we too, whether in this life or the next, may be "brought forth triumphant" and see for ourselves "the great Jehovah," Jesus Christ, the Son of God (Moro. 10:34).

NOTES

1. Marion G. Romney, *Improvement Era* 69, April 1966, 301.

2. Larry E. Dahl and Charles D. Tate, Jr., eds., *The Lectures on Faith in Historical Perspective* (Provo, Utah: Religious Studies Center, 1990), 65; hereafter *Lectures*.

3. Catherine Thomas, "The Brother of Jared at the Veil," in *Temples of the Ancient World*, ed. Donald W. Parry (Salt Lake City: Deseret Book and F.A.R.M.S., 1994), 394–95.

4. *Lectures*, 103.

5. *Lectures*, 51.

6. Bruce R. McConkie, *The Promised Messiah* (Salt Lake City: Deseret Book., 1978), 298.

7. Ibid., 298, 576, 586.

8. Neal A. Maxwell, *Ensign*, April 1993, 68.

9. Joseph Smith, *Teachings of the Prophet Joseph Smith*, comp. Joseph Fielding Smith (Salt Lake City: Deseret Book, 1976), 150.

10. Bruce R. McConkie, *The Millennial Messiah* (Salt Lake City: Deseret Book, 1976), 150.

11. Spencer W. Kimball, *Ensign*, June 1976, 4.
12. Ibid.
13. Joseph B. Wirthlin, *Ensign*, November 1990, 65.
14. Kimball, *Ensign,* 4.
15. *Lectures*, 93–94.

CHAPTER FOURTEEN

"EVEN THE FAITH OF ELIJAH": JOSEPH SMITH'S FAITH IN THE LORD JESUS CHRIST

DANEL W. BACHMAN

JOSEPH SMITH WAS an extraordinary man of extraordinary faith. During his thirty-eight and a half years, the Prophet accomplished amazing things in the world of religion. His achievements and greatness were due to the influence of the Lord and the gospel in his life, and that influence was present largely because of his "exceeding faith."[1] Yet, while many aspects of Joseph's personality and character have been studied, very little has been written analyzing the nature and depth of his faith in the Lord Jesus Christ.[2]

How does one know if another person has faith in God and his Son, Jesus Christ? It is difficult to determine even if the person is living, but the problem becomes more troublesome when that person is deceased because we are forced to rely totally on the incomplete record of written history. However, in the case of the Prophet, the records are relatively abundant and the study rewarding. We begin by looking at the interplay of foreordination and faith in relation to Joseph's first significant spiritual experience—the First Vision. We will then explore several of the attributes that attend or are a part of faith as they can be ascertained in his life.

Joseph Smith: Boy of Faith

At the age of fourteen, Joseph Smith saw the Father and the Son in heavenly vision. Fourteen! Can one have sufficient faith at such a tender age for such an account to be credible? Some have thought that perhaps his was an experience similar to that of Paul or Alma the Younger, apparently without antecedent faith, but given to fulfill the foreordained purposes of God and answer the prayers of others. Others feel that young Joseph possessed "great faith" when he saw God.[3] The question, then, is, Was Joseph's faith nonexistent at the time of the First Vision? Or, if he did have faith, was it a gift from God or something he had developed?

The Foreordination of Joseph Smith

Undoubtedly external heavenly influences played an important role in bringing about Joseph's early spiritual experiences. Like Paul, he was foreordained.[4] Like Alma he was the beneficiary of the prayers of others.[5] Indeed, Joseph's foreordination, based on God's foreknowledge, permitted others to speak prophetically of him and pray for him.[6] Significantly, there was more known and spoken of him by way of prophetic anticipation than any person in scripture other than the Lord himself.[7]

Anciently, the most extensive information about Joseph Smith was given to Joseph of Egypt (see JST Gen. 50; 2 Ne. 3). After reiterating these prophecies in his own writings, Nephi offered the opinion that "there are not many greater" (2 Ne. 4:2). While giving his namesake son a patriarchal blessing, Joseph Smith Sr. said that Joseph the son of Jacob "looked after his posterity in the last days." Weeping before the Lord because he realized that his descendants would be scattered and driven by the Gentiles, he "sought diligently to know from whence the son should come who should bring forth the word of the Lord, by which they might be enlightened and brought back to the true fold, *and his eyes beheld thee, my son*; his heart rejoiced and his soul was satisfied."[8] Commensurate with his petition, Joseph of Egypt learned that part of Joseph Smith's divine foreordination was to bring forth the Book of Mormon.[9]

It was revealed to him that the Prophet was to do a work for the House of Israel which would be of "great worth unto them" because it would bring them to the knowledge of the covenants which the Lord made with their fathers.[10] He was to be given power to bring forth the word of the Lord which included the writings of the people of both Judah and Joseph (2 Ne. 3:12). Isaiah likewise speaks extensively of Joseph Smith's role in bringing forth the Book of Mormon, which was to be an antidote to a spiritual famine which he saw coming upon the nations.[11]

Through the prophecies of Joseph in Egypt, Lehi, Nephi, and others also knew of Joseph Smith.[12] Thus Book of Mormon writers and compilers as well as the Saints of their generations prayed for the preservation of the book and the publication of its message in our day.[13] Saints on both continents prayed *about* him and, undoubtedly, *for* him. Moroni, in writing of the prayers of the Saints who possessed the land before him, said, not only did they pray "in behalf of their brethren," but "behold, *their prayers were also in behalf of him that the Lord should suffer to bring these things forth*" (Morm. 8:23–25; emphasis added).[14]

It was Elder John A. Widtsoe's view that Joseph Smith received a "magnificent education" from heavenly sources in the decade prior to the organization of the Church. "But," he said, "this education was possible *because of the innate qualities of his character.* Even the Lord needs good material, if a good and great man is to be formed."[15] Therefore, like others, Joseph Smith became one of the "noble and great ones" in the premortal existence by developing his spiritual talents there, thus qualifying for his special foreordination and assignment. The power and influence of that foreordination in his life was enhanced by the prayers and faith of many ancient Saints. It was probably a similar understanding that led Elder Orson F. Whitney to remark in General Conference in 1920:

> It was no accident, no chance happening—Joseph Smith's going into the grove that spring morning, one hundred years ago. It was an event predestined, heaven-inspired. I once thought that any good boy who prayed in faith could see just what Joseph saw. But I have put away that childish notion. I have learned that all boys are not Joseph Smiths. God hears and answers the prayers of the humblest of his children; but

> he answers them as seemeth him best, and not always in the same way. He gives according to the capacity of the one who receives.
>
> It was no ordinary man that went into the woods that morning to pray. It was a Prophet, a Seer. Joseph Smith was not made a prophet by the people who held up their hands for him on the sixth of April, 1830, when this Church was organized. He was already a prophet, chosen, as Abraham had been, before he was born; ordained, like Jeremiah, before he was formed in the flesh. The people merely "sustained" him in that position, manifesting by the uplifted hand that they were willing to follow him as their leader, and to accept of his ministrations in that capacity. He was already a prophet, already a seer; God had made him such in advance. But all men are not Joseph Smiths. He was a man like unto Moses. He was the rarest human being that has walked this earth in the past two thousand years. And why did he go into the grove that morning and pray for wisdom and light? It was because the time had come. *The Hour* had struck, and *The Man* was there—the man whom God had provided.[16]

The Faith of Young Joseph Smith

But does foreordination coupled with the prayers of faithful ancients account totally for the First Vision, or had Joseph developed, as Joseph Fielding Smith said, "great faith" by age fourteen?[17] As the Prophet himself was to say, speaking about another subject, the truth probably "takes a road between them both."[18] That is, his faith was likely the result of his own belief and trust in God combined with an endowment from on high.

There is compelling evidence that in addition to divine gifts, Joseph had a rare faith for such a young lad. Like fifteen-year-old Mormon, who "being somewhat of a sober mind" was "therefore . . . visited of the Lord" (Morm. 1:15), the records indicate that an uncommon maturity and solemnity were critical components of Joseph's religious inclinations prior to the First Vision. This comes out prominently in the 1832 account of the First Vision. At about age twelve his mind was "seriously imprest" with a concern for the welfare of his soul, which led him to search the scriptures, "*believeing* [sic] *as I was taught,*" he said, "that they contained the word of God." "Thus from the age of twelve years to fifteen," he wrote, "I pondered many things in my heart concerning the situation of the world of mankind."[19] At another time Joseph said he was about fourteen when he "began to reflect upon the importance of being prepared for a future state" which led him to inquire of others about the plan of salvation.[20] In yet another account he spoke of "deep" and "poignant" feelings aroused during the religious excitement preceding the First Vision when his "mind was called up to serious reflection and great uneasiness" (JS—H 1:8).

It is not, therefore, insignificant that he was attracted to the gospel early in his life. For a young man between twelve and fifteen to ponder the welfare of his soul and the condition of the world bespeaks a singular spiritual depth confirmed by his mother's recollection that he "always seemed to reflect more deeply than common persons of his age upon everything of a religious nature."[21] This and her comment that he was "less inclined to the perusal of books than any of the rest of our children, but far more given to meditation and deep study"[22] are echoed in his patriarchal blessing. "Thou hast sought to know [the ways of the Lord] and from thy childhood thou hast meditated much upon the great things of his law," his father said.[23] His parent's observations are reminiscent of Joseph's own statement about reflecting "again and again" on the meaning of James 1:5 (JS—H 1:12).

That this passage of scripture came to Joseph with such great power and entered with "great force into every feeling" of his heart implies the stimulating action of the Spirit prompting him to seek the divine guidance of which James spoke (JS—H 1:12). But faith was also present. "Believing the word of God," Joseph later told John Wentworth, "I had confidence in the declaration of James."[24] In a journal account of the First Vision, Joseph said, "information was what I most desired at this time, and with a fixed determination to obtain it, I called upon the Lord."[25] Thus, the First Vision apparently resulted from a combination of young Joseph's contemplative and resolute spiritual quest, the catalyst of the promptings of the Spirit, plus the gifts and blessings resulting from foreordination and the prayers of others in his behalf.

A significant element of faith undergirded all of Joseph's formative spiritual experiences. The same assurance, determination, and confidence attending the First Vision was present three years later. Before Moroni's visit, Joseph felt condemned for the "foolish errors" and "weaknesses" of his youth. He prayed for forgiveness and a manifestation to know of his standing with God; *"for I had full confidence in obtaining a divine manifestation, as I previously had one"* (JS—H 1:28–29; emphasis added). Oliver Cowdery's account of this same experience is laced with even stronger language of faith, which emphasized Joseph's great concentration and resolution. He asserts that Joseph's "heart was drawn out in fervent prayer, and his whole soul was so lost to every thing of a temporal nature, that earth, to him, had lost its claims." In his desire to contact "some kind of messenger who could communicate ... his acceptance with God," Joseph "settled upon a determined basis not to be decoyed or driven" from his purpose.[26] Similarly, before the conferral of the Aaronic Priesthood, Oliver Cowdery said, "[Our] souls were drawn out in mighty prayer to know how we might obtain the blessing of baptism and of the Holy Spirit." Like Abraham, the pair "diligently sought for the... authority of the holy priesthood, and the power to administer the same; for we desired to be followers of righteousness and the possessors of greater knowledge."[27]

This confidence, certainty, diligence, and faith exhibited in his early years remained with Joseph throughout his life. But Joseph was never complacent, believing the quality of his faith was adequate. There is an exquisite entry in his 1842 journal to this effect. At the time, Joseph was eluding officials then attempting to extradite him to Missouri for his alleged role in an attempted assassination of ex-governor Lilburn Boggs. His seclusion permitted him to reflect on trusted and loyal friends. He was determined to "prove faithful" to them, he said in his 23 August entry, until God called him "to resign up" his breath. Then he pleaded with his Heavenly Father to "look down upon thy servant Joseph, at this time; and *let faith on the name of thy Son Jesus Christ, to a greater degree than thy servant ever yet has enjoyed, be conferred upon him; even the faith of Elijah."*[28]

Joseph Smith Possessed the Attributes Associated with Faith

Like love, faith is composed of a number of other attributes. Both are rather like an orange: there is only one fruit, but it is made up of many sections. Pure love, or charity, exhibits itself in such things as long-suffering, humility, upright behavior, rejoicing in truth, believing, bearing, hoping, and enduring all things.[29] Similarly, one who has faith in God possesses a constellation of characteristics such as a repentant and prayerful heart, patience, optimism, courage, and obedience, among others. Any one by itself, or perhaps even two or three together, would not necessarily mean the one possessing them had faith in God. This is especially true if that person does not overtly profess an active faith in God or possess a religious nature or concern themselves with religious things. But in one who claims to be a person of the Spirit, all of these attributes and more will be present.

The *Lectures on Faith,* which Joseph helped prepare, deliver, and publish, teach that it is necessary for the human mind to understand and believe in the *correct* ideas of God's "character, perfections, and attributes" in order to develop and exercise saving faith in him.[30] This information is transmitted through the spoken and written testimonies of prophets—living and dead.[31]

Those with a correct understanding of God, who believe and act upon it, *behave* differently than those who do not. For example when a person comprehends and believes that God is truthful and cannot lie, he has the intellectual justification to trust God's promises. "[W]ith the idea of the existence of this attribute in the Deity in the mind," the lectures say, "all the teachings, instructions, promises, and blessings, become realities, and the mind is enabled to lay hold of them with certainty and confidence."[32] That assurance translates itself into trusting behavior. Similarly, understanding that God is perfectly merciful, long-suffering, gracious, and slow to anger does away with doubt caused by our individual "weaknesses and liability to sin." We are then enabled to repent with confidence that God will forgive.[33] Likewise, we can place ourselves under his guidance and direction when we understand the justice and judgment of God, knowing that he will do right by us. Conversely, when we do not understand and believe in the correct attributes of God, doubt exists. And since doubt is antithetical to faith, a person in such a condition will not trust God, repent of sins, or place themselves under his tutelage. Thus trust, repentance, and obedience are characteristic behaviors of a person of faith. Similar arguments could be made for courage, patience, sacrifice, scripture study, and other conduct.

Nephi and his elder brothers Laman and Lemuel provide a marvelous illustration of the relationship between a correct understanding of God and faithful living. Nephi said he *knew* that God would give no commandments to his children unless he prepared a way for them to "accomplish the thing which he commandeth them" (1 Ne. 3:7). Therefore, he asserted, "I will go and do the things which the Lord hath commanded." *Going* and *doing* were manifestations of Nephi's faith based on his understanding of God. Laman and Lemuel, on the other hand, "did murmur *because* they knew not the dealings of that God who had created them" (1 Ne. 2:12; emphasis added). *Murmuring* was a direct outgrowth of their ignorance about God.[34]

Therefore, in order to analyze the life and works of Joseph Smith we must examine his beliefs about God and the actions or works those beliefs produced. We can only satisfactorily see into Joseph's heart and soul to assess the degree and quality of his faith through the window of his words and life. When we do so it becomes evident that he possessed in abundance every meaningful trait associated with faith in God. We will discuss three examples in some detail.

Joseph's Faith Expressed through His Repentance

Repentance is the firstfruits of faith in Jesus Christ.[35] Joseph Smith maintained a lifelong concern about his spiritual condition and status before the Lord. "The salvation of my soul is of the most importance to me," he once wrote. "I must steer my bark safe."[36] Joseph understood and trusted in the Savior's atonement and perpetually sought its benefits in his life. From the vantage of hindsight, we know that throughout his life he excelled at repentance and maintaining open communications with his Heavenly Father; he was consistently repentant.

As is commonly understood, the first step in repentance is to face the reality that one is guilty of sin and offense toward God. For Joseph, such realizations began before the First Vision, as he tells us in his earliest account. Pondering over the condition of his soul at the age of twelve, he said, "My mind become [sic] excedingly [sic] distressed for I become convicted of my sins."[37] Reflecting on his "vices and follies" between the ages of ten and twenty, he told Oliver Cowdery that his imperfections "often" gave him "occasion to lament." It was with a "deep feeling of regret" that he publicly confessed his sins.[38] That he confessed them is further evidence of his genuine repentance.

Throughout his life Joseph acknowledged his transgressions. Time and again he taught the Saints and others that he was a man possessed of the weaknesses, passions, and frailties of all mortals, and it concerned him that so many thought he should be "something more than a man."[39] As we shall see, Joseph's transgressions were also frequently mentioned in the revelations he received. That he made no effort to conceal the Lord's chastisements is additional indication of his humility, sincerity, and integrity.

The next step in repentance is to seek the Lord's forgiveness. Throughout his life, Joseph endeavored, as the language of the Book of Mormon puts it, to "retain a remission of [his] sins" (Mosiah 4:12). Although he found mercy from God in 1820, a concern for clemency lay at the core of his petition that night three years later when Moroni visited him. "[A]fter I had retired to bed I... was meditating upon my past life and experience, I was verry concious [sic] that I had not kept the commandments, and I repented hartily for all my sins and transgression, and humbled myself before Him <whose eyes are over all things>."[40] In the 1838 version he says he often felt "condemned" for his weaknesses and imperfections. "I betook myself to prayer and supplication... for forgiveness... and also for a manifestation to me, that I might know of my state and standing before him" (JS—H 1:29). Faith attended these appeals. He told John Wentworth, "While I was praying unto God, and *endeavoring to exercise faith in the precious promises of Scripture*, on a sudden a light like that of day... burst into the room."[41] The Lord confirmed that his repentance was spawned in the hospitable environment of faith when he said that following the First Vision, Joseph "was entangled again in the vanities of the world." Nevertheless, "after repenting, and humbling himself sincerely, *through faith,* God ministered unto him by an holy angel" (D&C 20:5–6; emphasis added).

Even though by 1823 Joseph had received two manifestations in response to his supplications for mercy, he continued to battle weakness. Following the loss of the 116-page manuscript of the Book of Mormon, the Lord spoke of "how oft" Joseph had "transgressed the commandments and laws of God" (D&C 3:6). Racked by guilt Joseph feared for his soul during this trying time; he also lost the right to translate for a period. But he didn't give in to despair "I continued my supplications to God, without cessation." Later, with the restoration of his gift, Moroni also brought a heartening message: "[H]e told me that the Lord loved me, for my *faithfulness* and humility."[42] It is not insignificant that at least nine times the Lord told Joseph Smith in revelation, either individually or as part of a group, that his sins were forgiven.[43] Unquestionably the basis on which he received forgiveness was no different than for other people, and these statements demonstrate the thread of the repentance that wove its way through the fabric of his life.

Nonscriptural examples of the humble, dependant, and repentant spirit which permeated his life have also survived. One poignant illustration comes out of a small Indiana village in 1832. In June of that year, Joseph, Sidney Rigdon, and Bishop Newel K. Whitney were returning to Kirtland from Missouri. They had taken a stage from Vincennes on the western edge of Indiana heading southeast for New Albany on the Ohio River where they could catch a steamer upstream to Cincinnati. Near the hamlet of Greenville something caused the horses to bolt. In the excitement Bishop Whitney leaped from the stage and caught his foot in the wheel, breaking his leg in several places. Sidney continued on to Kirtland, but Joseph laid over in Greenville with Bishop Whitney.[44] With no basketball hoop, television, Walkman, or videos to occupy his free time, how did he spend it? In a private communication to Emma, never intended for the perusal of the Church, Joseph wrote:

> I have visited a grove which is Just back of the town almost every day where I can be Secluded from the eyes of any mortal and there give vent to all the feelings of my heart in meaditation and prayr I have Called to mind all the past moments of my life and am left to mourn <and> Shed tears of sorrow for my folly in Sufering the adversary of my Soul to have so much power over me as he has <had in times past> but God is mercif<ul> and has fo[r]given my Sins and I r[e]joice that he Sendeth forth the Comferter unto as many as believe and humbleeth themselves before him.[45]

Joseph maintained an almost childlike concern, though not an immature one born of self-doubt, to keep himself clean before the Lord, and he found joy in the principle of repentance. "My soul delighteth in the Law of the Lord," he journalized in April of 1834, "for he forgiveth my sins."[46] As the Lord continued to hone his prophet, Joseph harbored a penitent heart to the end. Lamoni-like, Joseph once told the Saints, "I am at all times willing to give up everything that is wrong, for I wish this people to have a virtuous leader."[47] His diligence bore fruit. His faith on the Lord Jesus Christ had led him in the paths of repentance continually, and the final verdict was glorious, for the Lord declared, "I seal upon you your exaltation, and prepare a throne for you in the kingdom of my Father, with Abraham your father" (D&C 132:49).

Joseph Smith and the Prayer of Faith

It is axiomatic that one who lacks faith in God will not be found praying much; conversely, a person of great faith petitions the Lord often. The experience of the brother of Jared illustrates that even a man of faith many occasionally neglect his prayers (Ether 2:14), but I am not aware that Joseph was ever rebuked for slighting his. He was diligent in prayer, and the "windows of heaven" were frequently opened wide to him. That itself is a testimony to the quality of faith attending his supplications.

Prayer was not a peripheral or ritualistic thing with Joseph. His was not a crisis approach to prayer, nor did he pray only at the times specified in the rituals and traditions of Christianity. Neither was he fanatical about it. His was a practical, sincere, yet lifelong commitment to prayer. He consistently communicated with his Maker for many reasons—to express thanks and gratitude, for answers to questions, for the benefit of others, for the things he needed, and many more. Moreover, he never questioned the power of prayer or whether he received answers.

Like Tevye in *Fiddler on the Roof*, Joseph talked to God any time, any place, and under any circumstances. Prayer was as natural to him as breathing and he encouraged his followers in the same practice.[48] One indication that prayer was at the core of Joseph's life is how often he includes petitions to God in his personal and private documents. How often do we moderns write prayers anywhere, let alone in our journals, letters, and private writings? Yet Joseph *frequently* did this. For example, his first journal covers the period of 27 November 1832 to 5 December 1834.[49] There are entries for approximately eighty-six days. In twenty-four of these, or almost twenty-eight percent of the time, Joseph records prayers or mentions them.[50] Similarly, his journal from 22 September 1835 to 3 April 1836 contains 196 entries and prayers are entered forty times and mentioned another thirteen, or twenty-seven percent of the time.[51]

Most of the petitions were only a line or two, sometimes only a phrase, but the wide range of concerns reflected in them is impressive. Joseph sought for direction, protection, deliverance from enemies, the safety and welfare of his family, the success of his missionary labors, the success of a printing business (one was even for the achievement of a goal of adding 3,000 new subscribers for the Church newspaper in three years),[52] the blessing of the Saints in Zion, prosperity, gifts of the Spirit among Church members, blessings for his brethren in their callings, keeping the Saints strong in the faith, aid in getting Church businesses out of debt, and mercy upon himself and his brethren. He also frequently expressed thanks and gratitude.[53]

Of the many excellent examples of the sincere and trusting nature of his communications with the Lord, a few must suffice as illustrations. A portion of the entry for 4 December 1832 reads, "Oh Lord deliver thy servant out of temtations [sic] and fill his heart with wisdom and understanding." A year later he wrote, "being prepared to commence our Labours in the printing business I ask God in the name of Jesus to establish it for ever and cause that his word may speedily go for [th to] the Nations of the earth to the accomplishing of his great work in bringing about the restoration of the house of Israel." Two weeks later: "O God let the residue of my fathers house ever come up in remembrance before thee that thou mayest save them from the hand of the oppressor and establish their feet upon the rock of ages that they may have place in thy house and be saved in thy Kingdom."[54]

Frequently financially strapped, Joseph was grateful for the assistance he received from others. But he also desired to help the poor; they were often on his mind and in his prayers. The day Noah Packard gave the Kirtland Temple fund raising committee a $1,000 loan, Joseph asked God to bless this brother with a hundredfold of the things of the earth for his righteous act. In addition, Joseph's heart was "full of desire" to be blessed with prosperity until he could pay all his debts, "for it is <the> delight of my soul to <be> honest. Oh Lord," he pled, "help me and I will give to the poor."[55]

When Joseph Smith Sr. fell seriously ill in the fall of 1835, his prophet-son worried for his father's life. On Sunday 11 October Joseph recorded:

> [V]isted my Father <again> who was verry sick <in secret prayer in the morning the Lord said my servant thy father shall live> I waited on him all this day with my heart raised to god in the name of Jesus Christ that he would restore him to health again, that I might be blessed with his company and advise.[56]

That evening David Whitmer assisted Joseph in administering to the elder Smith. They rebuked the disease and Joseph reported that "God heard and answered our prayers to the great Joy and satisfaction of our souls."[57] Joseph Sr. got out of bed and dressed himself. Two days later Joseph found his father "much recovered" and marveled "at the . . . power and condesension [sic] of our Heavenly Father in answering our prayers in his behalf."[58]

At about the same time, Joseph's sister-in-law Mary was in a dangerous situation attending the eminent birth of a child. Don Carlos was sent to nearby Chardon for Frederick G. Williams who practiced medicine among the Saints. While waiting for their return Joseph "went out into the field and bowed before the Lord and called upon him in mighty prayer in her behalf." He was answered that Williams would come and be blessed with "wisdom... to deal prudently" and that Mary Smith would deliver a "living child" and "be spared." Two hours after Williams arrived, Susanna Bailey Smith was born. "[T]hus what God had manifested to me was fulfilled every whit," Joseph journalized.[59]

Late in 1835 and in early 1836 the Prophet was anxious to prepare the brethren for the endowment which the Lord promised to give when the Kirtland Temple was completed. He labored diligently to cleanse and prepare them for the experience. Understanding the importance of the prayer of faith in these preparations, in January of 1836 Joseph gave the quorums of the Church instruction on how to offer such prayers. He explained the importance of private, silent supplication—prayer which concentrated and unified their thoughts and feelings. Next, one was to pray vocally; he called it a "sealing prayer," expressing the united petition of the quorum. At the conclusion of the prayer they were to confirm their agreement with three hearty "Amens." Then they were to pray silently again.[60] His counsel was productive. During this period many experienced remarkable spiritual manifestations in what Milton Backman has called a "pentacostal season"—perhaps the spiritual apogee of the early Church.[61] Following one such session, Joseph went home "filled with the Spirit," and while he slept he reported that "the visions of the Lord were sweet unto me, and His glory was round about me."[62]

The Optimism and Confidence of Joseph Smith

Joseph Smith constantly exhibited traits that are threads in the fabric of faith. His life was filled with challenges, difficulties, rejection, persecution, pain, prison, and enough trails to put men in awe of his stamina to see them through.[63] On several occasions he referred to himself as a "rough stone" and the only polishing he got was "when some corner gets rubbed off by... force against religious bigotry, priestcraft, lawyer-craft, doctor-craft, lying editors, suborned judges and jurors, and the authority of perjured executives, backed by mobs, blasphemers, licentious and corrupt men and women—all hell knocking off a corner here and a corner there."[64] But this isn't surprising. In July of 1830 the Lord cautioned his prophet to "be patient in afflictions," because he would have "many" and implied they would be more or less constant throughout Joseph's life (D&C 24:8). In the difficult drama of the Missouri incarceration, the Lord whispered "peace" unto Joseph's soul and reminded him his adversity and afflictions would be "but for a small moment" and if he would "endure it well" God would exalt him to triumph over all his foes (D&C 121:7–8).

Many afflictions! Indeed, it was true. It started in his youth when an attempt was made on his life by an unknown gunman.[65] A gut-wrenching leg operation at age eight left him on crutches for a long period, during which time his family moved from New England to New York and he was forced by the man his father hired to bring the Smith family to Palmyra to walk a considerable distance in inclement weather.[66] The litany of Joseph's trials is long, and he was literally long-suffering. The list includes, but is not limited to, persecution from the time of the First Vision; mobs wanting the gold plates surrounding his home; citizens of Palmyra boycotting the sale of the Book of Mormon; being tarred and feathered; confronting extreme internal dissent during the Kirtland apostasy; enduring endless litigious entanglements in two score or more lawsuits and trials;[67] fisticuffs with his quick-tempered brother William; losing in death siblings, a parent, grandparents, aunts, uncles, and several children in childbirth or infancy; carrying the weight of having close friends and followers wounded and killed for the religion he founded; facing overwhelming odds against a mob-militia at Far West in Missouri; suffering and languishing helpless for several months in putrid Missouri dungeons with all their attendant indignities while his people were driven from the state; surviving both legal and illegal attempts to extradite him from Illinois into Missouri; having his pleas for redress for losses in Missouri coldly rejected at all levels of government; meeting increasing political and social hostility in Western Illinois; and finally, willingly sacrificing his life for his people and his cause.[68]

Through it all Joseph remained buoyant, confident, and optimistic. He taught that believing in the justice and judgment of

God enables us to "wade through all the tribulations and afflictions" to which we are subjected, "believing that in due time the Lord will come out in swift judgment" upon his enemies.[69] Enduring afflictions well is a manifestation of great faith and is as important as enduring to the end. As in so many other things, his life was a testimony to his belief in that principle.

Joseph was seldom discouraged and never doubted his mission.[70] One can look in vain through competent biographies and monographs for evidence that his knees ever buckled, that he ever questioned whether his call was divine or his mission heaven-directed. "Think of what he passed through!" wrote George Q. Cannon, one who knew him well.

> Think of his afflictions, and think of his dauntless character! Did any one ever see him falter? Did any one ever see him flinch? . . . Notwithstanding all that he had to endure, and the peculiar circumstances in which he was so often placed, and the great responsibility that weighed constantly upon him, he never faltered; the feeling of fear or trembling never crossed him—at least he never exhibited it in his feelings or actions.[71]

In persecutions Joseph himself identified with Paul.

> [T]here were but few who believed him; some said he was dishonest, others said he was mad; and he was ridiculed and reviled. But all this did not destroy the reality of his vision. He had seen a vision, he knew he had, and all the persecution under heaven could not make it otherwise; and though they should persecute him unto death . . . all the world could not make him think or believe otherwise.
>
> *So it was with me.* (JS—H 1:24–25; emphasis added)

"I don't blame any one for not believing my history," he once said. "If I had not experienced what I have, I could not have believed it myself."[72] Nevertheless, he lived by the advice he once gave to his young cousin George A. Smith who was about to leave on a mission. "'Never get discouraged. . . . [I]f I were sunk in the lowest pit of Nova Scotia, with the Rocky Mountains piled on me, I would hang on, exercise faith, and keep up good courage, and I would come out on top."[73] And come out on top he did! On another occasion he said if he and the Saints ended up in hell, they would kick the devil out and turn it into heaven.[74]

Although space has permitted us to examine only three or four of the evidences of Joseph Smith's faith in some meaningful detail, it should be observed that similar treatments might be given to other relevant and important indices of his faith—things such as courage, obedience, sacrifice, and intense love for and study of the scriptures.

That Faith Might Increase in the Earth

In 1816 Solomon Chamberlain, later a convert to the Church, petitioned the Lord with a question similar to Joseph's which brought the First Vision. Chamberlain, too, had a heavenly manifestation. An angel informed him "*that faith was gone from the earth*, excepting a few and that all Churches were corrupt."[75] The Lord implied the same thing in a revelation to the Prophet. He explained that one of the reasons Joseph Smith was called was "that faith also might increase in the earth" (D&C 1:21). And Moroni, speaking of the purpose of ministering angels, wrote that they showed themselves unto those who were of "*strong faith* and a firm mind in every form of godliness." Angels declared the word of Christ unto these "chosen vessels" to enable them to "bear testimony of him." "And in so doing," Moroni writes, "the Lord God prepareth the way that the residue [remainder] of men may have faith in Christ" (Moro. 7:29–32, emphasis added).

As *the* witness to this generation,[76] Joseph not only possessed great faith, but his testimony of the reality of Jesus Christ and his mission was the starter leaven which would eventually "leaven the whole lump."[77] In an 1834 epistle to the Church at Kirtland, Joseph responded to some objections to the Book of Mormon. To the religionists of his day he asked a sharp, heart-stopping, thought-starting rhetorical question. "But we ask, does it remain for a people who never had faith enough to call down one scrap of revelation from heaven . . . to say how much God has spoken and how much he has not spoken?"[78] If there was so little faith in the earth at that time, what can we say of the faith of a man who was a Nile River of revelation? In his humility, in 1842 Joseph Smith aspired to possess the faith of Elijah. The witness of scripture suggests that his petition was granted.

> And there shall rise up one mighty among them, who shall do much good, both in word and in deed, being an instrument in the hands of God, *with exceeding faith,* to work mighty wonders, and do that thing which is great in the sight of God, unto the bringing to pass much restoration unto the house of Israel, and unto the seed of thy brethren. (2 Ne. 3:24; emphasis added)

The evidence leads one to conclude that Joseph Smith's faith may have equaled or perhaps transcended the ancient prophet Elijah's long before 1842, and because it did, faith has indeed increased in the earth.

Notes

1. 2 Ne. 3:24. It was John A. Widtsoe's opinion that Joseph's "unchanging faith and trust in God" was the first and foremost of five qualities that made him great. See John A. Widtsoe, *Joseph Smith Seeker after Truth, Prophet of God* (Salt Lake City: Bookcraft, 1957), 329.

2. Interestingly enough, in my survey of the literature about Joseph Smith in preparation for teaching classes about him and for this article, I have not come across a single article devoted to the subject of his faith. Thus the justification for this introductory essay.

3. Concerning the First Vision, Joseph Fielding Smith wrote, "Great was his faith—so great that he was able, like the brother of Jared, to penetrate the veil and behold the glory of those holy beings." *Essentials in Church History* (Salt Lake City: Deseret Book, 1961), 47.

4. On the foreordination of Paul see Gal. 1:15. Alma, although not speaking of his own foreordination, clearly understood the doctrine; see Alma 13.

5. Prayers on behalf of Alma are mentioned in Mosiah 27:14 and similar prayers are found in Alma 6:6. Although we are not specifically told so, it is entirely possible prayers of others may have been a factor in Paul's vision as well.

6. Joseph Fielding Smith, comp., *Teachings of the Prophet Joseph Smith* (Salt Lake City: Deseret Book, 1967), 365; hereafter *TPJS*. See as examples of

the comments of others about his foreordination: Brigham Young, in *Journal of Discourses* (London: Albert Carrington, 1854–86), 7:289–90; hereafter *JD*; John Taylor, *JD* 26:106; and Wilford Woodruff, *JD* 18:118.

7. The following individuals were known by name *before* their birth: Jesus Christ; Isaac; Josiah, king of Judah; Maher-shalal-hash-baz; Cyrus, king of Persia; John the Baptist; Noah; Moses; Aaron; John the Revelator; Mary, the mother of Jesus; Joseph Smith Sr.; and Joseph Smith Jr.

A tradition existed among the ancient Jews about a messiah ben Joseph. For an LDS view of this subject see Joseph Fielding McConkie, *His Name Shall Be Joseph* (Salt Lake City: Hawkes Publishing Inc., 1980), 153–84.

8. Joseph Smith Sr., cited in Archibald F. Bennett, *Saviors On Mount Zion* (Salt Lake City: Deseret Sunday School Union Board, 1950), 68; emphasis added. Compare 2 Ne. 3:4–5.

9. The connection between the petition of Joseph in Egypt that one from his posterity would bring forth the "word of the Lord" and Joseph's assignment to translate the Book of Mormon may be direct and tangible. Inasmuch as we know that the brass plates of Laban contained a larger record in some respects than our present Old Testament, including the genealogy and prophecies of Joseph, and that they were recorded in Egyptian (1 Ne. 5:11–16; 2 Ne. 4:2; Mosiah 1:1–4), it is probable, even likely, that they were begun by Joseph in Egypt and brought to Israel during the Exodus. These same brass plates could have been the first source book of many from which the Book of Mormon is derived.

10. Compare also the last portions of 2 Nephi verses 12 and 21. The Book of Mormon was a principle vehicle in restoring this knowledge. In Moroni's title page to the Book of Mormon he said one of the reasons the book was written was "to show unto the remnant of the House of Israel what great things the Lord hath done for their fathers; and that they may know the covenants of the Lord, that they are not cast off forever." Compare 2 Ne. 29:1–2. Lost and changed covenants were associated with apostasies throughout history. See Isaiah 24:5; Ezek. 44:7; 1 Ne. 13:20–14:17 (especially 13:23, 26; 14:5, 17); and D&C 1:15.

11. The account in Isaiah 29:11–12 is greatly expanded in 2 Ne. 27:6–27.

12. Jacob: Gen. 49:22–26; Moses: Moses 1:41; Joseph: JST Gen. 50:24–34; 2 Ne. 3; Isaiah: Isa. 11, 29:11–13; 2 Ne. 27:6–27 (and perhaps others); see also Monte Nyman, "Isaiah's Many Prophecies of Joseph Smith," in *A Symposium on the Old Testament* (Salt Lake City: The Church of Jesus Christ of Latter-day Saints, 1983), 126–30; and Victor L. Ludlow, *Isaiah: Prophet, Seer, and Poet* (Salt Lake City: Deseret Book, 1982), 407–10; Jesus: Matt. 13 (see Joseph's interpretations of this in *TPJS*, 98–105), Matt. 24:14 (see footnote 75 below); Moroni: Ether 5:1–3; the brother of Jared: Ether 3:28. Probable references include: Jer. 30:21; Mal. 3:1; John 1:19–21, see JST John 1:22 and

Andrew F. Ehat and Lyndon W. Cook, comps., *The Words of Joseph Smith* (Provo, Utah: Religious Studies Center Brigham Young University, 1980), 370–71; Jacob 5:70–72; 3 Ne. 21:10–11; see also *Times and Seasons* 5 (2 Sept. 1844): 635.

13. See D&C 10:46; Enos 1:11–18; Mormon 5:15–21; 8:23; 9:36.

14. This may also be *one* of the meanings of the part of D&C 128:18 which says: "For we without them [the dead] cannot be made perfect; neither can they without us be made perfect. Neither can they nor we be made perfect *without those who have died in the gospel also*" (emphasis added).

Truman Madsen offered a similar answer as to why Joseph received the First Vision. "One response is that the visitations received by the Prophet Joseph Smith weren't an answer just to his own prayer, but to the prayers of literally millions, maybe even those beyond the veil, who had been seeking and reaching for generations for the restoration of the gospel—fulfillment, in fact, of a phrase offered by billions, 'Thy kingdom come.' (Mt. 6:10). That is an important insight. You and I pray not alone. We pray as part of a great modern movement and are empowered in that very process." Truman G. Madsen, "Prayer and the Prophet Joseph," *Ensign* (Jan. 1976), 18.

15. John A. Widtsoe, *Joseph Smith Seeker after Truth*, 329; emphasis added. He also said, "From his boyhood Joseph Smith's character displayed the elements of greatness." It is not clear what Elder Widtsoe means by the word *innate,* but he seems to be suggesting that Joseph had developed his character in the premortal existence and brought those qualities with him into mortality.

16. Orson F. Whitney, in *Ninetieth Annual Conference of The Church of Jesus Christ of Latter-day Saints* (Salt Lake City: Deseret Book, 1920), 122–23.

17. Joseph Fielding Smith, *Essentials,* 47.

18. *TPJS*, 338.

19. Joseph Smith, 1832 history, in Dean C. Jessee, ed., *The Papers of Joseph Smith,* 2 vols. (Salt Lake City: Deseret Book, 1989–1992), 1:5; emphasis added.

20. Joseph Smith to John Wentworth, 1 March 1842, Joseph Smith, *History of The Church of Jesus Christ of Latter-day Saints,* 2d ed rev., ed. B. H. Roberts, 7 vols. (Salt Lake City: Deseret Book, 1959–60), 4:536; hereafter *HC.*

21. Lucy Smith, Biographical Sketches of Joseph Smith, preliminary manuscript, 40, 43, cited in Dean Jessee, "The Spirituality of Joseph Smith," *Ensign* (Sept. 1978), 17.

22. Lucy Mack Smith, *History of Joseph Smith* (Salt Lake City: Bookcraft, 1979), 82.

23. Joseph Smith Sr., Patriarchal Blessing Book no. 1:8–9, Ibid., 17.

24. *HC,* 4:536.

25. Jessee, *Papers,* 2:69, entry for 9 November 1835; emphasis added.

26. Oliver Cowdery, "Letter IV, to W.W. Phelps, Esq.," *The Latter-day Saints Messenger and Advocate* 1 (Feb. 1835): 78–79; emphasis added; hereafter *M&A*.

27. Oliver Cowdery, Patriarchal Blessing Book no. 1:8–9, cited in Jessee, "The Spirituality of Joseph Smith," 18; emphasis in original. Compare Abraham 1:2. The author is grateful to Alma Allred for pointing out the similarity of the language of these two passages.

28. Jessee, *Papers,* 2:441–42; emphasis added. For the background of this entry see Dean C. Jessee, ed., *The Personal Writings of Joseph Smith,* (Salt Lake City: Deseret Book, 1984), 542–43, 530; hereafter *Writings.*

29. 1 Cor. 13:1–8; see Gal. 5:22–24 for the source of the fruit analogy.

30. Joseph Smith, *Lectures on Faith* (Salt Lake City: Deseret Book., 1985), Lectures 3–5. (Hereafter cited with appropriate lecture and paragraph number, i.e., Lecture 1:1.) See particularly Lecture 3:2–5.

31. Smith, Lecture 4:2. See also Rom. 10:13–17 and Joseph's reworking of the critical verse 17 in *TPJS,* 148; Acts 10:34–43; Moro. 7:30–32.

32. Smith, Lecture 4:16.

33. Smith, Lecture 3:20.

34. Given the importance of these principles it shouldn't surprise us that the one thing we are told about the Liahona, in addition to the fact that it served as a guide for Lehi's family through the wilderness, is that writing also appeared on it from time to time "which did give [them] understanding concerning the ways of the Lord" (1 Ne. 16:29).

35. See for example Alma 34:15–17; 3 Ne. 7:16; Moro. 3:3; D&C 3:20.

36. Joseph Smith [to Emma Smith, 21 March 1839, cited] in Richard Bushman, "The Character of Joseph Smith," *Ensign* (April 1977), 11.

37. Jessee, *Papers,* 1:5.

38. Joseph Smith to Oliver Cowdery, *M&A,* 1 (Dec. 1834):40.

39. Joseph told the Twelve he did "many things <inadvertently> that are not right in the sight of God." To the Relief Society he said, "The wrong that I do is through the frailty of human nature, like other men. No man lives without fault." One visitor to Nauvoo later reported in a newspaper that Joseph said he "did not profess to be a very good man, but acknowledged himself a sinner like other men, or, as all men are, imperfect; and it is necessary for all men to grow into the stature of manhood in the Gospel." These quotations make it clear that Joseph's sins ensued from the common frailties of man rather than from rebellion or, as he said, a "disposition" to commit "great or malignant sins." References: Jessee, *Papers,* 2:66, 76; *HC,* 5:140, 408; JS–H 1:28. Compare his remarks to Oliver Cowdery: "I have not, neither can it be sustained in truth, been guilty of wronging or injuring any man or society of men." Joseph Smith to Oliver Cowdery, *M&A,* 1 (Dec. 1834):40.

40. Jessee, *Papers,* 2:69–70.

41. Joseph Smith to John Wentworth, 1 March 1842, *HC*, 4:536; emphasis added.

42. Lucy Mack Smith, *History of Joseph Smith*, 135.

43. See, D&C 29:3; 60:7; 62:3; 64:3, 7; 82:1; 84:60–61; 90:1; 110:5; 132:50.

44. *HC*, 1:271–72.

45. Joseph Smith to Emma, 6 June 1832, Jessee, *Writings*, 238. A few years later, Mary Fielding Smith, who visited Joseph during a life-threatening illness in the summer of 1837, wrote to her sister, "He feels himself to be a poor Creature and can do nothing but what God enables him to do." Mary Fielding Smith to Mercy Thompson, July 1837, cited in Jessee, "The Spirituality of Joseph Smith," 20.

46. Jessee, *Papers*, 2:28, under date 1 April 1834.

47. *HC*, 6:412. Compare Alma 22:18.

48. Orson F. Whitney, *Life of Heber C. Kimball* (Salt Lake City: Bookcraft, 1967), 69–70. Truman Madsen asserted that "The hallmark of the prayer-life of Joseph Smith is intimacy." Truman G. Madsen, "Prayer and the Prophet Joseph," 18. See, for example, the experiences of Daniel Tyler, "Recollections of the Prophet Joseph Smith," *Juvenile Instructor* 27 (15 Feb. 1892): 127; hereafter *JI*; Mary Elizabeth Rollins Lightner, Diary of Elizabeth R. Lightner, 3, cited in Madsen, "Prayer and the Prophet Joseph," 20; and William F. Cahoon, "Recollections of the Prophet Joseph Smith," *JI* 27 (15 Aug. 1892): 492–93, who all observed and testified of the intimate nature of his prayers.

49. This particular journal is a good example because, as Dean Jessee has written, "Although small, this first journal merits attention because it contains more of Joseph Smith's own handwriting than any of his other journals. It reveals personal feelings and a sensitivity not reflected in the journals recorded for him by his scribes." Jessee, *Papers*, 2:1. The student, however, should be advised that even much of this journal is in the handwriting of scribes and individual entries must be checked in Jessee's work to determine which statements are holographic. For examples of prayers included in letters, see Joseph Smith to Emma Smith, 13 October 1832, in Jessee, *Writings* (Salt Lake City: Deseret Book, 1984), 253; *TPJS*, 25, 27, 30, 34, 35, and 37.

50. He actually records prayers twenty-two times and mentions it three times, but records a prayer once on the same day as he mentions it. See, entries for the 27, 28, 29 November; 4 December 1832; 6, 13, 20, 25, 28 October; 1, 13, 19 November; 4, 18, 19 December 1833; 11, 16, 31 January; 1, 3 March; 7, 19 April; 21 August; and 29 November 1834, in Jessee, *Papers*, 2:2–35. Interestingly, the five lengthiest entries each occupy approximately one-and-a-half to two-and-a-half pages of printed text; one of them records a list of seven petitions Joseph and his brethren unitedly took to the Lord. Jessee, *Papers*, 2:18–19.

51. Jessee, *Papers,* 2:39–210. Again one of the longest entries in this section is the dedicatory prayer of the Kirtland Temple.

52. Jessee, *Papers,* 2:21, under date of 31 January 1834.

53. My experience parallels that of Truman Madsen who said: "Joseph demonstrated an innate and striking capacity for gratitude for even the slightest favor from the Lord or from his fellowmen. I have wept while reading in his journal prayers for his brethren. Even the smallest favor called out stirring warmth and gratitude." Madsen, "Prayer and the Prophet Joseph," 21.

54. Jessee, *Papers,* 2:5, 14–15, and 17.

55. Jessee, *Papers,* 2:39–41, under date of 23 September 1835.

56. Jessee, *Papers,* 2:51.

57. Ibid.

58. Ibid.

59. Ibid, 2:55.

60. *HC,* 2:386, 391.

61. Milton V. Backman, *The Heavens Resound, a History of the Latter-day Saints in Ohio, 1830–1838* (Salt Lake City: Deseret Book, 1983), 284–309. It should also be mentioned that certain ordinances such as washings and anointings undoubtedly facilitated the spiritual preparations the brethren were making.

62. *HC,* 2:387.

63. Thomas F. Rogers has written " . . . upon leaving the grove and for the rest of his life, Joseph never again knew a moment's respite from either persecution or misunderstanding on the part of his closest friends, even his wife, Emma. One unwittingly asks how he or anyone could have borne it and still maintained all he did if he did not know with a surety that the cause he pursued was 'well pleasing' in God's sight." "Thoughts about Joseph Smith: upon Reading Donna Hill's *Joseph Smith: The First Mormon,*" in John M. Lundquist and Stephen D. Ricks, eds., *By Study and Also by Faith* (Salt Lake City: Deseret Book, 1990), 2:593.

64. *TPJS,* 304; *HC,* 5:401; see also *HC,* 6:21; *TPJS,* 307.

65. Lucy Smith, *History of Joseph Smith,* 67.

66. "Howard drove me from the wagon," he said, "and made me travel in my weak state through the snow 40 miles per day for several days, during which time I suffered the most excruciating weariness and pain." LDS Historians Book A-1, note A, 131–32, LDS Church Archives.

67. Seventeen lawsuits were filed against Joseph in Chardon, the county seat, between 1837 and 1839. Others were filed in nearby Painesville. One particular day six suits were brought against him in Painesville. It is estimated that Grandison Newell alone may have filed as many as thirty legal actions against the Prophet. See Karl Ricks Anderson, *Joseph Smith's Kirtland* (Salt Lake City: Deseret Book, 1989), 37–39.

68. See a similar list in the autobiographical verses of D&C 122:4–7.

69. Smith, Lecture 4:14.

70. There are few times when his words betray possible discouragement but some of them are debatable. One is his petition to the Lord recorded in D&C 121:1–6, after spending a long, cold winter in Liberty Jail. He might be forgiven for being discouraged if he was; given the conditions it would be understandable. But such a petition is not *prima facie* evidence of discouragement. Nevertheless, even if he was discouraged, it didn't last long, because as in Nephi's psalm (2 Ne. 4), in the midst of his introspective prayer, optimism and courage returned. See D&C 121:7–12, 33; 122:1–9.

71. George Q. Cannon, discourse of 29 October in 1882 in *JD*, 23:362.

72. *TPJS*, 361.

73. John Henry Evans, *Joseph Smith an American Prophet* (New York: The Macmillan Co., 1946), 9.

74. *HC*, 5:517.

75. Solomon Chamberlain, *A Short Sketch of the Life of Solomon Chamberlain,* 11 July 1858, 2–4, LDS Church Archives, cited in Susan Easton Black, "'I Am Not Any Longer to Be Alone,'" *Ensign* (Jan. 1989), 51. The angel further told Chamberlain that the Lord would soon raise up a church after the "Apostolic Order" with its same gifts and powers and a book like the Bible would come forth for the guidance of the people.

76. See Joseph's comments about Matt. 24:14 in *HC*, 6:363–64.

77. See Joseph's interpretation of the parable of the leaven hidden in three measures of meal (Matt. 13:33) in *TPJS*, 100.

78. The Elders of the Church in Kirtland to Their Brethren Abroad, 22 January 1834, *HC*, 2:18. In Far West, Missouri David Osborn heard Joseph declare, "You may hug up to yourselves the Bible, but *except through faith* in it you can get revelation for yourself, the Bible will profit you but little..." David Osborn, "Recollections of the Prophet Joseph Smith," *JL* 27 (15 March 1892), 173; emphasis added.

CHAPTER FIFTEEN

WOMEN OF EARLY MORMONISM: A STUDY IN FAITH

CAROL CORNWALL MADSEN

> Hath not God chosen the poor of this world rich in faith, and heirs of the kingdom which he hath promised to them that love him?
>
> James 2:5

I HAVE FOLLOWED no cunning devised fable," wrote Mormon convert Ann Hughlings Pitchforth with stunning conviction. "Facts are stubborn things; they cannot be beat down nor be annihilated by clamour.... I dare not barter my eternal peace for man's opinion.... I can rejoice in the Lord all the day long, and smile at the taunts of the ignorant.... Truth cannot be destroyed by persecution." Ann's ringing declaration of faith had separated her from her husband, who would not believe, from her parents, who could not understand, and from her beloved English home, which she would never revisit. It had brought her, full of hope and anticipation, to a new life with new friends in a new land. Nauvoo, Illinois, was the center of all that mattered to Ann and her children. They had made the long journey from England together and shared an irrepressible faith. Ann died a year later in a camp a few miles east of Winter Quarters and was buried in an unmarked grave, but her dream lived on.[1]

No tales beyond those of that first generation of Latter-day Saints can better illustrate the power of faith or show that faith is primarily a matter of the spirit, not the mind or heart, since both logic and emotion so frequently yield to faith. Faith is an elusive element in the historical record because it transcends the material world and is not subject to the same tests of verification as social and natural phenomena. It can be measured only in the lives of the faithful for whom it is directive and defining. It was a genuine "leap of faith" that separated Ann Pitchforth from the personal comforts and attachments that made up her life in England. It was faith that held Ann Crookston and her mother to the Church when Ann's father and brothers died after emigrating to Nauvoo. Left alone "in a hovel on the Mississippi" to support themselves in loneliness and unfamiliarity, Ann and her mother had to find work for which neither of them was trained. Yet they somehow managed to gather sufficient resources to make their way west when the Saints left Nauvoo—just one evidence of the enabling power of faith.[2] Only a determined faith could explain the acceptance by so many women, after mental, emotional and spiritual searching, of a principle of marriage that assaulted their most feminine sensitivities. For these early Saints, faith mediated between their conversion and the life that followed.

Paradoxically, faith is both humbling and empowering. Even as it necessitates a total yielding, almost a self-abnegation to the object of one's faith, it also becomes an enabling and motivating drive capable of changing lives. Similarly, while it serves as a powerful driving force in the lives of the faithful, it is also a source of refuge, a comforting presence amidst uncertainty and instability. And always it is a product of the self, the result of an individual inward searching, its meaning understood best by the person of faith. Many people today, however, have allowed the technology and abundance of modern times to render faith, and religious belief of any kind, anachronistic, a superstition from the past. Clearly, faith speaks a language and portrays a worldview that eludes the nonbeliever.

While faith is the foundation of religion and beyond the scope of most historians, it is nevertheless as much a category of the historical as of the sacred. The secular approach of historical writers along with the "super-natural" quality of faith, however, has either marginalized or excluded it as a historical element.[3] But religious faith has always been a causal factor in the human story, as much of an identity-constructing element as class, race, or gender, the axes of contemporary historical analysis. Certainly it was for the women in this study. Their Mormon consciousness dominated the other defining elements in their life.[4]

Faith has also engendered compelling social visions that have had the capacity to create and transform communities as well as alter individual lives. The Mormon experience speaks to this reality. It offers its adherents not only new spiritual concepts but a reordered social arrangement in which unity, commitment, and community are fundamental. Mormonism from the beginning created a new cultural identity for its followers which distinguished them both religiously and socially from other religious believers.[5]

Despite the lack of attention given to religion by historians, nineteenth-century American women are best understood if religion is added to the traditional paradigm.[6] Though they were not all "believers" or attached to a religious denomination, religion was, in effect, their domain in the larger social commonwealth. It was ceded to them by a society that was becoming more and more secular and a clergy that recognized a natural ally in the struggle against the materialism, acquisitiveness, and worldly tenor of a nation stirring to its own potential wealth and power. Biblical injunctions ordered women's temporal universe and the churches defined their spiritual one.[7] Christian values were a dominant thread in the social fabric of nineteenth century America, generating a set of shared assumptions that gave a sense of cohesiveness to a rapidly changing American society. The moral authority granted women helped to hold the disparate social strands together. Though the gendered religious scheme of that period gave men the ecclesiastical positions, it ascribed to women a natural spirituality. They expressed their religiosity through church membership and its duties, through benevolent service, and through religious devotion in the home.

Despite their "natural" spirituality, however, many women sought for and experienced an overt religious conversion expressed in several ways. For some it took the form of a palpable sense of forgiveness of sin; for others, an increase of piety. Occasionally conversion meant a new religious affiliation, but always it signified a "change of heart" or a charge of spiritual energy. Conversion spiritually empowered women, initiating a strong sense of mission which manifest itself in a variety of religious activities.[8]

Converts, either to Mormonism or to renewed religious devotion, came from both the churched and the unchurched, but seldom from nonbelievers.[9] A distinguishing feature of many early Mormon converts was a dissatisfaction with the existing sects. Rather than turn away from religion altogether, however, they became "seekers," waiting for a religion that fulfilled their own particular religious quest. Most were seeking not only for a personal witness of God's love or Christ's saving power; they were waiting until the Spirit testified that truth, authority, and revelation had been restored as the foundation stones of Christ's gospel. Many of Mormonism's early converts were "seekers," and when the message they awaited arrived by way of the missionaries, they were open vessels, receptive to the witness of the Spirit. "I believed it right off and obeyed it in the spring," wrote Mary Gibbs Bigelow about her conversion, an assertive act that altered every facet of her long and eventful life.[10]

Nancy Naomi Alexander Tracy also found that Mormonism, unlike any other religious claim, filled the spiritual void in her life. She had always been of a religious bent but had resisted joining any sect. When a Mormon elder came to her village in Jefferson County, New York, curiosity—to see if all the disparaging words she had heard about the Mormons were true—took her to hear him preach. To her surprise she saw a "tall stately looking man with piercing black eyes;...when he began to speak it was with such force and power before he was half through," she remembered, "I could have borne my testimony to the truth of the Gospel and the doctrine he was preaching. I believed with all my heart."[11] Conversion could be swift and sure, a powerful, permanently transforming spiritual charge.

Though numerous spiritual autobiographies exist from centuries ago that show how women struggled with their sinful natures before converting to Christ,[12] many Mormon converts seem to have been spiritually prepared to receive the unique Mormon message. Newel and Elizabeth Ann Whitney of Kirtland, Ohio, for example, had received a spiritual manifestation that messengers bearing the authority and truth they were seeking would soon reach them. When the missionaries did indeed come, the Whitneys eagerly embraced the gospel they were prepared to receive.[13] Similarly, after hearing the elders preach in their Illinois town, Sarah Pea Rich and her family hoped to hear more, but the elders left the vicinity soon after. Six weeks later, however, Sarah dreamt that they would return and saw them in her dream walking together down the long lane that led to her house, then greeting her on the porch. Her dream became reality when she saw the elders walking toward her home at dusk the following day. "I have been looking for you to come," she said to them. "Why?" they queried. "Had you heard we were coming?" Then she told them of the dream. Their response fulfilled the revelation: "Well," they said, "we had a vision that we were to return here and baptize you and build up a Church in this region." Sarah was the first one baptized and within weeks there were seventy members and a new branch of the Church.[14]

Discouraged by cultural norms to seek vocations other than domestic, many young women found the religious life to be fulfilling and life-affirming. During the revivalist period, particularly, women found new outlets for religious expression such as praying in the revival meetings, conducting prayer circles, and evangelizing family and friends. Thus, Phoebe Carter was not so unique when she left her family in Maine to become a Latter-day Saint. Too emotional to say her good-byes in person, she chose to write them. "Had it not been for the spirit within," she noted, "I should have faltered at the last." But the spirit prevailed and she prepared to join the Saints in Kirtland, promising her mother before she left that if she became disillusioned and her faith was misplaced, she would return home. Phoebe's faith didn't falter and in time her parents accepted the gospel as well.[15]

Charlotte Carter also broke her familial ties to follow the promptings of her newfound faith. As a domestic servant in London, she was intrigued when two Mormon missionaries came to the home where she worked. They were rejected by her employer, but Charlotte was interested and attended their meetings. She was soon converted. After earning the necessary funds, she traveled to

Utah, meeting on shipboard a fellow convert who would become her husband. Her faith that the Church would confirm her selfhood and provide power and meaning to her life propelled her to make this life-changing decision.[16]

Mary Brannigan was another young woman who traveled to Zion alone. Converting to the Church in her native England without her family's knowledge, she taught school to earn enough money to pay her passage to the United States. But emigrating allowed no fond good-byes or promises. Her parents would never have consented to her conversion nor her emigration, and so she left without their knowledge. But she loved the gospel and was determined to find her place in Zion, arriving in Iowa in time to join a handcart company. When the company resupplied at Fort Bridger she chose not to borrow the proffered money to replace her shoes. "My shoes are almost as good as new," she told the captain of the company, "and I do not propose to go into Salt Lake City in debt." Mary was physically worn but spiritually exhilarated by the experience. When she finally reached the valley, she declared herself "as happy as could be" having reached "Zion safe and well" and ready to begin a new life among the Saints.[17]

These women and thousands like them who became Latter-day Saints did not make such dramatic and assertive life choices on whims or fancies. They knew that the costs of their decision were simply too great to be borne without a deep and total commitment. Conversion was life-disrupting and all encompassing, and they had willingly yielded themselves to its uncertainties because of the sureness of their conviction. Eliza Cheney counted those costs and made her decision: "I did not embrace this work hastily," she wrote. "I came into it understandingly, I weighed the subject, I counted the cost, I knew the consequences of every step I took."[18] There was no looking back to the road not taken.

* * * * *

> *...a religion that does not require the sacrifice of all things never has power sufficient to produce the faith necessary unto life and salvation....*
>
> Lectures on Faith 6:7

In reviewing the lives of these women we can only be amazed at the strength and durability of their conviction. They were "far above the average," one admirer wrote of them. "One cannot but feel they were called and in fact chosen to assist in ushering in this last dispensation."[19] The sense of being in the vanguard of a new and final religious era gave significance to their sacrifice and transcendent purpose to their labors in establishing Zion—first in Ohio, then in Missouri, again in Illinois, and finally in Utah. Conversion palpably demonstrated the operation of God's grace in their lives. This was the Lord's work and they had been miraculously chosen to be the vessels through which his kingdom would be established, "no more to be throne [sic] down," Zina Young asserted during the dark days of Nauvoo.[20]

How did conversion change the lives of the early members? It did not mean simply responding to a dormant religiosity or affiliating with a traditional religious group, behavior which characterized the spiritual awakening of many people in the wake of the religious revivals of the early nineteenth century. For revivalists, there was no need to pull up stakes and travel across an ocean or half a continent to join with other believers. There was no need to possess the kind of faith that accepted the contemporary existence of a prophet, the personal manifestation of Deity to a farm boy, or a new volume of sacred scripture. Nor did they need to suspend their sense of moral propriety and accept a way of life that demanded total unselfishness in their closest relationship.

Conversion for Latter-day Saints meant both religious and geographic relocation. The principle of gathering clearly distinguished the conversion experience of early Latter-day Saint women from that of their Protestant counterparts. This principle, one of the most distinctive characteristics of nineteenth-century Mormonism, enabled the Church to establish the numerically strong and materially secure foundation essential to building the spiritual kingdom. But it also meant painful separations, tedious if not tragic journeys, and repeated uprootings, personal sacrifices that challenged the staying power of that first surge of religious zeal. Conversion, therefore, had to include a tenacious commitment to the spirit of gathering for Mormonism to survive. The truly converted had testimonies as firm as that of Phoebe Chase, who wrote to her unconverted children in New York her reason for leaving them to join the Saints in Nauvoo in 1840:

> The Lord has blest us in obeying his commands in gathering with the Saints and helping in the work of the latter-day which you think is not the work of the Lord but My Children it is the work of the Lord for no man ever could bring about so great and so marvelous a work and now I tell you I am stronger in the faith of the work than I was when I was there.[21]

In the earliest years, and particularly for many immigrants, deprivation—of homes, supplies, and comforts, especially the loss of loved ones—marked their entry into Mormon life. Like the Tracy family, many converts traded a life of predictability and security for one of instability, insufficiency, and uncertainty. "We had not as yet learned to deprive ourselves of comfort," Nancy Tracy wrote as she remembered her family's move to Kirtland, "and little did we realize what we would have to endure for the Gospel's sake."[22]

Nauvoo, like Missouri before it, laid innumerable challenges before the Saints. For much of the time that it was home to the Church it offered inadequate housing and insufficient food and supplies while providing an abundance of disease and death. The newly arrived Field family confronted all these. Not long after their arrival, the father and two daughters succumbed to malaria, leaving the mother alone with six children in her care. For several weeks their food consisted of one pint of cornmeal a day. "Mother worked very hard to provide for us and keep our family together," Mary Field wrote. "The Saints were very kind to us and tried to help us the best they could." Despite such daunting trials, the Fields did not regret their decision to settle in Nauvoo and were sustained by something more than their small supply of cornmeal. "We did not complain," Mary Field explained, "as we were too thankful to be at Nauvoo with the other Saints of God and to be acquainted with our prophet and leader, Joseph Smith, and listen to his teachings."[23]

Jane Benbow and Hannah Kington, British converts, also sacrificed to gather with the Church. The Benbows and the Kingtons had been instrumental in opening the way for the gospel to spread in Great Britain. Jane Benbow opened her home in Herefordshire for the preaching of Wilford Woodruff and other missionaries; Jane and Hannah, both childless, lodged and fed them; and the Benbow's pond became the site of hundreds of baptisms. Members of their religious group, the United Brethren, followed the Benbows and Kingtons into the Church, most of them emigrating to Nauvoo, some with the financial help of the Benbows. As yeoman farmers, John Benbow and Thomas Kington were comfortable, productive, and respected. Jane and Hannah had little reason to leave their homes or change their way of life. Nevertheless, using a small legacy from their fathers, Jane and Hannah contributed to the printing of the first Book of Mormon in England, a hymnal, and the *Millennial Star.* They also agreed to join the Saints in Nauvoo. After struggling to adjust to the hardships they encountered there, both died in the exodus from Illinois, little noted for their selfless service to the Church.[24] Yet the sacrifices of these first-generation Mormons honed and strengthened their faith and the faith of their families and made them ready candidates for God's grace.

* * * * *

> *...it is expedient in me that they should be brought thus far for a trial of their faith.*
>
> (D&C 105:19)

Zion was elusive in those early years. Kirtland, Missouri, and Nauvoo had all held promise, but the Church was not yet large or strong enough to offset the threats and harassment that its unconventional claims and cohesiveness drew upon itself. The trail west to a place where the Saints could once again gather, this time "unmolested and unafraid," added one more trial of the stability of their faith in the work. It was difficult for everyone but especially hard for women. Birthing on the trail took a heavy toll on mothers and infants, and families were often broken by death and then reformed with new members before the journey's end. Every hand was needed, and women without husbands or sons took over their tasks or depended on others to assist. Traveling in large wagon trains, however, mitigated the difficulties. It was a collective venture, survival depending on cooperation, sharing, and looking after one another. "Everyone helped everyone else," Priscilla Merriman Evans remembered of her trip across the plains.

"Strong men would help the weaker ones until they themselves were worn out...."[25] While the geographic destination had no visible form in the travelers' minds, their spiritual vision was clear. They were headed for a new Zion, another gathering place, and material characteristics were secondary to the spiritual. They were sustained by the conviction that they were on the Lord's errand, doing their part to establish Zion wherever it was to be.

Unlike most other westering travelers, the Mormons were seeking a place of collective refuge, impelled by a shared vision. Those who died along the way were seen as martyrs to a cause, not victims of a risky venture. They were not after riches or adventure. They accepted their trials as refining elements that would make them Latter-day Saints in deed as well as in name. "We waded streams, crossed high mountains and pulled through heavy sand, leaving comfortable homes, father, mother, brother and sister to be where we could hear a prophet's voice and live with the Saints of Zion," wrote Mary Ann Jones Ellsworth at the end of her long journey.[26] Their trials were rites of passage that tested their faith and their worthiness to attain their ultimate, eternal destiny.

Creating new settlements in the West that would provide a material setting for the growth of the kingdom compounded the uprootedness of the early Saints. Drusilla Hendricks, an early settler of the Salt Lake Valley, remembered the hardship of those early times. Arriving in the valley in 1847, the Hendricks were fortunate enough to secure a log house in the old fort, and by killing one of their trusty oxen, they were able to have meat for their table and tallow for candles. But they had no wheat or flour for bread. A friend, Adeline Benson, seeing their plight, saved a little of her rations, and when she had secured enough for a meal, took it to the Hendricks and said, "Have something good." The Hendricks declared it good, a change from the diet of boiled beef and cornmeal on which they had subsisted. But Salt Lake City was only a temporary home for the Hendricks. In the 1860s they were called to begin again in Richmond, Utah, where they repeated the whole process.[27]

When the Tracy family reached the Salt Lake Valley it was only a temporary resting place for them also. Moving on to Ogden, they were happy to find plentiful timber, "so we had a cabin thrown up as soon as we could," Nancy Tracy wrote. "The next thing was to secure something to live on through the winter." They sold a yoke of cattle for a large beef ox and then sold the ox for twelve bushels of wheat which was "scarce and hard to get at any cost." She carefully husbanded it to make it last through the winter. "I would cut the children a slice of bread," she wrote, "make some cruit coffee with a little milk in it, and tell them to thank the Lord for it, and they were satisfied."[28]

Crickets, grasshoppers, Indians, disease, shortages, and the weather conspired to add to the challenges of carving a community out of a wilderness. Yet the growing stream of settlers answered the call to build homes in the unlikeliest of places, submerging their own preferences to the needs of Brigham Young's colonizing design. Obedience has always been an evidence of faith and the early Saints had manifold opportunities to prove theirs. It was obedience to the call to gather that brought converts from out of the world to make a united Church. It was obedience that drew the first pioneers to an unsettled western desert after the Church was driven from Nauvoo. It was obedience to their leader's call to answer the nation's military needs that deprived the western-bound Mormon companies of husbands and fathers. It was obedience that fragmented families, sometimes for years at a time while husbands served missions and performed other long-term Church service. And it was obedience that took families into inhospitable areas to create outposts of the kingdom, which they had committed to serve.

These were not male undertakings. They were wholly dependent on the willingness of *families* to uproot themselves and settle again and again. Women sustained the community building, suffering all of the deprivations and the emotional and physical dislocations of colonizing while contributing in the same degree as their husbands, sons, and fathers. But their names are generally unrecorded in the histories, their contributions to the great colonization achievement of the West unheralded. If the official records leave them out, their diaries tell their story, a story that runs across the pages in vivid, unembellished detail. Women provided a continuity—in their families as they raised their own children and often their grandchildren, and in their communities as they created networks that provided the health care, education, and culture that gave a settlement cohesion and identity and often determined its quality of life. None of this was easy. The Lord had promised that he would try their faith, and they were willing to meet the challenge. From her conversion on, Nancy Tracy experienced all of the trials that tested the faith of that first vanguard of Saints. "My life, ever since I became a Mormon, has been made up of moving about, of persecutions, sacrifices, poverty, sickness, and death." Her faith was the shield that protected her from the piercing thrust of total despair and her "hope of salvation" was the "helmet" that kept her from succumbing to her trials (1 Thes. 5:8). For those early Saints, eternal life was their holy grail and they were willing to confront any challenge to win the prize. Their power to do was in their assurance that God would fully compensate their suffering and their steadfastness. At the end Nancy Tracy was able to say, "I have drunk the bitter cup to the dregs, yet the Lord has sustained me and has been merciful and not forsaken me."[29]

* * * * *

> *And Christ hath said: If ye will have faith in me ye shall have power to do whatsoever thing is expedient in me.*
>
> (Moro. 7:33)

In the early years, there was a fine line between service and sacrifice. A calling to act as a ward or stake auxiliary president, after the Saints were settled in the West, often meant thirty years or more in the position, certainly pushing the boundaries between selfless service and sacrifice. One wonders if Isabella Horne ever entertained the notion of refusing one of the many calls that came to her in overlapping regularity. For twenty-six years, while bearing and mothering fifteen children, Isabella served as president of the Salt Lake Stake Relief Society. She also officiated as president of the Senior Cooperative Retrenchment Association and treasurer of the central board of the Relief Society. She was a member of the Deseret Hospital committee, a counselor in the presidency of the Deseret Silk Association, and president of the Women's Cooperative Mercantile and Manufacturing Institution.[30] Such multiple—and long—callings were not unusual. Sarah

M. Kimball guided the fifteenth ward Relief Society for forty years during which time she also served as secretary of the central Relief Society Board and president of the Territorial Woman Suffrage Association. Jane Molen served thirty years as stake Primary president in Cache Valley. While traditional female reticence kept many other capable and faithful women from assuming these visible positions, they formed the supporting army of female workers who sustained the work of kingdom-building. Like Jane Benbow's and Hannah Kington's contributions, theirs were vital but unheralded.

While some women officiated in the organizations, other women ministered in more personal ways, their service to the kingdom expressed as doctors and midwives, among other occupations. Responding to the urgent need in early Utah for trained medical help, women throughout the territory accepted calls to travel to Salt Lake City or even to the East to learn midwifery, nursing, and even doctoring. These were not always favored callings. When Mary Ann Maughan was appointed midwife of the new settlement in Tooele, Utah, she resisted the calling, knowing its demands. With a large family to care for she had little time to care for others. But the blessing that set her apart for that task also promised her the well being of her children during her service. It was a contract she couldn't refuse.[31] Sarah Jane Lewis was even less enthusiastic about her new calling. "I said plenty of mean things about the ones who thought I could go," she wrote. "I was leaving nine children, the youngest eighteen months old…I thought that there were plenty of others who could go easier and do better work than I." She determined to visit Brigham Young when she arrived in the city and tell him that the calling was a mistake. But when she did, his response to her long remonstrance was to give her a blessing, promising that her children would be well and she would be blessed in the work. The words were magic. She took the course, returned home, and faithfully served her community for thirty-three years as its primary medical resource, "never sorry for the knowledge" she had attained through this calling. "I always thought of myself as a missionary," she recalled.[32]

Emma Liljenquist was another who left a young family behind to answer the call to learn midwifery and obstetrics. Like the others she also had faith in the blessing given to her upon completion of her studies and depended on it to enable her to raise her own large family and care for the health needs of Hyrum in Cache Valley, Utah. "It made my heart ache when I had to leave my babies," she remembered, "...but I had to go with a smile on my face and bring happiness into the sick room.... You might ask why I left them, but I had been called by the Church to perform this service, and I felt that it was a special calling."[33] It is little wonder that Emmeline Grover Rich, a midwife in the Bear Lake Valley, felt "pretty used up" at the end of a forty-year stint. But they all had three things in common—their faith in the inspiration of the call, in the promised blessings to follow, and in the value of their service to the kingdom. Their faith empowered them to fulfill the difficult tasks that were their share of kingdom-building.

When the Relief Society was reestablished in 1869 in Utah, more opportunities to serve presented themselves to the sisters. Not only were they to perform the Society's original charge to provide compassionate service, but they were to be a part of Brigham Young's broad-based economic program to keep the Saints financially and materially independent and continue to build a strong material base for the Church. This required total commitment from the Saints. Brigham Young explained the parameters of kingdom-building in 1864: "...everything that pertains to men [and women]—their feelings, their faith, their affections, their desires, and every act of their lives—belong [to the Kingdom], that they may be ruled by it spiritually and temporally."[34]

Shouldering their delegated responsibilities, women answered another unique call to the faithful. Being a Mormon was like nothing else their former life offered. From Idaho to Arizona women "retrenched," making their own straw hats instead of buying manufactured bonnets, wearing homespun dresses instead of fancy silks "from the states," and making simple meals and refreshments rather than elaborate repasts for their families and friends. "A reformation is needed among us," Retrenchment Association president Isabella Horne told the sisters, "and we come here together to bring about this reformation."[35] Home industries became the watchword of the Saints, and when the sisters felt that the sacrifice of silk dresses was asking too much, Zina D. H. Young, a wife of Brigham, was appointed head of a new home industry—sericulture. For many fashion-conscious but retrenchment-minded women, the home production of silk, which included nurturing the tiny silk worms with a continuous supply of mulberry leaves, was worth the effort. When the industry faltered and then failed, it was not for lack of effort by Zion's sisters.

While the silk industry may not have caught the fancy of every Relief Society member, virtually all were involved in saving grain, a preeminent task of early Mormon women. As nineteenth-century gleaners, they gathered the abandoned grain from the fields and gradually accumulated large stores of it for families in need and for less prosperous times. It meant hard work and much responsibility, but it grew into a successful welfare program carefully administered by the women of the Relief Society until subsumed by the general welfare program of the Church. The grain-saving mission became synonymous with the Relief Society, a sheaf of wheat symbolizing its charge for compassionate service.

* * * * *

> *Let us hold fast the profession of our faith without wavering;...*
>
> (Heb. 10:23)

Sacrifice challenged these women's faith, but for the steadfast such offerings strengthened and refined it. For most of them their endurance evoked gratitude and humility, not pride or self-congratulation. But the spirit needed constant refreshment. Discouragement and disillusionment lurked enticingly around the edges of their daily rounds. They turned to testimony meetings, temple worship, patriarchal blessings, and the gifts of the Spirit to nourish their faith and help them fight against such spiritual assaults. They were highly sensitive to the Spirit's presence and felt that they were living guided lives.

Professing their conviction through the demonstration of the gifts of the Spirit characterized the spiritual experiences of many women in the early Church. Offsetting her unhappy memories of difficult days in Nauvoo was Elizabeth Heward's recollection of the cottage meetings held in each other's homes. As a newcomer to the city she was slow to participate but vividly recalled the prayer meeting where "Sister Wheeler sang in tongues" and Elizabeth was given the gift of interpretation. "We had a joyful time indeed," Elizabeth wrote. "I never missed a meeting when it was in my power to go." During a period of particular discouragement, she read a passage in the Book of Mormon that described the people raising their voices in song "for the Lord hath comforted His people" (Mosiah 12:23). "When I read these words," Elizabeth recalled, "my whole soul was filled with joy and hope in the great mercy and goodness of God in the redemption of the human family." Then Elizabeth raised her own voice in song, singing several verses in tongues. "This was the first time I had that gift," she wrote, "so I truly rejoiced in the Spirit and praised the Lord."[36] These spiritual manifestations, gifts to the faithful, were like antidotes to the potentially poisonous effects of unrelenting hardship.

Winter Quarters became another proving ground of faith. The Saints were suspended in the most primitive of conditions between a beautiful city to the east, which they were forced to abandon, and an unknown, unsettled desert to the west. They were stretched both physically and emotionally. "The absence of the pioneers [the vanguard company] on their journey to the Rocky Mountains," wrote Emmeline B. Wells years later in the *Woman's Exponent,*

> was a time of great anxiety to those who remained behind, and especially to those whose fathers, husbands and brothers were members of that memorable company. The sisters held regular meetings to pray and exercise faith for the pioneers.... These seasons of refreshing among the sisters helped them to endure the weary days and almost sleepless nights, while those they so tenderly loved were plodding the sandy plains, wending their way through an unknown country to their "promised land."[37]

Patty Sessions, among others, made a record of these "seasons of refreshing" in Winter Quarters. She noted in her diary the many times women met together, uniting their faith and thereby enjoying the comfort and spiritual uplift of the gifts of the Spirit, prophesying, speaking in tongues, and blessing one another through the power of their faith. "We prayed prop[h]esied and spoke in tounges and interpreted and were refreshed," she wrote on April 24, 1847. She relished feasting on "the good things of the kingdom" in such gatherings, the good things being the power of their faith to invoke the presence of the Spirit.[38]

The trail west offered more occasions for women to gather together. Eliza R. Snow records a time on the trail when the women in her company met in a grove for prayer. "We have a time not to be forgotten," she wrote of the spiritual hour they shared.[39] How often such notations concluded with those words, "not to be forgotten." They are significant in understanding the durability of these sisters' faith, for it was the memory of such spiritual moments that guarded them against the inevitable periods of doubt and discouragement. These collective professions of their individual faith buoyed their spirits and comforted women in the most trying of circumstances. As evidence of the reality of the restored gospel, the spiritual gifts did indeed follow these true believers, reassuring them of the divinity of the work in which they were engaged.[40]

Through the nineteenth-century female ritual of "visiting," women kept their ties close, their relationships current, and their interdependence strong. When such warm, affectionate connections are overlaid with a spiritual veneer, strong and enduring bonds inevitably follow. Professing faith through the exercise of spiritual gifts became a central feature of many of their informal gatherings, such as the prayer meeting held for Mary Ann Freeze, president of the Salt Lake Stake Young Ladies Mutual Improvement Association. She was suffering from a tumor and her board members had gathered to unite their faith for her healing. It was "one of the most heavenly meetings ever enjoyed by the Saints," Mary Ann recorded. "The Spirit of God rested down upon us in such mighty power that it was difficult for the sisters to control their emotions so as to be able to speak," she wrote. "The prayers and remarks of the Sisters were so full of love and pleading for my welfare that it humbled me to the very dust of the earth."[41]

A gathering at Zina Card's home in 1884 of women who served together in the Logan Temple was another example of such seasons of spiritual renewal and shared sisterhood. The women spoke in tongues and interpreted and blessed one another, embraced by the spiritual union fostered by their holy calling in the temple. One of the group, Jane Molen, noted that "the spirit of the Lord was made manifest in many ways. It was a day long to be remembered."[42]

Romania Pratt Penrose, one of Utah's early women doctors, also cherished such spiritual meetings, like the one held in the home of her friend Emmeline B. Wells. Thirteen women, friends and co-workers in the Church, each "spoke by the power and spirit of the Holy Ghost," she remembered, never having witnessed "such a rich flow of the spirit of God as was manifested on that occasion.... We truly had a time of feasting the soul and rejoicing."[43] All of their social gatherings did not take on such spiritual dimensions, but religious devotion underscored their lives, and the manifestation of their faith through the exercise of spiritual gifts enhanced their feelings of self-worth and acceptance in the kingdom.

The temple also reinforced women's sense of value to the Church. Temple service meant a surcease, if only for a while, of the emotional and physical claims of everyday life. It linked the heavenly with the earthly and for many was "the evidence of things not seen" (Heb. 11:1). Temples were the most tangible symbols of God's relationship with his children and his desire to unite them once again with him. Temples not only received the faithful but revitalized their faith. Temple service connected women with the most sacred rituals of the gospel, a means of giving and receiving blessings of eternal consequence. Women temple workers were honored for their service, often called priestesses because of their holy work and earning the title "mother in Israel."

In the early years in Utah, the Saints not only performed the saving ordinances in the temple but also set aside certain days for a practice since discarded—rebaptism—and blessings for the restoration of health. Women frequently engaged in these rituals. Lucy Bigelow Young, Eliza R. Snow, and Zina D. H. Young were three of the many who officiated in these ordinances in the Endowment House and later in the St. George, Manti, Salt Lake and Logan temples. One Manti temple worker, Christina Willardson, lamented missing the opportunity because she did not work on that day of the week. "Tuesdays being the day for baptism and waiting on the sick and infirm," she wrote, "I have not had the opportunity of seeing the sick healed instantly or waiting much on them in the temple."[44] But it was the privilege of Minerva White Snow to witness many healings while serving in the Manti Temple. "I have seen the sick healed, the lame made to walk, and the blind to see, and I wish to repeat my testimony...that Joseph Smith was a Prophet, and that this gospel was established by divine revelation."[45]

One who benefitted by a temple healing blessing was Ellen B. Ray Matheny. When she was thirty-one she had an accident that left her partially paralyzed for six years. In the seventh year of her disability she went to the St. George Temple to be baptized for her health. "From that time I rapidly improved, and in one year I was called to go to the St. George Temple as a regular worker, where I worked for three years without losing a day on account of sickness."[46] Temple worship both proved and sustained their faith.

Adding to the rich spiritual life that temple service and spiritual gatherings provided for faithful Latter-day Saint women were their patriarchal blessings. These spiritual guides were unique to Latter-day Saints and invested Mormon women with specific responsibilities and blessings. They were a source of spiritual empowerment as well as a declaration of women's place in the covenant. Though offering conditional blessings and promises, they revealed the spiritual dimensions of the woman of faith. The foundation of the blessing was the declaration of lineage, emphasized in great detail and force. "The blessings of holy men and Patriarchs even from days of old are upon thine head," Lovinia Dame was told in her blessing. The patriarch explained that because of her royal lineage through the line of the ancient patriarchs, "None can stay the fountains of knowledge that shall be opened unto thee."[47]

Angelina Packer learned that even if she stepped aside "from the faith of the Gospel" she would be redeemed "because of thy blood, thy stock, and the royal family unto whom the promises made by Abraham pertain."[48] Such promises did not fall on indifferent ears. They had the power to bolster the most fragile ego and to give assurance of God's ruling hand. With such disclosure of one's spiritual lineage, it is little wonder that through these blessings women were charged to teach, to testify, to counsel and to bless other members of the Church and promised the ability to do so.

Elizabeth Thompson learned from her patriarch that she would be granted a gift of "wisdom, knowledge, light and also faith, hope and charity." "Many," he said,

> shall come to thee for counsel and advice and they shall go away happy and contented and thou shalt have great influence with thy sex for good, also shall the young and rising generation come to thee for advice and instructions and thou shalt bless them and they shall bless thee and thou shalt go forth and do much good.[49]

Patriarch Zebedee Coltrin told Martha Riggs that she would be numbered among the mothers in Israel, for, he said, "thou will become mighty in the midst of thy sisters...and thou shall have a knowledge by which thou shall teach the Daughters of Zion how to live, for it shall be required unto thee from the heavens." She was also promised that none would surpass her in wisdom and many would seek knowledge at her hands.[50] Like the declaration of their lineage, such promises linked women with the essential purposes of the Church and created for them a viable and necessary function independent of an organizational calling. All of these spiritual resources safeguarded their faith and helped to create unwavering testimonies.

* * * * *

> *And we know that all men must repent and believe on the name of Jesus Christ, and worship the Father in his name, and endure in faith on his name to the end, or they cannot be saved in the kingdom of God.*
>
> (D&C 20:29)

For early Saints the boundaries between the spiritual and the temporal were fluid, and thus they avoided the contradictions of compartmentalized lives and conflicting claims. All aspects of their lives were centered on establishing Zion and preparing for the Savior's eventual reign. But such religious consecration did not promise these early Latter-day Saints saintly lives. They were not free from dissension in the wards, nor from disagreement with leaders and assignments, nor disputes among co-workers and neighbors. Their faith did not blind them to human weakness, and they often struggled with the demands, directions, and discourses that did not always suit their own sense of right. Their conviction, however, made them pilots of their own destiny. Religion is, after all, invited into one's life. At any point, had their faith wavered, they could have taken another road, and some did. At any time they could have rejected each new demand on their time and resources, and some did. At any point they could have challenged the wisdom of their leaders, procedural changes, and organizational developments, and some did. Most did not. As Ann Pitchforth discovered, faith can be a stubborn thing. Maintaining faith meant facing up to the challenges from within oneself as well as those from without. It is clear why the accolade most often accorded the deceased drew upon the battle imagery of Timothy: "She has fought the good fight of faith and earned her reward" (1 Tim. 6:12).

Faith and commitment did not come to all in a distinct pattern. For some, like Mary Gibbs Bigelow, conversion was instantaneous. But for others, like Eliza R. Snow, one of the most zealously devoted of that generation, it came slowly. She yielded to baptism only after years of study, prayer, and deliberation. Recalling her moment of commitment in poetic form, she wrote:

> ...I listened to the Sound
> Counted the cost, and laid my earthly all
> Upon the altar, and with purpose fixed
> Unalterably, am determined now to be a Saint."[51]

Her long life seasoned and matured that commitment. Her faith in the Church was the pillar of her life.

Others were not as articulate, but grammatical lapses did not diminish the sincerity of their testimonies. Remembering the disaffections of some of the members in Nauvoo, Desdemona Fullmer Smith remained firm despite pressure to renounce her testimony. "Olover Coddery with others would say to me are you such a fool as still to goo to hear Joseph the fallen prophet.... I said the Lord convinced me that he was a true prop[h]it. and he has not toled me that he is fallon yet." Then she added, "I belong 30 years in this Church and the longer I live in it the better I like it."[52]

Surviving the physical challenges, the emotional upheavals, or ecclesiastical demands that marked the lives of the early Saints somehow strengthened rather than diminished their commitment to the gospel. Most could endorse the sentiments of Caroline Crosby when many of her friends lost faith in Joseph Smith in Kirtland, "I felt very sorrowful, and gloomy, but never had the first idea of leaving the church or forsaking the prophet."[53]

A reading of these accounts may help explain the neglect of historical attention to religion. The traditional tools of scholarship are simply inadequate to fully interpret the essence of religious faith, as demonstrated by these women. Their own accounts are our best source of understanding the power of personal faith.

Although individual faith is always subject to constant reassessment, the personal writings of these pioneer women show that for them it was never negotiable. In their own words, each conveyed the conviction expressed by Ellen Douglas Parker: "I still feel to rejoice and to praise my God that I at so early a period was called to obey the Truth, and I feel determined by the grace of God to endure to the end, and I would be glad to have all my friends go with me."[54]

Notes

1. From a letter written to the Saints on the Isle of Man published in the *Millennial Star,* 20 vols., 8 (15 July 1846): 12–15. See also "Ann Hughlings Pitchforth," a brief life sketch, Archives, Harold B. Lee Library, Brigham Young University, Provo, Utah.

2. "A History of Ann Welch Crookston," typescript copy, LDS Church Archives.

3. Historian Linda Kerber attributes the lack of attention by women historians to women's religious experience to the fact that "religious history was...something women were expected to do." American history has generally neglected religion, she adds, because "the main lines of American development were understood to be elsewhere." See Linda Kerber, "Women's History for the 1990s: Problems and Challenges," in Susan Ware, ed., *New Viewpoints in Women's History: Working Papers from the Schlesinger Library 50th Anniversary Conference, March 4–5, 1994,* 38.

4. Nancy Cott elaborates on this concept by categorizing women's self-identification as feminist (a consciousness that confronts the inequalities in a woman's life), female (a consciousness that emphasizes the commonalities of women's traditional experience), and communal (a conscious identity a woman shares with men and children of her class, race, ethnicity, religion, region, etc.). See Nancy Cott, "What's in a Name? The Limits of 'Social Feminism'; or, Expanding the Vocabulary of Women's History," *Journal of American History* 76 (Dec. 1989): 827.

5. Eliza R. Snow, as a case in point, can better be understood as a nineteenth-century Mormon than a nineteenth-century Victorian American woman and would so identify herself that way. In the 1994 Tanner Lecture to the Mormon History Association, Patricia Nelson Limerick examines this distinctiveness and places Mormonism within the category of ethnicity. See Limerick, "Peace Initiative: Using the Mormons to Rethink Ethnicity in American Life," *Journal of Mormon History* (Spring 1995).

6. A recommendation urged by Kerber and other historians. See Kerber, "Women's History for the 1990s: Problems and Challenges."

7. In the Judeo-Christian tradition, the subjection of Eve because of her disobedience in the Garden of Eden and her creation after Adam have defined the temporal status of all of Eve's female descendants. The religious argument against the expansion of women's rights during the nineteenth century, based on Genesis and the proscriptions on women in Corinthians, was one of the strongest deterrents to expanding women's opportunities. Yet the various denominations concurrently preached a spiritual equality of men and women, eventually reversing the balance in favor of women. Gerda Lerner traces the history of this debate and women's attempts to contradict the concept in *The Creation of Feminist Consciousness* (New York: Oxford University Press, 1993), 133–66. The nineteenth century debate over Eve is chronicled in Donna A. Behnke, *Religious Issues in Nineteenth Century Feminism* (Troy, New York: The Whitson Publishing Company, 1982).

8. Virginia Lieson Brereton analyzes the language of nineteenth- and twentieth-century Protestant women's published conversion narratives in *From Sin to Salvation, Stories of Women's Conversions, 1800 to the Present* (Bloomington & Indianapolis: Indiana University Press, 1991).

9. The terms *churched* and *unchurched,* respectively, designate those who were at least nominal members of a religious denomination and those who professed religion but did not hold membership in any denomination.

10. "Autobiography of Mary Gibbs Bigelow," typescript, in Marvin M. Witt Papers, LDS Church Archives.

11. "Autobiography, Life and Travels of Nancy M. Tracy," *Woman's Exponent* 38 (Aug. 1909): 16.

12. Examples can be found in John Ferguson, ed. *An Illustrated Encyclopedia of Mysticism* (London: Thames and Hudson, 1976); Martin Buber,

Ecstatic Confessions, trans. Esther Cameron, ed. Paul Meades-Flohr (San Francisco: Harper and Row, 1985); and Walter Hollen Capps and Wendy M. Wright, eds., *Silent Fire: An Invitation to Western Mysticism* (San Francisco: Harper and Row, 1978).

13. Edward W. Tullidge, *The Women of Mormondom* (New York: Tullidge & Crandall, 1877), 42.

14. Journal of Sarah Pea Rich, typescript copy, in possession of author.

15. As quoted in Tullidge, 411–14.

16. Joseph Alexander Cornwall, "Romance of the Sea" (The Story of Charlotte Carter Cornwall), in possession of author.

17. "Mary Brannigan Crandall," in *An Enduring Legacy,* 10 vols. (Salt Lake City: Daughters of Utah Pioneers, 1987) 10:143–46.

18. Eliza A. Cheney, "Letter to Parents," typescript, LDS Church Archives.

19. Emmeline B. Wells, "LDS Women of the Past," *Woman's Exponent* 36 (April 1908): 57.

20. Zina D. H. Young, Nauvoo Diary, 24 May 1845, LDS Church Archives; a published version is "'All Things Move in Order in the City': The Nauvoo Diary of Zina Diantha Huntington Jacobs," edited by Maureen Ursenbach Beecher in *BYU Studies* 19 (Spring 1979): 285–320.

21. Phoebe Chase to her Children, ca. 1840, in Charles Marsh Correspondence, Nauvoo Restoration, Inc., materials, LDS Church Archives.

22. "Autobiography, Life and Travels of Nancy M. Tracy," *Woman's Exponent* 38 (Sept. 1909): 17.

23. Mary Field Garner Collection, typescript, Special Collections, Harold B. Lee Library, Brigham Young University, Provo, Utah.

24. See James B. Allen, Ronald K. Esplin, and David J. Whittaker, *Men with a Mission, 1837-1841, The Quorum of the Twelve Apostles in the British Isles* (Salt Lake City: Deseret Book, 1992), 124, 151, 248 n. 46.

25. "Handcart Companies, The Edward Bunker Company, Priscilla Merriman Evans," in Kate B. Carter, *Heart Throbs of the West,* 12 vols. (Salt Lake City: Daughters of Utah Pioneers, 1945), 6:354–55.

26. "Ellsworth Company, Mary Ann Jones Ellsworth," in Kate B. Carter, *Heart Throbs of the West,* 6:358–59.

27. Historical Sketch of James Hendricks and Drusilla Dorris Hendricks, typescript, LDS Church Archives.

28. "Life History of Nancy Naomi Alexander Tracy Written by Herself," typescript copy, 43, Harold B. Lee Library, Brigham Young University, Provo, Utah.

29. Ibid., 51, 62.

30. Susan Arrington Madsen, "Mary Isabella Horne," in Daniel H. Ludlow, ed., *Encyclopedia of Mormonism,* 4 vols. (New York: Macmillan Publishing Company, 1992) 2:657–59.

31. "Journal of Mary Ann Weston Maughan," in Kate B. Carter, *Our Pioneer Heritage,* 20 vols. (Salt Lake City: Daughters of Utah Pioneers, 1959) 2:381.

32. "Pioneer Midwives," in Kate B. Carter, *Our Pioneer Heritage,* 6:483.

33. "Pioneer Midwives," in Kate B. Carter, *Our Pioneer Heritage,* 6:444–46.

34. *Journal of Discourses* (Liverpool, England, 1853–1886) 10: 329.

35. Minutes of the Senior & Junior Cooperative Retrenchment Association, 20 February 1875, LDS Church Archives.

36. "A Sketch of the Life of Elizabeth Terry Heward," typescript, LDS Church Archives.

37. *Woman's Exponent* 10 (15 Dec. 1881): 107.

38. Patty Sessions, Diary, 30 April 1847, LDS Church Archives.

39. *Eliza R. Snow, An Immortal* (Salt Lake City: Nicholas G. Morgan, Sr. Foundation, 1957), 337, 339, 346, 355, 356, 358.

40. 1 Cor. 12:1–11; Morm. 9:24; Moro. 10:8–17; D&C 46:11–26. See also Joseph Smith, *History of The Church of Jesus Christ of Latter-day Saints,* 6 vols. (Salt Lake City: Deseret Book, 1951), 1:322–23, which quotes Joseph Smith as saying: "The gifts which follow them that believe and obey the Gospel, as tokens that the Lord is ever the same in His dealings with the humble lovers and followers of truth, began to be poured out among us, as in ancient days."

41. Mary Ann Freeze, Journal, 23 May 1895, Special Collections, Harold B. Lee Library, Brigham Young University, Provo, Utah.

42. Jane Molen, Diary, 18 August 1883, LDS Church Archives.

43. Romania Pratt Penrose, "Memoirs of Romania B. Pratt, M.D.," typescript, 10–11, LDS Church Archives.

44. "Temple Workers," *The Young Woman's Journal* 4 (April 1893): 304.

45. Ibid., 302.

46. Ibid., 303–4.

47. Blessing given to Lovinia Dame by William Smith, n.d., Nauvoo, Illinois.

48. Blessing given to Angelina Avilda Packer by William Smith, 6 June 1845, Nauvoo, Illinois.

49. Blessing given to Pamela Elizabeth Barlow Thompson by Israel Barlow, no other data given, LDS Church Archives.

50. Blessing given to Martha A. Riggs by Zebedee Coltrin, 11 November 1876, LDS Church Archives.

51. "Evening Thoughts of What it Means to Be a Saint," *Poems, Religious, Historical, and Political* (Liverpool: Latter-day Saints' Book Depot, 1856), 4.

52. Desdemona Fullmer Smith, Reminiscence, Written 7 June 1868, LDS Church Archives.

53. Reminiscences of Caroline Barnes Crosby, Utah State Historical Society, Salt Lake City, Utah.

54. Ellen Douglas Parker to her mother, 16 July 1848, from St. Louis, Missouri, photocopy of original in possession of author.

Notes on the Authors

Linda Aukschun was born and raised in Utah, and she graduated from Brigham Young University. She has taught seminary for ten years and is currently assigned to the Brighton High School Seminary. Linda and her husband, Carl, have two grown sons, Ben and Bradley.

Danel W. Bachman was born in Twin Falls, Idaho. He completed a bachelor's degree in psychology at Brigham Young University and a master's degree in history at Purdue University. He has taught in the Church Educational System for twenty-seven years. He and his wife, Pat, are the parents of four children. They currently live in Logan, Utah, where he is a member of the faculty at the Logan Institute. Brother Bachman has published articles in the *Ensign* and scholarly journals.

John K. Challis is a seminary and institute instructor. He was born in Salt Lake City and raised in Cedar City, Utah. He holds a degree in public relations and advertising from Southern Utah University, and he worked in those fields and in graphic design prior to joining the Church Educational System. He currently teaches in Afton, Wyoming, and he has served in many capacities in the Church. He is married to Julie Maxwell and is the father of five daughters. Brother Challis is currently pursuing a Master's degree in history.

James A. Carver was born and raised in Nephi, Utah. He completed his education at Brigham Young University, obtaining a bachelor's degree in psychology and secondary education and a master's degree in religious education. He has taught in the Church Educational System for thirty-one years. Brother Carver has published in the *Ensign* and has written a pamphlet entitled *The Mormon Faith Un-Decker-ated* and *The New Mythmakers*. He and his wife, Merilyn, are the parents of ten children and currently live in Cedar City, Utah.

Richard D. Draper received his M.A. from Arizona State University, and his B.A. and Ph.D. in history from BYU, where he is presently an assistant professor in the Department of Ancient Scripture. He has, at various times, served as an Institute director, seminary principal, and member of the Church Education System's college curriculum writing committee. His publications include articles for the *Ensign, Encyclopedia of Mormonism,* and *Studies in Scripture* vol. 5, and *Opening the Seven Seals: an Analysis of the Message of the Book of Revelation,* published by Deseret Book. In the Church he has served as a bishop, a high councilor, and a scout master. He and his wife, Barbara Ellen Johnson, have six children.

Audrey M. Godfrey holds an M.S. degree in history from Utah State University and presently serves on the board of directors of the Utah Historical Quarterly. She has published a number of articles on historical topics and is a co-author of *Women's Voices, an Untold History of the Latter-day Saints,* and *Studies in Scripture,* published by Desert Book. In the Church she has served as a Relief Society President, Primary president, and a gospel doctrine teacher, as well as serving with her husband, who was president of the Pennsylvania Pittsburgh Mission. She and her husband, Kenneth, have five children and five grandchildren.

Kenneth W. Godfrey is director of the Logan Institute of Religion and has directed institutes in California and in Ogden, Utah. He has been employed by the Church Educational System since 1958 and has served as an area director in California, Arizona, and Northern Utah. Brother Godfrey holds a Ph.D. from Brigham Young University, is a past president of the Mormon History Association, and has served on the board of editors of *BYU Studies*. He has published more than one hundred and sixty articles and six books. He is a former bishop and mission president and has served on the Instructional Development Committee of the Church. He is married to Audrey Montgomery, and they have five children and five grandchildren.

Gerald E. Hansen Jr. was born in Munich, Germany but his most formative years were spent in Nebraska, Iowa, and Arizona. He served a mission in France and Switzerland. He received his B.A. in English from Eastern Oregon State College and his M.A. in English from BYU. Brother Hansen taught seminary for five years in Kuna,

Idaho, then became the Institute Director at Purdue Univesity, and finally became a teacher in the religion department at Ricks College in 1988. He and his wife Sharlene Wilderson have eight children.

Carol Cornwall Madsen was born and raised in Salt Lake City, Utah. She completed her Ph.D. in American History at the University of Utah and is currently a professor of history at Brigham Young University as well as an associate research professor in the Joseph Fielding Smith Institute for Church history at Brigham Young University. Author of *In their Own Words, Women and the Story of Nauvoo* published by Deseret Book, Sister Madsen has also won five awards for various articles about Utah women. She is married to Gordon A. Madsen and they are the parents of six children and grandparents of five. She and her husband enjoy acting as guides on Church History Tours in the United States and Great Britain.

Robert J. Matthews was born in Evanston, Wyoming, and received his B.S., M.S., and Ph.D. degrees from Brigham Young University. He has been with the Church Educational System since 1955 and has taught in Idaho, California, and at BYU. For several years he was also assigned as a course writer, editor, and researcher for seminaries and institutes of religion. He served for eight and a half years as Dean of Religious Education at Brigham Young University and is professor emeritus of ancient scripture there. Brother Matthews is married to Shirley Neves, and they are the parents of four children.

Daniel C. Peterson received a doctorate from the University of California at Los Angeles and teaches Islamic studies and Arabic at Brigham Young University. He is a member of the board of directors of the Foundation for Ancient research and Mormon Studies (F.A.R.M.S.) and the committee that oversees operations at BYU's Jerusalem Center for Near Eastern Studies. He edits the semiannual *Review of Books on the Book of Mormon*. He is the author of *Abraham Divided: An LDS Perspective on the Book of Mormon* and a co-author of *Offenders for a Word: How Anti-Mormons Play Word Games to Attack the Latter-day Saints,* both published by Aspen Books. He is married, the father of three boys, and currently serves on the high council of the Brigham Young University 11th Stake.

Stephen D. Ricks's educational background includes both a B.A. and an M.A. from Brigham Young University and a Ph.D. from the

University of California, Berkeley, and Graduate Theological Union. He is currently a professor at Brigham Young University, where he teaches courses in biblical Hebrew and Book of Mormon. He also teaches in the Honors Program. His numerous publications include books and articles on topics ranging from scriptural allegory to temples in antiquity. He has served as acting president and chairman of the board of directors of the Foundation for Ancient Research and Mormon Studies and Associate Dean of General and Honors Education at BYU. He and his wife, Shirley Smith, are the parents of six children.

John G. Scott was born in Winnemucca, Nevada. He was baptized into The Church of Jesus Christ of Latter-day Saints in Pullman, Washington, while attending Washington State University, where one year later he completed a four-year institute program. After serving in the Flordia, Ft. Lauderdale Mission, he received a B.S. in history and a secondary educational endorsement from Utah State University. He has also earned his M.Ed. degree from Brigham Young University and received a special certificate of achievement in post graduation studies from the Logan Institute of Religion. Brother Scott has taught in the Church Educational System since 1984 as a seminary and institute instructor. He and Valene Joyce Haralson are the parents of six children and currently own and operate a small farm in west central Wyoming.

Philip C. Wightman was born and raised in the Provo area. He was called as a missionary to the Great Lakes Mission, and is a graduate of Brigham Young University with a bachelor's degree in math and a master's degree in the history of religion. He has also completed his classwork towards a Ph.D. in junior college administration. Brother Wightman had been with the seminaries and institutes for five years when he joined the religion faculty at Ricks College. He has recently been released as the chairman of the religion department at Ricks and now serves as the chairman of the Division of Religious and Family Living. Brother Wightman has served in a number of Church callings, including high counselor and bishop. He and his wife, Pat, have six children—five sons and a daughter—and six grandchildren.

Scripture Index

Subject Index